Currant Bread ...

Michael John Bird

Grosvenor House
Publishing Limited

Michael John Bird is hereby identified as author of this
work in accordance with Section 77 of the Copyright, Designs
and Patents Act 1988

The book cover picture is copyright to Michael John Bird

This book is published by
Grosvenor House Publishing Ltd
28-30 High Street, Guildford, Surrey, GU1 3HY.
www.grosvenorhousepublishing.co.uk

A CIP record for this book
is available from the British Library

ISBN 978-1-907211-98-0

"There is no point in telling your story,
if you are not prepared to tell the truth"

Preface

The first thing a reader may ask, when faced with an autobiography, is "Who is he? Why does he think his story is worth telling?" And then, "Is he telling the truth?" In fact, I am nobody special, and certainly not famous. But really, haven't we all something to say about life, as we find it? And there have been millions of unsung heroes who could have told us dramatic and heart-rending stories of their lives. Autobiographies should not be the prerogative of only the rich, or the famous - or even the infamous. There is plenty of room for Mr nobody in this world of endless variety. Us Mr nobodies make up the vast majority of the human race! Let us not demean ourselves or our own importance! So here is the story of a little man (or rather, a little boy). May you enjoy reading it as much as I have enjoyed writing it. Here is my testimony of how I, personally, found the world I was born into, in the year of our Lord, nineteen hundred and thirty three. It wasn't until 1939, from the age of six, that I started to try and make sense of my unhappy predicament. The span covers roughly the next ten years of my life, while I consciously tried to understand and control my muddled, restless and increasingly mischievous emotions and escapades, in preparation for that more serious and adult world, that I began to perceive I must eventually face and come to terms with, and to learn to live by its stern governing and controlling rules.

Contents

Foreword

It was 1939. I was approaching my seventh birthday. The Second World War had broken out and southern England was about to receive the first of Hitler's Luftwaffe bombs...

Thousands of kiddies, from all walks of life, were evacuated to supposedly safer parts of the country...

Though many families were broken up, and brothers and sisters separated, they all had one thing in common: they all had to attempt to settle down and try to adapt to living with strangers, in a new strange environment. It is a little known fact that many lone evacuees were forgotten, and left to live out their lives with their new adoptive families, and in their new environments. Their fate and the rest of their lives were dependent on this throw of the dice of life.

Most lone evacuees came from orphanages and children's homes. They had already suffered traumatic family break-ups, before the war started. I was one of these unfortunate victims.

We were never officially adopted. Indeed, we seemed to have been conveniently forgotten or purposefully ignored by the authorities of that time (and, in some cases, by our own parents) in the more immediate urgent priorities of the war. In a way, we were thrown to the wolves of fate.

A few lucky, lone evacuees found themselves in homes of love, where they were genuinely accepted as one of the family. Others, more unfortunate, were used as skivvies and unpaid labourers...or worse. And it is here lie the many sad and untold stories of their lonely childhood, youth and juvenescence.

I was evacuated from a children's home in Kent, to a slaughterman's family in a small village in rural Staffordshire.

Here I was to grow up. As far as I was concerned, I had no Mum, or Dad, or family. Don't believe the saying "What you don't have, you don't miss". It is not true, as my following story will testify.

For reasons that you will read, I found I could not call my foster mother "Mum". And it was here my troubles began...

It is almost winter, 1939. I am sitting shivering in a huge, unfamiliar armchair, clutching a large glass of ice-cold milk in my small hand, and balancing two chunky slices of currant bread on a plate, on my knee.

And this is where my story begins...

CHAPTER 1

Wide eyed and Wondering

When I was seven years old, early 1940, due to the danger of Hitler bombing Southern England, I was evacuated, along with a large group of other kids, from a childrens' home in Ramsgate, Kent, to a small village in Staffordshire called Blythe Bridge. By bus and by train we were dispersed throughout the Midlands, U.K.

I ended up with a family, name of Batesons, in this village five miles from the market town of Uttoxeter and about ten miles from the County town of Stafford.

Any recollections of my troubled life before this exodus are very faint and sketchy, and hang in my clouded memory like fading photographs. For the purpose of my autobiography this forgetfulness doesn't matter: indeed, it is better so, for I suspect those early years were very unhappy and traumatic ones for me, and are best forgotten anyway. As far as I am concerned, my life and my propelled juvenescence began at this age of seven, when I alighted from the train at draughty Stafford railway station. It's as far back as I can, and wish, to remember.

For the sake of continuity, I will sketch in briefly, a few of those 'fading photographs', recalled always with pain, a sense of fear, and sorrow, gleaned from barely remembered very early childhood and filled out with a few facts told to me since, to bring the reader up to the time I arrived, wide-eyed and wondering, at the rail station in Stafford town.

1

Apparently, some time before the war, my Mum and Dad split up and two of my brothers and I ended up in care in separate childrens' homes. The eldest third brother Bob was old enough to take care of himself, and to help Mum, so I have learned since. Very, very vaguely I remember violence in our family, especially to myself (from Dad apparently, I was to learn later). I can remember great fear, and being threatened, assaulted and physically hurt; and that is all. Time has mercifully blotted out the details but terrible nightmares over the years give me a fearsome inkling. I suppose this is the period when most damage is done to our psyche, at that very early age, before conscious memory begins.

In the childrens' home it must have been a strict regime, as here I also have memories of fear, discipline, cruelty and regimen. Some sort of prefect sat us younger ones on the toilet at set times, and stood over us until we 'did something'. It we couldn't evacuate our bowels then we were shouted at and bullied and occasionally clouted by the teenage overseers, then taken outside to the quadrangle where we were made to run round and round until we agreed we were ready to 'do it'.

Every Friday we were given a strong dose of thick and horrid peppermint medicine mixture...if you couldn't swallow it willingly your nose was gripped tightly, your head was held well back and, "OPEN MOUTH!" and down it went, force fed. An unpleasant experience for a five year old in a strange orphanage. I have hated the taste of peppermint ever since, in sweets, drink or food.

Breakfast was either heavily salted porridge or chunks of lard-spread bread, or occasionally beef dripping but more often lard. You were not allowed a drink until you'd eaten the bread. Many children, including myself, couldn't swallow this indigestible dry mixture and would sit chewing it round and round in our mouths. Eventually our hair would be grabbed from behind and we would be told to spit out the dry masticated food back onto the plate. We were then not allowed to leave the table, or have a drink of water, until we had eaten the horrible chewed lumps from our plates.

I have faint recollections of going to infant school and of a kindly teacher...the only kind person I can remember from those days. I also remember air-raid drills and having to run to underground shelters...and oddly, and more clearly and indelibly than anything else, I can remember carrying my gas-mask everywhere with me. It was in a little square box, covered with a type of crinkled dull silver oilcloth.

For some reason (was it a pathetic Teddy Bear substitute...or the equivalent of a comfort blanket?). I was very attached to this case and clung to it all the time. It is one of my clearest memories. It travelled with me to Staffordshire. It remained the only link with my unhappy orphanage childhood and my new life in Staffordshire for some years, and I can recall feeling lost, bewildered, frightened and finally abandoned as through the following years it became worn and battered and tatty. The silver skin faded, cracked and got dirty, and the war ended, and the case was tossed finally and unceremoniously into the dustbin by 'Em, my new 'Mum' (whom you will soon meet). It was an omen of what had gone and what was to come...

I might have been praying this one and only weak link with my past would never break...

And thus, with the demise of my gas-mask, all traces of my past were finally severed and destroyed and gone forever, and my new life began. In the event, it was to turn out not much better than before, but, in retrospect...from the moment I was given that Currant Bread and that large glass of cold milk in Mrs Batesons' living room, in the reality it was no worse than many others suffered during the austere war years. It could have been worse.

The Batesons owned a smallholding, consisting of a few fields, an assortment of animals, many sheds and outbuildings, an outside shit-house (it didn't warrant being called a lavatory) no laid-on water (a well down the field provided all our water) and no gas or electricity supply. The lighting was by an Aladdin paraffin lamp, the heating and cooking came from a large cast-iron black-leaded range, and the water was hand-carried in buckets from the said well down the field, where the cattle drank.

Blythe Bridge could hardly be called a village: to use an old word, it was more of a hamlet. It lay in a valley at the bottom of a steep hill, along which meandered the River Blythe, a tributary of the Dove. There was Batesons' house, an old mill, a pub, and directly across the road from us, a Blacksmith's shop, or Smithy. Strangely enough, the Blacksmith was named Mr Smith. He had a wife and two daughters, and also took an Evacuee. The River Blythe ran past the Smithy, about a hundred yards from our house, its tinkling and twinkling waters forked and passed beneath two narrow road bridges. The village was surrounded by rolling fields, woods, low-lying marshland, and interesting 'pit-holes' (which were rumoured to be old bomb craters, but I don't think so), and the odd outlying farmsteads.

It sounds an idyllic place, described like that. And I suppose it should have seemed a green pastoral wonderland for a seven year old evacuee from the concrete prison of the city orphanage I had just come from. I came just at the right time and age: but it didn't appear to me like that. That is the rose-coloured view that only happens in romantic novels. The war years, though hard and severe, brought their own brand of experiences, and the countryside seemed almost to belong to me alone, as most of the village men were away fighting, and the women and those that remained were too old, or busy and careworn, to bother about me roaming about the place. I was just another of "those damned evacuees, who caused trouble and would come to no good". There was more than a grain of truth in this surly comment often made by the local village folk ...for like the Bible says: "Some seed fell upon stony ground, and gave forth bad fruit". Many evacuees did indeed come to no good (probably due in part to their inauspicious start to life). Some evacuee families scuttled straight back to "The Smoke" as soon as possible, preferring their previous

CURRANT BREAD

crowded existence in the polluted air and terraced houses of the cities, and even Hitler's bombs, to the unfamiliar and disturbing quietness of the countryside, and the perceived unfriendly quirkiness and small-mindedness of its 'peasants'. Others, like myself, had no choice but to remain, and to attempt to make sense of their sorry start to life, and to just get on with it, eventually marrying local girls and raising families. But it was all a big gamble, and many lost their way and fell by the wayside, as you might guess.

Exact dates are immaterial. The account spans the war years from 1939 to 1945 and beyond. The names of those still living have been changed to protect their identities. As far as memory allows, the truth will be told, warts and all. Brutal, sad, strange, immoral and amoral, funny or quaint: I have tried not to take sides or to be prejudiced, but to tell it as I saw and felt and thought about it, from juvenescence, to adolescence. Interesting and turbulent years. Due to my overriding desire to be totally honest, I can take no account of readers' sensibilities. This is not a work of fiction, meant to please and tease. I apologise in advance for any shock or affront, or any other emotional, mental, judgemental, or spiritual reaction felt by you, who peruse my most intimate and innermost thoughts, memories and experiences. If you don't like what you read, then it is not your type of book so put it back on the shelf. I also apologise for any episodes or recollections inadvertently clouded or tinged by the passing of time. Time is a great liar and colourist as well as being a great healer. Part of the healing process is the grateful forgetting of pain.

5

CHAPTER 2

Evacuation

As already mentioned, my memories of being evacuated to Staffordshire are pretty scant. Certain images remain. We were each 'ticketed' like cattle in transit, with labels attached to our coat lapels telling our age and name. The popular images of lost, dejected and bewildered war evacuees, standing on a windswept railway station, is certainly true. We carried various tatty bags and suitcases, and perhaps a greasy brown paper bag containing the residue of our packed 'lunch': half eaten, dry bread jam sandwiches. Us child evacuees could be picked out by our boxed gas-masks which were compulsory, swinging around our necks. I had a smelly black rubber mask, but some of the younger children were issued with Micky Mouse or Donald Duck gas-masks, as the standard issue type looked so grim. It looked like a grotesque black rubber mask and frightened them. They were scared and upset enough as it was. Many tots were terrified when it was forced over their faces. They could hardly breathe and felt they were being forcibly suffocated. If they were fitted wrongly or the filter became blocked your breath escaped at the sides and the thing made rude snorey wobbly noises.

A gaggle of us were transported to the long wooden Womens' Institute hut at Kingstone village, about a mile from my future (as yet unknown) home. We stood around feeling insignificant and apprehensive, pale-faced and pitiful. Local farmer-types inspected each of us in turn, like livestock. They could take whomever they liked and I remember one red-faced farmer jocularly inspecting a boy's teeth by peeling his lips back like he would a cow at a cattle market. I suppose he wanted a healthy, sturdy specimen to work on his farm as cheap labour. It happened. Thus, the weakly weedy pale-looking ones (who often came from inner city environs) were the last to be chosen. I must have been a passable looking sample and was picked by proxy by a large and laughing farmer who treated it all as a joke and guffawed at my tremulous worried face. "Cheer up lad, nothing's that bad, I'm sure" he chortled. He explained to his equally amused and portly companion that "Mrs Emily Bateson has asked me to pick her one out. Poor devil doesn't know what he's in for. She didn't feel like coming out on such a cold night. This one doesn't look too bad. A bit pasty-like around the gills, but he'll do" Unfortunately for me, this highly amused farmer sealed my fate for the next twenty odd years, and indeed, for the rest of my life. He must have thought he was picking me out of the village fete bran-tub.

From Kingstone Village Hall I was taken the mile or so to Mrs Batesons' smallholding at the hamlet called Blythe Bridge. There I was dropped off and left with my new 'Mum'. It was here this story begins with that glass of cold milk, and the currant bread (wherecame the title of this tale).

I was to learn in later years that, due to a severe stomach ulcer, Mrs Bateson ate large quantities of currant bread for breakfast, dinner, tea and supper. For some reason it didn't upset her tummy. I was to become a currant bread expert (buyer and sampler). It became a two or three times a week chore for me over the years to fetch it from wherever we could obtain it, and I grew to hate the stuff for this reason alone.

I can remember only two other evacuees who were 'farmed out' in the same locality as myself, although of course there must have been many more. Robert Able went to the Smith's house, over the road from us. Arthur Smith, the Blacksmith, liked his ale, and he could be violent when drunk: so poor Robert was one of those who landed on stony ground. Many evacuees were very sad and sorry creatures and would be described today sympathetically as disturbed children from broken homes, but were viewed then as naughty and disobedient, or even as irrevocable rogues and villains, or worse. 'A thoroughly bad lot' was a popular local description. I was myself (not intrinsically I hope) branded in the ensuing years as 'evil' and a 'bad lot' and a 'hard-faced little sod' and a lot of other nasty spiteful names, by the ever inventively invective and bullying Mrs Emily Bateson.

Arthur Smith, our neighbour over the road, despite being an alcoholic, was a brilliant Blacksmith, and we kids would stand and watch him fashion a horseshoe from a white-hot piece of iron, just like moulding a piece of plasticine. All he used was a pair of tongs, a glowing furnace, and a bouncing hammer on a ringing anvil.

Why did the horse not scream and kick out with pain, we wondered, as Mr Smith deftly took and wedged the horse's foot between his legs, apply the smoking hot iron shoe to the hoof, take a nail from his lips and hammer it skilfully into what we kids thought was the animal's foot, and then file it with a rasp.

Sunday then was always big boozeup day for the man of the family. While the motherly Mrs Smith dutifully cooked the Sunday roast, Arthur took his traditionally well-earned pints at the Blythe Inn a short walk away (and a long concentrated wobble back) to the Smithy. It seemed traditional too for the dinner to be thrown straight onto the back of the fire on Arthur's return. He would shout at his wife and smack the kids around a bit, and then go to bed to sleep away the long Sabbath afternoon. This performance took place almost every Sunday. And the same thing happened no doubt in many households across the land. The man in those days was usually the main bread-winner, and, rightly or wrongly, the rest of the household had a certain respect for this,and this 'right' of the breadwinner to his holy day of booze.

Robert, the other 'bad-un' evacuee, who was placed with the Smiths, was accused one day of stealing a necklace that had gone missing, and was hoisted by Arthur, this particular Sunday, up to his neck in the icy water of the fifty gallon wooden rain tub that graced the outside wall of most of the houses then. The necklace was eventually found and hadn't been stolen at all. Poor Robert suffered many more indignities and thrashings, due more to Arthur's drink problem and the Smith's daughters' spitefulness, than to Robert's waywardness.

It is small and seemingly unimportant recollections and events like this that we seem to remember more than important happenings. Perhaps I remember them because these things weren't (at that time) happening to me, but were portents of things I feared would happen later. (They did!)

Where are you now Robert Able? Did you survive?

Johnny Locke was another evacuee I remember. A sinewy, wiry, sallow-skinned, rat-faced and extremely resilient and tough little tyke he was too. Rumour had it that he had to live in the barn, and slept in straw, at the farm where he had been taken.

Johnny used to 'play up' at Kingstone Infants' school, and the teachers were almost in fear of him. One day he took the best part of an hour-long math's lesson physically fighting and wrestling with the woman teacher, and I was very grateful to him for wasting unvaluable teaching time (I hated sums) and, incidentally, entertaining the rest of the class. I have never seen a teacher and a pupil actually intertwined on the classroom floor in a seemingly life or death struggle before or since. He must have been ahead of his time, for pupil-teacher violence seems almost commonplace now. She was an unpopular vindictive teacher (well, that's how us kids saw her), so Johnny became the school hero.

He also unbunged the huge hundred gallon galvanised rain tank that was strictly out-of-bounds in the school playground. They couldn't stop the water gushing out and the following morning there was a hard frost and we made the best and longest slides ever. Thanks Johnny. Where are you now? Did you manage to iron out your problems and stay out of gaol? 'Cos they all said that's where you'd end up. Are you still out there, in the land of the living? It'd be nice to hear your story too!

CHAPTER 3

'Em was for Mum

During my first few months at Mrs Bateson's I was encouraged and urged to call her "Mum". I was much too young, confused and scared to understand the significance of this. I suppose, from her point of view, if I was to live with her for as long as it took - the war that is (there was no fixed period for our stay agreed by any authorities), then it was desirable for both of us to feel at least some sort of friendly bond, and to make me feel a part of the family.

It was a noble aspiration if it worked out, but that was a big IF. But it was both new to us: we were both 'feeling our way': charting in unknown waters, in a situation neither of us had experienced before. Like many well intentioned ideas, in the event, it was not as simple as that. Real feelings will eventually show through no matter how we pretend, or wish things to be.

Even then, at seven years old, I felt intuitively awkward using the term Mum to this, as yet, unproven and 'untested' stranger, and I almost instinctively avoided using it whenever I could. It is obviously extremely rude, hurtful and unkind (from an adult's point of view) to never use a person's name or appellation: and it will be assumed you are thinking of and treating them as a non-person, and therefore they will feel deeply affronted and insulted - and this is probably true unless they are saints and can rise above such natural and personal feelings and emotions. But try explaining this to a seven year old kiddie, especially an uprooted and disturbed one who

11

cannot even remember his own Mum. The lines of friendly communication between me and 'Em were already blurring. We were already getting off on the wrong foot.

Not only that: it is harder still for a youngster to call an adult anything respectful if he feels he is being treated unkindly or abused. A natural feeling of reciprocated love and trust has to be earned over a prolonged period, sometimes for many years. The more damaged a child is, the longer it takes. If there is no love at all forthcoming, only hostile coldness, spitefulness, retaliation and abuse, then that child will draw deeper than ever into its shell.

Constant abuse from an adult will only meet and engender suspicion, fear, non-co-operation and sadness in a child. Later, as the child begins to feel and understand the concept of hate, hate will follow. As time went on, I was progressively subjected to bullying, scolding, nagging, intimidation and the occasional beating. From Mrs Bateson's point of view I might have deserved this treatment. I don't know. But that is not my contention.

Perhaps worse than the physical beatings (which many kids would prefer, if they had a choice) were the cruel tongue-lashings and demoralising criticisms. She cast pernicious hints and aspersions on my innate character and nature, and slandered my unknown family, which, at this time, as far as either of us were aware, might not even be existent. "Your Dad must have been a wrong 'un and your Mum couldn't have loved you or she wouldn't have washed her hands of you" 'Em postulated. "She couldn't have been much good anyway, else she wouldn't have deserted you" she carried on. "I think she's in trouble with the police and the authorities, otherwise why is she hiding?" "Why doesn't she come out of the woodwork and show herself?" And so on and so forth.

These remarks cut deep and wounded and hurt me, which of course they were intended to do. I had no family there to defend me or protect me, or themselves, and I didn't know where they were anyway, so how could I protest or deny her accusations?

All this compounded the situation. In my misery and defiance, I mumbled replies and wouldn't call her Mum. It was the only form of protest I knew at that age: a refusal to co-operate with anything she said or did. This made her angrier still, and the whole situation became self-perpetuating. Looking back, this would account for one of her most used accusations... "You wouldn't treat a dog the way you treat me". She would pout and purse her lips spitefully.

I was told in later years that Emily Bateson's main reason for accepting an evacuee into her life and home was as a companion to Tommy, her only child. If this was true, it didn't work out (does it ever?). Tommy was much younger than me and a very spoilt child...and, as the years passed, it turned out that we had nothing in common at all anyway. We were as different as chalk from cheese.

During these early days I had to act as his nursemaid and look after him and play with him. I soon showed an inherent distaste for this enforced chore of looking after her spoilt son and was sulkily chided by his doting mother. "Why won't you play with him Michael?" she would whine, sounding quite hurt and insulted. "He's done nothing to you". Then she would ORDER me to play with him. I would silently and surlily obey, but was very soon bored out of my mind.

It soon became obvious to me, even as a seven year old, that I was not going to receive the same attention as her son. I was clearly going to be a second-class member of the household.

Why did I feel like this, you may ask?

Well, I was a lonely and deserted war Evacuee, bereft of my natural parents and already twice uprooted and dumped with unsympathetic strangers. Surely an understanding guardian could have made an effort to be patient, loving and fair? I have debated this question with myself many times because I believe it was during this period my generally rather jaundiced and cynical view of life was formed. Our outlook on life is not formed when we are toddlers or babies, but when we begin to 'grow-up' and start to feel and think and analyse the world around us for ourselves.

Be that as it may: it soon became apparent that I would be treated as second-class and the skivvy of the household. I was not immediately conscious or aware of this, not for many years: it just happened that way, and knowing no better, I did as I was told.

At this age I carried heavy buckets of water to the house from the well down the field, and fetched the daily milk in a white enamelled milk can from the farm over a mile away across several fields (later we would have our own cow). I daily black-polished all shoes and goose-greased the leather farm boots and clogs, in the shed outside. I broke the large lumps of coal, riddled the slack, and sawed logs, splitting some into sticks. Two or three times a day I filled the brass coal bucket and scuttle (which I had earlier polished) at the side of the fire-range, and stacked the oven with sticks, ready that I might light the fire the following morning. This preparation for maintaining a fire was almost a full time job in most houses then when there was no gas or electricity laid on (now they are lit by the flick of a switch, and sometimes not even that).

Fires were lit by screwed-up twists of newspaper, and the sticks had to be thin and bone dry, and obviously in plentiful and endless supply. Later, ironmongery shops sold packets of tar-smelly firelighters (small blocks impregnated with flammatory substances) which were guaranteed to light any fire, and flared sparkily and brightly.

The price of coal, which had been relatively cheap for a long time, started to soar, so I spent hours riddling the mountains of slack (coal dust) and salvaging what scraps of coal I could find. Previous to this, slack was considered waste and was often thrown away. Through the years many households had accumulated mountains of the black, dusty stuff. As the price of coal increased yet further, this slack was at first riddled and then riddled again, to extract the bits of coal, and finally burnt as a fuel in its own right. To help it lump up, it was mixed with old tea-leaves etc and used properly could make a fire equal to any coal-fed combustion.

Bolstering slack with logs was a good method. Cinders from the grate, which had long be thrown out to make garden paths, were also recouped and recycled again as fuel, which perhaps is why coke was now being delivered along with the coal (it was cheaper...for awhile). There is a 'cinder-path' in almost every town and this is where it got its name. The days of waste of natural resources were coming to an end (though this idea had hardly been conceived then). Now, only sixty years later, whatever coal remains in the ground is too expensive to mine, and even the coal mines are closing.

On winter nights the fire was stacked high. First a large log was installed into the already glowing embers, then well backed up with the tealeaf-sodden lumpy slack. With a bit of skill this generated more heat than the coal itself, and many's the time I've sat hunched over the fire watching the log burn away and the mountain of glowing slack crash down into the grate, like the lava from a miniature volcano. There was no television then, so we watched the fire burn instead! (Debatedly more interesting than television!) It generated a certain cosy sense of comfort and security away from the tough and bleak trials of life at the time, and the war, and the long, dark, cold winter evenings. A pensive child might imagine he sees moving pictures in the glowing pulsating depths of a winter's fire.

It was prudent to make your supper-time toast with a couple of wedges of home-made bread, speared on the long-handled three-pronged toasting fork, before this fire-crash occurred, for sometimes it almost put the fire out, which had to be rebuilt. The toast was spread thickly with either home-churned salted butter, or beef or pork dripping, heavy with its residue of delicious dark brown gelatinous gravy. It's odd now I think about it, that there seemed to be no shortage of these nourishing natural foods during the rationed war years (though remember, the Batesons where cattle slaughterers). Pork dripping is an expensive luxury today (it used to be given away along with the

Sunday joint) and is nothing like that which I remember, being rock-hard, insipid, and tasteless compared with what we ate then. It had been obtained from the home slaughtered pig that now hung, drawn and quartered, from the iron hooks on the kitchen or larder ceiling, and from which you sliced your heavily salted bacon as and when you wanted it. The old pig had lived a happy life routing in the fields and living off the fat of the land. And now we lived of the healthy pork and fat of his uncontaminated and unscientifically treated carcass. Not like today.

As the dancing shadows from the flickering flames of those evenings of yesteryear rekindle in our ageing memories, we might do worse than pensively muse for a moment on this fading still-life memory of that time, not so long ago. These old homely pleasures and bounties are mostly lost for ever. Today's young folks might scoff at an old man's dreaming. Undoubtedly, those 'good old days' had many grim downsides, but also many pleasures and benefits that today's youngsters will never know, understand or enjoy.

Here I will begin to refer to my foster mother as 'Em, for that is what I called her for most of the twelve odd years that I lived in her house. It's funny now I come to think of it, because her full name was Emily Mary Bateson. But I called her 'Em because I couldn't bring myself to call her Mum, not because her name was Emily. 'Em was for Mum.

Although her son's name was Tommy her pet name for him was Billy Bunting. It was derived from the old nursery rhyme "Billy Billy Bunting, your Daddy's gone a-hunting, to get a little rabbit skin to wrap the Baby Bunting in". It's just one of those daft old rhymes with meaningless lyrics, from times of yore. Yes, I know. I never understood it either. Surely they never wrapped their babies in rabbit-skins - or did they? Mrs Bateson would sing this lullaby to Tommy while she was rocking him to sleep on her knee.

I confess without shame, I was soon to become and always remained, jealous of Tommy Bateson. He was forever bestowed with anything and everything he ever wanted and was spoiled to death, as they say. His Mum had a photo taken of him and put in a golden frame. It showed him with an unruly mop of curly blonde hair. He looked like a rosy-cheeked little female cherub.

One of the things that stuck in my craw was his money box. He had one of those expensive-looking shiny metal boxes that the banks of the day gave away free to encourage youngsters' (mothers') to save. This particular one was a heavy oval Lloyd's Bank affair with slots for sixpences, half-crowns, florins, shillings and pennies. Once you'd pushed the coins in, an ingenious spring-loaded catch came up and you couldn't get them back out without a key.

Well, I could. Later, my jealousy engendered my inventiveness as I pushed a knife blade into the slot, pushing back the catch and carefully sliding a coin out. As long as I didn't do it too often, or take too many coins, it was never noticed. I think this was probably my earliest mean trick to get even with a life I felt had cheated me. The habit and the feeling would remain with me for many years.

I was never given a money box although they cost nothing. You only had to ask the bank for one. The worse thing was, throughout the years, family visitors and friends were blatantly encouraged to donate coins for Tommy's money box. It was purposely displayed in a prominent position on the mantelpiece where you couldn't hep but notice it. It was an expected tradition that guests would ask "Is that Billy Bunting's money box there?" Then, "yes" 'Em would cringingly smile. "He's saving up for a new bike" (or a pedal car or whatever). The visitor would rummage in her purse, or pocket, and into the slots would go the silver half-crowns or florins, while I cowered, unnoticed and jealous, in the corner, watching.

During the war years friends came from the cities to visit the Batesons.

They were fair-weather friends, who appeared at the outset of the war and vanished when the war ended, and fell into the category of spivs amd black-marketeers. There were a lot of spivs about during the war. They came for the fresh country goodies they couldn't get in the towns. There was a thriving black market and the Batesons, involved in the family business of slaughtering animals, were never short of meat and its many by-products. We could also supply eggs, milk, cream and butter, rabbits, fruit, firewood, fresh field mushrooms, watercress and many other country products that, in season, grew wild in the surrounding countryside. These were the years of abundance, when Tommy's money box was filled to overflowing. At an early age he grew comparatively rich and, when he became a teenager, immediately on leaving school, bought a gleaming new motor-bike from the proceeds of his money box.

This, despite the fact I had 'milked' it over the years, ever since he was a baby!

Of course I was jealous!

Sometime during these early years at Mrs Bateson's her husband Henry got called up to fight in the war...and I have little recollection of him at this time. It was to be just myself, Emily, and Tommy Bateson, in the house. Of course, I met Henry after the war ended, when he was demobbed. I'll introduce him to you later.

So you now have the setting. Me, a war evacuee. Emily, my 'foster mother' or 'guardian', with her husband gone to the war. And her spoiled son, Tommy Bateson. Ahead of us stretched the war years. Tough, mean and lean times. With two children, Mary Bateson had to keep the smallholding ship afloat. It must have seemed a worrying prospect from her point of view.

But then there was Old Grandad Bill Bateson, the one who'd begat the whole Bateson dynasty. He was another eccentric member of the family who later came into and influenced my life. As far as I can recall, he had many sons but no daughters. Thanks to the knacker business, founded by Old Bill (as he was known locally) the whole family and their descendants, due to the trickle down of inherited wealth, were to enjoy a relatively well-off bucolic life-style for many years

... although they were all rough, ordinary, very hardworking and frugal country folk.

Grandad had lost an arm. He'd speared his wrist one day with a steel, the pointed instrument used to sharpen the knives whilst skinning the cows in the slaughterhouse. First, his hand went septic and the surgeons had to amputate it. Then, a couple of years later, his arm went, and they removed that at the elbow. Grandad used to say he could feel his amputated 'invisible' arm throbbing, and would sit on a bench in the yard just rubbing thin air where his arm used to be. Fascinating to us kids to watch. Eventually, they fitted him up with an artificial arm and a snap-on hand and hook.

He couldn't skin the cows any more, so he passed the knacker business on to his eldest and favouite Son, Zac, and bought and ran the local pub, The Blythe Inn. Accordingly, Henry (my 'Dad'), the youngest son, who was a naive, simple and very easy-going but hard-working sort of chap, after the war went to work in the slaughterhouse for his brother Zac. Henry would earn the money, while his elder 'Boss' brother, the spendthrift debonair and woman-loving Zac, would spend it.

The scene is now set for the rest of my story.

Imagine me, an observant but rather down-trodden, sad and puzzled little evacuee, with emotional and mental problems of my own, plonked down amongst this family Bateson set-up. Grandad, who had always liked his booze, settled into his role as Landlord of The Blythe Inn, like a duck takes to water (or a Landlord takes to whisky!) Zac, the married slaughterhouse boss, who liked big cars, big women, and big money because it would buy these things, but didn't like work, became the much gossiped-about village rake and womaniser. His meek, mild and easy-going brother Henry (his job interrupted by his years as a soldier) slaved away patiently down at the slaughterhouse, singing, killing, and butchering the cows. Meanwhile his houseproud and puritanical purse-lipped wife Emily sniffed in disapproval at her hardworking husband's brother Zac's wayward, debauched and drunken lifestyle. She often confided in little me (who, at that age hadn't a clue what was going on) that 'that Uncle Zac of yours is a right womanising drunken bastard". She didn't shy away from a bit of colourful language when it suited her. Country folk don't.

Strangely, secretly, my sympathies sided with Zac.

Henry was the most harmless and the least trouble of the bunch. An amazingly hard grafter, he went about his business slightly nervous of his eternally dour, sour, grumbling and nagging houseproud wife, and the mischievous family goings-on around him. All he wanted was a peaceful life. He seemed determined to appear happy, untroubled and contented with his lot (which, in truth, was not a happy one). His apparently tolerant, placid and diplomatic nature was the perfect foil for Emily's whingings and complaints, particularly about his brother Zac's love-affairs and drunkenness.

Although very hard working, poor Henry suffered from the family's hereditary illness, tuberculosis. Gaunt and rangy in appearance, his thin boney face and pale complexion was flecked by tributaries of broken blood veins. Yet he never gave in to his illness and stuck to his arduous and bleak job cheerfully day in and day out, summer and winter. And, believe you me, the slaughterhouse, especially in winter, was a pretty grim place to work, and that's an understatement. Surrounded by icicles of blood and frozen carcases, with no way of warming himself, he worked alone in huge tin sheds with concrete floors in a clearing in the woods: but you could hear him humming or singing to himself long before you entered this woodringed quadrangle of animal death.

Henry was always humming and singing, but I suspect it sprang from deep wells of frustration and unhappiness at his lot in life. My clearest and most abiding memory-picture is of him striding home down Blythe Bridge Bank after a hard day at the knackeryard. He is carrying home a young heifer's heart for his wife Emily to stuff, or a cow's tongue to press. Or some piece of offal for their blackmarket friends. He is singing his favourite song "Don't laugh at me because I'm a fool" and he sings these same words over and over again, and hums the rest because it is all he knows. Was it an unconscious thing? Did he remember these particular words because he guessed he was being taken for a fool? I've often wondered...

But he is now dead and gone along with his wife Emily who pouted herself through life. He was Mr Happy and she was Mrs Sourpuss, and Uncle Zac was Mr naughty. Grandad would appear later as Mr evil to me. And, surprisingly, gone also is son Tommy Bateson, the spoilt Billy Bunting. His money-box fortune didn't save him. I have outlived them all, and will follow soon in my own good time.

But not until I've finished my Currant Bread!

CHAPTER 4

Twas me, and 'Em

Even now, at sixty three years of age, though she is long dead and gone, the ghost of 'Em hangs over my very soul like a residual shadow, a cloud that I cannot shake off, and I am still at a loss what I should call, or should have called, with genuine honest feeling, my 'foster' Mum: (you see, I still have to put it in inverted commas. I can't even write it with an easy conscience). I can sense within myself a subconscious distaste of the word mother, and this is all because of the spiteful and dour Mrs Emily Bateson.

The reasons for this 'mental-block' would, no doubt, give a field day to a psychoanalyst.

I was never officially adopted by 'Em: she was merely supposed to be looking after me for the duration of the war. It was an emergency situation, all done in the name of expediency. Everything was being rushed through. It was anticipated that Southern England was about to be badly bombed and they moved as many people as quickly as they could. The dictionary defines the word 'foster' as 'to bring up and cherish' ... well, I was brought up, in a fashion, but I certainly never felt 'cherished' (to protect and to treat with affection). So, strictly speaking, I do not even feel like using, nor did she merit, the courtesy title of 'Foster Mother'.

Perhaps the old fashioned 'Guardian' (one who has the care of another) is the nearest I will allow myself. This word smacks of Dickens and the Victorian era, and so be it. We were a bit

Dickensian in our household. My apologies for this long, drawn-out pedantry - but in this particular respect, and for the sake of accuracy in this account of my relationship with Emily Bateson, and for my own wish to be getting at the truth, and also for my own peace of mind and integrity, I need very much to be precise here.

Even the use of the word Guardian makes me feel guilty, because I honestly believe she never took proper care of me. So what should I call her, apart from a waste of time? And now I feel guilty again, because what she was and what she did, I now realise, happened because it was her nature to be like that! And also, the thought must occur to me, as it might to you, what WOULD have happened to me if I had had to stay in southern England, to face Hitler's bombs?

She knew no better. So I must excuse and forgive her in the end.

You see, many people expected us evacuees to feel grateful to the good country folk who took us in during the war - and, I suppose, in a perfect story-book world, we would have. But real life is not like that. Workers don't feel grateful to their bosses for giving them jobs; kids don't feel grateful to their parents for having and nurturing them; citizens don't feel grateful to the politicians for taking on the problems of running the country. Maybe they should, it's debatable: but they don't.

All this is sad, but true.

As I said earlier, I began innocently enough, on the subtle prompting of Mrs Bateson, to call her Mum. This artificial attempt to win my trust, didn't last long... it just didn't feel right to me, even at that tender age. Remember, I was a very confused and unhappy seven year old. The first sign that I wasn't happy was the tendency for me to lower my voice (and my head) when I had to address her and to mutter or mumble the word "Mum". I obviously didn't want to say it. She understandably resented this sullen response and not being a very patient type of woman, she took her resentment out on what she thought was the cause of her anger, little me. This made me less inclined than ever to call her Mum, or anything else for that matter, and thus a vicious circle began. It is at crucial times like this that lifelong habits and attitudes are formed. Strong feelings put down deep roots, and like pernicious and erradicable weeds, they run wild. In later years they are almost impossible to root out, sort, and eliminate. And so we all have our 'complexes' and 'hang-ups', and psycho analysts have to use regression therapy to try to root out, and rid us of these deep-rooted 'weeds' in our psyche.

As time passed 'Mum' dwindled to 'Mm' and 'Mm' dwindled to 'Em. And, as I grew old and bolder (a bare-faced, or hard-faced little bastard, as she often called me) I didn't even bother to call her anything at all (polite, that is!) Call me an ignorant ungrateful little swine if you like. 'Em did, and worse, many times. I got used to it (and even started to believe it myself). So she advanced it to an ignorant, ungrateful and hard-faced little sod. But that's the way it was. It was an adult expecting a child to behave in a way she thought I should behave. Like a piece of plasticine, she was trying to mould me into the shape she thought a little evacuee boy should be. Well, I was not plastic and never would be. I was behaving in the way I felt. At that age I was not aware of the politics and conventions of expected behaviour, which are questionable anyway.

Over the years the interrelationship between myself and Mrs Bateson deteriorated to one of subtle warfare. This story was not going to have a happy ending. In a nutshell, what happened was, while I was young she exploited the natural dominion of adult over child, by bullying and abusing me to get her own way. But, innately, I was not the type to be forever intimidated (thank God) and as I grew up I gradually began to understand the situation a little better, and reacted with ever growing resentment and confidence. One day I would have the sense and find the courage to strike back. This is how it goes. It is why revolutions happen.

Somewhere along the way, as I grew more aware of my unfortunate predicament in life, the gnawing worm inside me began to turn. Later, at a given moment in time, as though it was written in the wind, there came a watershed, fuelled by an onrush of years of seething angry frustrated emotion and misery. This only needed the daring of nerve, and a catalyst, to erupt at last in explosive protest and resistance. You can only hold the lid on a simmering pot, or a valve under pressure, for so long. And that, finally, is what happened. As you will see.

Mrs Bateson was extremely and unusually houseproud. She was notorious far and wide around the village for her obsessional cleanliness. She was sniggered at in the bar-room talk in the Blythe Inn, remarked about over the fences of gossiping neighbours, and a figure of fun among more liberal and more easy going relatives. You took your shoes off when you entered her house whether you were the butcher, the baker,the doctor or the candlestick maker or you got a serious pout. Everyone knew that if you didn't you would be the one who'd caused her to be ill and you would be blamed for starting one of her diabolical headaches or her famous bad backs (and who would want that on their conscience?) This could lead to weeks in bed for her and the beginnings of a nervous breakdown, and you'd be treated to one of her long-faces or a haughty, sulky silence and puckered tut-tutting lips when next you called. So you took your shoes off.

My slippers were kept just inside the door, and my boots were left outside whenever I entered the house, even if it was only for a drink of water.

On her hands and knees she red-polished the quarry-tiled floor from back to front every single day of her life. With her set, flushed and determined face, like a child in a seething mood, she knelt on rags and with polish-sodden other rags buffed the floor with unbelievable vigour and non-stop energy.

I, (and her husband Henry - before he'd escaped to the war) knew to keep well out of her way during these set and sacred cleaning hours (about 9am,'till 11.30) and woe betide anyone who didn't. She used Cardinal Red Tile, or Mansion Polish. When she had finished it was said you could shave yourself in the reflection from the polished floor. Any tradesmen doing jobs in the house had to traverse a pathway of newspapers laid end to end to the job in hand.

Once, when 'Em was confined to bed suffering from one of her bad backs (the builders had been in and dust was everywhere), the unpolished state of her red-tiled floor worried her so much she kept me off school for over a week to do the housework and polishing and cleaning for her. I remember feeling annoyed about this for a chart of the pupils' attendance register was pinned to the classroom notice board, and it marred my otherwise excellent record. As I was so rarely off school, the teachers were suspicious of the note she sent in. In any case, I hated doing the housework. It was not my scene: I was an 'outdoor' person through and through. I disliked the smell of the polish (which I'd had to tolerate for years) and couldn't understand what all the fuss over a simple thing like a floor was about. She sobbed when she got up because she said I hadn't polished the floor properly.

An amusing incident from this time that stuck in my mind, was when the doctor visited 'Em. He was an eccentric chap (as many doctors are - or were, then) and like Henry Bateson was given to humming tuneless dah-deh-dah tunes when he was visiting patients in their homes. (What makes them do this? Is it nerves or embarrassment? I've never liked hummers since). This particular day, as he climbed the creaky narrow stairs to Mrs Bateson's bedroom he gave out a short staccato fart on every single step, in tune to his dah-deh-dahs. I was giggling to myself in the living room downstairs. How odd it is that we remember such trivial distant hilarities. I just thought I'd share it with you.

The only perk for me being kept off school was having the run of the house, and like most kids I made full use of the opportunity to run wild. I could raid Billy Bunting's money box yet again, at my leisure, or suck the cream off the milk that was 'settling' in a large bowl ready to make churned butter. (No wonder Mrs Bateson complained the milk was not creamy enough for churning! (The cows got the blame for producing 'thin' milk). I dipped my finger into the condensed milk tin (delicious) or had a tablespoonful of golden syrup or black treacle - all favourite targets of mine. I sometimes experimented by mixing them all together with lashings of sugar and ate the sweet sticky mess with a teaspoon. I also liked to drink neat vinegar, but not too much as I was told it dried up the blood! (I never did know whether this was true or not. Is it?) I sampled a hidden bottle of whisky but didn't like it. The savoury pork-fat jelly gravy from the bottom of the basin was another favourite of mine: there was always plenty of this because of the slaughterhouse. And the large brown jar of sticky malt would stand a raid or two. (All households kept malt, or cod-liver oil and malt during the war. It was an essential food supplement for the young, and at one time was supplied by the welfare organisations). Though with our abundance of knacker meat, garden produce, wild fruits, farm and country products, I would have thought we had no need of artificial supplements.

During these home-alone escapades I also explored out-of-bounds areas like the 'front room', which was hardly ever used (because it needed heating and that cost money). When Mrs Bateson was out (which wasn't often) I searched her bedroom where I first discovered various mysterious adult sexual paraphernalia (it was the era of the douche-bag) and this stirred my immature imagination into intriguing realms of what went on in adult bedrooms.

I also found the 'secret' drawer in the oak desk where her husband Henry kept a huge cigarette, whisky and matches cache. (Due to the black-market we were short of nothing in our house during the war). This particular discovery kept me in cigarettes for years ... he had so many they were never missed.

To return to Mrs Bateson's houseproud fussiness. It was this obsession with tidiness and cleanliness (and also her moaning company) that drove me to spend more and more time out of doors...until I was more out than in, even during the winter.

I would mumble, "I'll have my dinner in the shed. It'll save me taking my boots off". We can get most of our own way in life by telling little white lies, partly to avoid hurting people, but more often for our own ends. A blend of subterfuge, apparent consideration, and a touch of flattery, can work wonders. Starting out as an underdog meant I had to learn these little tricks early in life (they have served me well ever since!)

Army style, clean sheets folded back, pillows square, 'Em had all the beds made by 8.30 am. There is a certain amount of useful good to be found in most people's habits, even if much of their behaviour is alien to our own: I grew to like the crisp, ultra-clean (and cold) white sheets. 'Em installed in me a healthy lifelong habit of making my own bed and ensuring it was always clean and hygienic. And that can't be bad. Good can come from bad.

Once 'Em started cleaning the house, nothing barring an earthquake could stop her. She clenched and firmset her mouth and puckered her forehead in a concentrated cross frown, and this was the sign for we who knew her to put down the newspaper and to clear off smartly outside, to get out of the way.

You can imagine the performance on Mondays for this was traditionally washday throughout the land. (Why? I have never understood).

Washday was a hectic laborious day-long business then, nothing like today when an automatic machine does it all in one go. The breakfast porridge and the beds still had to be made, and the floor and furniture polished, before she started the washing. And remember also, that we had a smallholding of animals that had to be seen to. And these were the days of boiling clothes in large outdoor coppers or boilers (cauldrons) and dolly tubs and pegs, scrubbing boards and iron mangles etc.

Many youngsters today, seeing these laundry implements of yesteryear, might be forgiven for thinking the world had been inhabited by giant women: so huge, heavy and clumsy were the tools used to do the weekly wash (and everything else). Most houses had an outhouse of sorts, the luckier ones a scullery or proper laundry room. Ours was a humble corrugated-roofed galvanised tin shed, that housed a large built-in brick-enclosed 'copper' that would hold maybe sixty gallons of water. A deep fire flue ran underneath this copper. It was my job, as early as possible on wash-day, to get a glowing fire lit, and to refuel it throughout the day to keep the clothes boiling merrily in the copper (a good warm job in winter).

As you can imagine it might take over three hours to get sixty gallons of water to the boil, so I had to rise by about 5 am. A strong through-draft ensured that, once well established, the fire would burn anything, and large quantities of old wood, coal, coke, cinders and clinker, bones and even dead rats were burned. I burnt anything I could lay hands on. It was an excuse to burn all rubbish in sight.

In our arrangement the red-hot boiled clothes were conveyed across the muddy yard to another shed (the old dairy) where we kept the corrugated zinc dolly-tub and the wooden dolly-peg (for agitating the washing) and the huge castiron wooden-rollered mangle. For those too young to remember the hectic chaos of wash-day history, the steaming-hot boiled clothes were sploshed in the dolly-tub, and vigorously hand 'dollied' about with the dolly-peg (a clumsy three-pronged wooden instrument with two sticky-out handles). This was the equivalent of the mechanical stirring of the clothes with the modern washing machine's agitator, with the difference of course that it was done by hand. Then the clothes, sheets and blankets were energetically scrubbed on the ribbed scrubbing board, and rinsed before being rolled through the massive mangle. No wonder those illustrations of old washerwomen all have bright red faces and muscular biceps!

I particularly remember the bleached-white boiler stick, used for stirring the washing in the boiler. And I had very good reason to! It had two uses, one to stir the washing and the other to whack me with when 'Em considered I had been wicked or naughty. As I was the one responsible for replacing worn out boiler sticks I soon changed it with one designed not to hurt so much (another trick I was quickly forced to learn). It was shorter and thicker and made of softer wood. I tested it out on a sack of grain first, the nearest I could find to the human bum. A poor test, granted, as a sack of grain doesn't yelp and feel the pain of a real posterior - and I had only the cloud of rising dust to indicate the strength of hit. But you have to make use of what you can get.

Sweet are the uses of adversity: there is nothing like a good whacking for getting the old brain-box working, as Billy Bunter knew when he stuck a book in his trousers. Billy Bunter and his mates, and Lord Snooty and his gang, taught me a lot of evasive ruses, and plausible excuses. The comic stories were full of useful tips.

The big cast-iron mangle was a monstrous machine, and required an Amazon to turn the handle and to mangle the clothes. Women seemed stronger and more muscular then, and it was no wonder. I used to think Mrs Bateson got her considerable arms from turning the mangle and from chasing and hitting me! The roller had two massive wooden rollers through which, by operating the creaking awkward iron-geared handle contraption (which sometimes pinched your hand) with the other hand you fed and guided the soaking redhot laundry through the wringers. Your fingers came very near to being mangled also, and there were in fact many accidents. A Strongman contortionist from the circus would have come in handy on washday.

The heavy floor standing mangles were eventually superseded by light-weight metal fold-away mangles with small rubber rollers. But they were still quite cumbersome and you still had to find room to store them. Later came smaller mangles that clamped to the edge of the kitchen table. Then came electric-operated washers with integral rollers, and finally came automatic washers that spun and dried the clothes and did the whole lot for you and made mangles totaly redundant. Ah, the march of progress...and I saw it all. But what do we do with all that time saved (or all that redundant machinery, for that matter?) Watch television?

Although, on washday, 'Em's increasingly sweaty and reddening face heralded near apoplexy...I quite enjoyed helping her: for all the wrong reasons of course, as kids are wont. I enjoyed lighting and stoking the boiler fire: it was a challenge to get it white-hot and roaring away and to see, at long last, the water beginning to boil. I would sit on a log in the shed, eating my dinner (mashed spuds, cold meat and pickled red-cabbage, which was our staple diet), the while feeding the fire with bits and pieces, and, more often than not, my dinner. There was a certain sickly soapy smell to the washing that I liked (remembering it now, I can rekindle that washday scene of so long ago). I can see 'Em, rushing across from the boiler shed to the dairy shed, cross-faced, panting and perspiring, carrying a steaming, dripping, water-laden blanket in the tight grip of the wooden tongs, to slosh it into the dolly-tub...

Enjoying myself, and having a quiet giggle (for I found the whole affair hilarious) but still mindful of 'Em's unpredictable temper, dodging and weaving to avoid bumping into her, I would be rushing the other way, perhaps with the white enamelled bucket to fetch more laundry from the boiler shed. Between gasps and grunts she would bark out orders: "Take these over to the copper Michael, while I mangle this blanket". Or, "Dolly those clothes while I go and check the dinner". While the rest of the world has always called me Mick (with many unprintable variations) she insisted on always using my proper name (which I regard as rather prim and cissy - we all have our preferences). I suppose it is possible that because 'Em used my proper name (and I eventually developed great hate for 'Em) that by association with her I didn't like my own name. I have never thought of this before. But it is from such complex feelings as this, formed when we are young, that many of our aversions (and preferences) are decided. Who knows? If this is so, and we are nothing but a bundle of our early feelings and experiences, how can we ever really know ourselves? She probably didn't like me either, for calling her 'Em.

What's in a name?

Quite a lot, it would seem.

Before I conclude this character sketch on Mrs Bateson's habits, foibles and idiosyncrasies (and, necessarily, in relation to her, my own) - seen through my eyes as a child, a few more brush strokes may help to clarify the nature of this houseproud, rather embittered, revengeful, hard and obstinate woman.

It is worth reminding the reader again here, that at the time I am writing about we had no mains water, electricity, or gas. It is easy to forget in this modern day and age, that this meant no electric or gas cookers or fires, and their attendant central heating systems (we had no water anyway), no electric light, no washing machines, electric dryers, airing-cupboards, vacuum cleaners, electric kettles, and no televisions and telephones, and many other things we now take for granted. The age of instant 'switch-on' help, comfort and entertainment was still a fair way off.

Pause, and think carefully for a moment. Modern man is in need of a good pause to stop his headlong race to ...where? People worked longer hours then and often didn't get home 'til dusk or dark. Today, if you fancy a cup of tea after a hard day at the factory, office or farm, it is ready in minutes.

Then, because it was dark when you got home, before you could do anything at all, you had to have light, otherwise you couldn't even find your way around the house. So first you lit a candle. If you had run out of matches or candles, you couldn't even do that.

If you hadn't taken the trouble, or had the foresight, to fill lamp reservoirs with oil, meths, or paraffin, or check that wicks were not burnt out, and that lamp mantles were not broken, while it was still daylight - these jobs had now to be done by candle-light. If you had foolishly forgotten to stock extra supplies of paraffin, spare wicks and mantles (because you had run out of money) you were jiggered anyway. Apart from candles (if you had any) there would be no light that evening, and probably no cup of tea either.

So you'd topped up the main tablelamp with paraffin by torchlight, candlelight or hurricane lamp* (the paraffin lamp we used to trek to the outside loo on a dark night) then lit it up (which, incidentally, gave a softer and better light than many modern electric ones). Some houses had lamps that hung on hooks from the ceiling, fuelled by methylated spirits, called Gas, Spirit or Tilley lamps. The lamp-flame took a while to settle down, and needed constant adjustment.

Now you could think of boiling the kettle for that longed for cup of tea, but the house was icy cold. So first you had to light the fire, to warm the place and to boil your kettle.

On a dark damp November's or winter's evening, this was not an easy task anyway. In the flickering light of the Aladdin's Lamp, you check that you have laid aside ready stocks of dry paper, sticks, coal and matches.

Bone dry, dead wood was essential. The previous day (or whenever it was light and you could find the time) you should have gathered, chopped and stuffed the still warm oven with sticks. If you didn't, it is doubtful now whether you can light a fire at all. If you have sticks in the shed, they will probably be too damp to light. You are still thinking of that cup of tea after that long, long day at work. And you haven't been properly warm all day.

So you stuff the grate with paper and sticks, and a few small lumps of coal (if you remembered to fill the coal bucket) and, hopefully, with fingers crossed, you set fire to the paper.

Coal fires were notoriously hard to light then, due to a number of factors. Damp sticks, poor quality coal, poor design of grates, or lack of a 'through draft" (the wind outside might be blowing the wrong way) to draw the fire. Or more often, a combination of all of these. To light a fire quickly to the point of boiling a kettle of water was quite a skill.

Most fires needed 'drawing' by placing a sheet of tin (or more commonly and dangerously, paper) across the front of the chimney, to cause a narrow inlet that would suck in the air below the fire. At this point the sheet of newspaper often caught fire and burnt your fingers. You'd let it go and it would disappear flaming up the chimney, or up the flaming chimney more like for it sometimes set the chimney on fire and you'd rush outside to see if flames were coming out of the roof. Imagine the problems this might cause on a dark damp night, out in the country far from anywhere!

O.K. So far, so good. At last you have your fire lit, and it seems to be going moderately well. Now for that cup of tea.

Damn! The bucket's empty. You've got no water!

So it's a trip in your wellington-boots carrying your bucket and a flickering hurricane lamp down the muddy field, to fetch water from the natural spring well where the cows drank. It's gone half-past-nine at night and you're still dying for that hot drink.

When you get back, all being well, IF the lamp isn't playing up, IF the fire hasn't gone out, you have the luxury of warming your frozen hands in front of the crackling flames while you wait for the kettle to boil...at last.

During the war, while her husband was away, Mrs Bateson (and myself) sweated it out round the farmstead. I think it was mostly this period that had made her hard and rather bitter. There was only me and her (Tommy was too young to help) to harvest the hay, and to feed, milk, clean out and care for the animals, and to run the house. We also helped Grandad Bateson out at the Blythe Inn. We owned a few fields and a meadow, and kept a barn stocked with hay - winter fodder for the cows.

Anyone who has done hay-making and harvesting the old fashioned way, knows what hard graft it is. I remember when the fields used to be cut by scythe. (Both Mrs Bateson and myself could use a scythe. A knack and a skill in itself and requiring great strength and stamina). The whole field of dried hay was raked and turned with a wooden pronged rake, then stacked. Later it was loaded by pitch-fork onto horse and cart and taken and stacked high in the barn in the rick or barn-yard, all by hand, where in a while it settled down to half its original height. Later it was topped up again, ready for winter feed, when it would be sliced out in chunks with an odd-shaped giant 'hay-knife' (another practised skill requiring great strength - which personally, I never mastered). During winter, the animals were kept inside because of the inclement conditions in the fields, the weather, and the lack of pasture.

The idyllic country scenes of artists and illustrators, of rustic cottages and haywains, and the carting of the harvest may awaken in us nostalgic memories of the quaint and simple lives of not-so-long ago, but, get real, those times were, at best, full of long hours of drudgery and worry, and at worst shortened your life in real terms. It was that hard. The saying "Hard work killed no man", is not true. Life expectancy was shorter then.

In between times 'Em and I reared our own chickens, geese and ducks. We kept a couple of pigs and, for a short while, a cow. We had the obligatory cat and dog, and tried a few fan-tailed pigeons, bantams, a cade lamb and a goat. We grew our own vegetables in our large garden where there were apple, pear, black and red-currant trees. We churned our own butter and attempted to make cheese, jam, chutneys and preserved fruits. Surely life can't have been as bad as I seem to remember?

Apart from an occasional visit to church on Sunday, 'Em hardly ever went out. The highlight of her year was the Church Fete at Kingstone village about a mile away. Then out came her rare going-out outfit, posh hat and coat, smelling of moth-balls. I would watch in awe as she did a sea-change into a different person: an impeccable, perfumed matron figure. As she did her final checks in the mirror and got me to brush the hairs from her coat-collar and shoulders, she looked more intimidating than ever. But I would soon be raiding the house for fags, a sup of whisky, and making myself a sickly sweet cocktail of condensed milk, sugar, malt, cream and syrup and whatever else I could find, washed down with a tot of neat vinegar! So who cared!

Because Mrs Bateson rarely went anywhere she missed out on local gossip, much of which was exchanged in the village pub, The Blythe Inn. But, like many housebound and agoraphobic people she had her own mysterious antennae-like means of picking up the gossip, seemingly out of thin air; and probably knew just as much if not more than the gregarious types who visited a lot, or went to the local public house. No passing pedestrian, cyclist, motorist, nor cat nor dog or even the first single flake of falling winter snow, was missed by her ever watchful, beady, nosy eyes.

Indeed, her continual boring observations, every few minutes, on the state of the weather, drove me crackers. "It has stopped raining". "The sun is coming out". "The fog is dropping". "The mist is clearing". I would mumble "Mm" in my agonized reply. My boredom was so acute, so weary was I of hearing these hackneyed obvious comments on the weather, a physical knot formed in my Adam's Apple and hurt my throat.

Mind you, she was not alone in these inane remarks: it is the main topic of conversation of the British people. Myself among them. Thank God for our lousy climate, I say. Otherwise we'd have nothing to talk about.

She seemed to know where every passing car or person was going and with whom, and at what times they entered and came out of the pub (we could just about see the Blythe Inn from our house). She would voice these thoughts aloud to me. "Mm" I would intone, just falling in to satisfy her.

I was genuinely not interested and these nosy habits of her made me less so.

Another thing that deeply affected me as a child, were our meals. In retrospect, now I am older, I realise times then were extrememly hard for everybody. Mrs Bateson's husband was away at the war. She was alone with two kids to feed and provide for, and severe food rationing was in force. There was a lack of a variety of things available. Exotic, imported fruits were rare. Many kids at that time had never seen a banana, or a peach. Santa Claus bought you your annual orange in a stocking at Christmas. I'd never tasted ice-cream, nor many other modern delicacies now taken for granted.

Nevertheless, we lived extremely frugally, even by war standards. After all, meat was plentiful and free from the family slaughterhouse and we had our farm animals to provide the best natural products of the country. I suspect much of the produce, the home-made butter etc, went to the city spivs who visited us at the weekends, in exchange for hard cash (a more - perhaps mistakenly, pressing commodity).

Apart from her currant bread, 'Em bought little from the shops. I was jealous of schoolmates who talked of egg and bacon breakfasts (we had salted porridge) and beans and sausage suppers. I surreptitiously and enviously perused their school lunch-time sandwiches to see what modern shop delicacies their doting mothers had packed for them. I'd never tasted chips or tinned beans (and rarely sausage) until I joined the RAF at eighteen. Then I made a glutton of myself at the piles on offer and have loved them ever since because of this deprivation when I was a kid. Epicures may scoff, but chips, beans and sausage are the stuff little boys are made of (not slugs and snails). These may seem petty grievances, but tasty food made more sense to kids than worries about shortages and the war, at that age.

It was the sameness and the monotonous daily menu that got to me. Dinner most days consisted of mashed potatoes, gristly cold meat, and pickled vinegary red-cabbage. Occasionally stale currant bread pudding, or Semolina or Sago followed which Pete my mate once likened to frogspawn, which turned me off it for life. Nothing wrong with that diet, you say? True. Indeed, good nourishing food ... unless you have it every day for years; which I did, until I was sick of it. I was glad I ate most of my meals outside, or in the shed, as I took to throwing most of it away, even if I was hungry.

I could always go round the fields later and fill up with apples, damsons, pears or sugar plums from the orchard.

Or dig up some pig-nuts. Or fill my gob with fresh watercress (I once ate a slug in watercress, which put me off it for a while). For 'afters' it would be wild strawberries, or blackberries, and a few hawthorn leaves and primrose heads to finish off. A meal fit for a King. Better than mashed potatoes and pickled cabbage any day. I even preferred the cubes of cow-cake and the molasses that I pinched from the cowshed that were fed to the animals at that time. It couldn't have done me any harm as I always seemed fit and healthy.

Breakfast was a huge bowl of inedible, solid, lumpy, lukewarm salted porridge, cold before I'd unwillingly forced it down. Tea was mostly lettuce, watercress or gristly beef sandwiches, or dry bread and jam. There's nothing worse than knowing what's on the table each and every day of the week, year in, year out. Now I have the freedom of choice I eat what I like when I like. I was glad to escape from 'Em's regimen, timetables and unimaginative fare. Adult often rebel against many of the habits forced on us when we were young, by parents who thought they knew best.

Mrs Bateson was years after other households in having a modern electric cooker fitted (and many other things). Even then she was scared to use "The new-fangled thing" and didn't want to get it dirty. It stood unused in the corner of the kitchen for months, although she proudly cleaned it thoroughly every day.

Eventually the old "Range" firegrate was ripped out. The workmen had to traverse the usual path of laid newspapers through the house to the living room. It was realised now that the grate was too big (and used too much fuel) and we'd got fed up with the dirty job of 'black-leading' it two or more times a week. All these years it had been an unnecessary chore and a waste of materials and labour. It also burnt a lot of coal and the price of all fuels was soaring. For these reasons small tiled grates became the fashion, but still with oven doors into hot areas at the top, and much smaller, and therefore more economical fireplaces at the bottom.

The old black-leaded Range of yesteryear was a classic of its kind. Most country houses had them. It had provided us with warmth, open-fire cooking and capacious oven facilities. It was the centre-piece of the living room, around which many activities took place. Many old folks of today almost had withdrawal symptoms when all they found in their new homes were flat, one-dimensional, uninteresting wall-mounted radiators. Who could sit round them on a cold winter's evening, making toast and roasting potatoes in the coals, and drying your boots out? The old Range was a Jack of all Trades. Constant hot water was drawn from a brass tap on the boiler at the side of the fireplace. The large curved fire-guard stopped the sparks, protected the kids and dried the towels, the washing and smelly socks. High over the fire swung a rise and fall drying rack on a pulley contraption, more often than not also draped with washing. So what if it filled the house with condensation and yellowed the walls? It seemed part of the mellowness of the age.

For most of the winter months a cauldron of constantly simmering stew, known locally as lobby, hung on a hook above the quietly glowing coals giving one a feeling of peace, security and warmth as you entered the room from the biting winds and snow outside. This is also missing with modern gas fires and radiators. The thick and highly seasoned, nourishing 'lobby' ran not a little risk of giving you food poisoning, as it was topped up every day with whatever meat scraps, of any age or kind, were available (no fridges or freezers then of course). Many an unfinished meal was scraped back into the pot. (Is this why it was called lobby, because bits of nondescript food were 'lobbed' into it at random? I don't know, but I wouldn't be surprised). If the fire went out overnight and the stew cooled, a half-inch thick layer of pork, bacon, beef and mutton dripping (blended fat) lay on top of the congealing stew. We picked the fat off to fry our rare eggs in, or to spread on the toast made in front of the fire. I've even eaten the congealed set dripping raw. It was delicious. Today's heart doctors and diet-fanatics may shudder in revulsion and horror but I can never remember us worrying about heart disease and cholesterol then! "Get some of that down you" old Grandmothers would chant. "It'll stick to your ribs and is just what you need in this freezing weather". It stuck to our ribs all right, and probably killed some of us.

On bath nights we brought in the long frost-covered tin bath that hung on a nail on the wall outside, and bathed naked in front of the roaring fire. The bath would be red-hot on one side, and freezing on the other. Then, after the fire-toasting ritual, made with home-made bread and smothered with dripping from the top of the lobby and liberally sprinkled with salt, we would sit for a while swathed in towels while we munched the smoke-flavoured toast. Then it was up the wooden hill to our freezing cold bedrooms and beds, clutching the oven shelf, or a hot brick wrapped in an old blanket (that was often singed with the heat!) to cuddle in bed. What more could one desire? Oh, happy, happy, but untrue days. How time plays tricks with our memories.

CHAPTER 5

Village School

It is now 1940. I am eight years old. I have been living with Mrs Bateson for over a year and we are a year into the Second World War. Mrs Bateson's husband Henry has been called up, along with millions of other husbands ... and people are realising the growing significance of the seriousness of an escalating world-wide conflict and that times, even in dear old insular England, are going to get hard. And harder still.

Despite momentous world worries Mrs Bateson's main worry at the moment is shoes. Shoes are one of the most expensive items for a growing boy. I have one half-decent pair for school and she decides to buy me a pair of clogs for use around the farmstead. I must look after them she tells me, and black-polish them every evening, in the shed (so as not to spatter 'Em's Mansion-polished floor) and even though they hurt my feet, I must wear them until they are completely worn out. The leather on the clogs is as stiff as a board and cuts into my ankles leaving red painful sores, and because of the wooden soles and metal cappings they are very heavy and awkward, clumsy, and noisy to walk in. They are fastened by thick greasy stiff leather laces.

Most times I must wear them without socks, but they chaff and damage my feet so badly 'Em finds me an old pair more darn than sock, and I use these with my clogs. I try to keep them from disappearing down into my clogs with tight elastic garters that cut into me and leave red weals in my white skinny legs.

Small problems maybe, but of more concern to an eight-year-old of the day, than the incomprehensible talk of war.

If you are born into a world at war, or near enough, you are inclined to take it for granted. You think it has always been like this, and hardship and doing without is part of life: so I accepted my clogs and the pain and the discomfort that came with them.

To save on my school shoes each evening I have to change into my clogs. And the same goes for my school clothes. I still change when I come home from work today nearly sixty years later, from that habit that was firmly instilled into me when I was a boy.

Wearing my clogs and my 'playing-out' clothes and my favourite shabby old ex-bus-conductor's hat (where did I get that hat?) you can hear me clopping down the village street like the sound of a horse, long before you see me. The clogs wear well on the hard gritty roads but are useless in the muddy fields or the winter snow for they gather up huge wedges of mud or sludge and I end up like a man with skinny legs, trying to balance on stilts, almost breaking my ankles as I hobble along.

Today is a school day. It is early morning and is snowing heavily. It is already inches deep. On 'Em's instruction I stand at the window watching for my pals struggling through the snow on their way to Kingstone Village School: a tough trek this particular winter's morning of well over a mile. Very little traffic passes through our remote village to blaze a trail for our weak little legs plodding laboriously through the almost untrod deepening snow.

I have belly ache. Is it because I don't like school or is it because I was forced to finish the large bowl of lumpy porridge that 'Em insists I need these cold mornings? Probably a bit of both. I have not yet learnt to question 'Em's dictates, and accept everything she says as gospel. "Don't forget your dinner bag" she calls as I see my friends coming down the lane, and prepare to leave. What has she put in my sandwiches today I wonder. Something yukky I bet. It'll be either Lemon Curd, Heinz sandwich spread, or condensed milk, or even sugar sandwiches, as usual. "Ta-ra Mmm" I shout as I step out into the deep snow to join my pals wending their way to school.

Within a couple of years a yellow school bus will be organised to pick us up and save us the walk (the march of progress?). Then we will kick our heels waiting outside the village shop longer than it takes to walk to school. But what the heck? It's free and saves us the exertion of going by Shank's Pony. But for now, in these 'primitive' times, we have to walk. Go on 'Shank's Pony' and exercise our muscles.

Certain memories and events of those early years at the village school, because of their deep impression on me at the time, are easily recalled. Others, by far the bulk, are forgotten for ever. Compared to most of today's modern halls of education, it was a toy-town school with a miniscule playground and primitive outhouse toilets. Of course, it didn't appear at all like that to me then (Big school, small boy). I was in awe of it...and the toy-town teachers. The age of sophisticated and hard-nosed youngsters had not yet fully dawned (apart from Johnny Locke that is!). The school is still in use today.

It had long metal and wooden desks with inkwells and conjoined bench seats that accomodated about six or seven school kids in a row together. The long grimy oak surface was pen-knife etched with many autographed names and initials, twinned or arrowed love-hearts, daggers and first-loves of long-gone pupils whose story will never be told. What tales of classroom boredom these elaborately carved doodlings and dreams could tell. They must have taken weeks of dedication and patience to gouge out. The teachers might have wished their charges could have given the same degree of dedication to learning their lessons. Now I come to think of it, where were the teachers while this early graffiti was being carved into the desk tops?

We had to trek through the snow, wind and rain to visit the toilets on the other side of the playground. At least it gave us an excuse to dodge part of the lesson. In summer we sat on our jackets on the hot concrete playground to eat our dinner-time sandwiches. In winter we stayed in the classroom and ate our food at the desks...which I hated. It felt like we hadn't had a break at all: I was never one to just sit and talk. At first playtime we were given a free bottle of milk which in winter was often frozen solid. Prime Minister Mrs Thatcher the milk-snatcher stopped this some years later.

If we didn't like the fillings in our sandwiches we tried to swop them with each other. I soon got fed up with 'Em's fillings which seemed to consist of boring stuff like fish-paste, jam, Lemon Curd, beetroot, or lettuce. A thick slice of the inevitable currant bread, or gristly meat sandwiches with the bread spread with pork dripping. During one exceptional desperate war period it was plain sugar, or condensed milk, or syrup on dry bread. The syrup and the condensed milk soaked into the unbuttered bread which curled and went hard, or spilled out and mixed with the fish-paste sandwiches. A small detail, but sufficiently sickly enough for me to remember it. But I liked Red or Brown Sauce sandwiches, and remember the sauce seemed to have a much superior flavour and quality than that which is available today. Perhaps it was made with the real thing, whereas today it is probably seasoned with artificial flavourings and bulked with God knows what.

The gristly meat sandwiches (the meat came from our slaughterhouse) were completely unswoppable. They were so thick, fatty, dry and unchewable that I threw them away over the hedge on the way home. Cheese was cheap and plentiful and tasted better too. Bread and cheese was the poor man's staple diet then. Most men took a piece of bread and a chunk of cheese to work with them. It was cut from large blocks in the village shop and you could afford to make a fat chunky sandwich with it too. It is almost a luxury today. Spam or polony sandwiches weren't bad. There were also various home-made chutneys and piccalillies of questionable tastes. We swigged our sandwiches down with lemonade, cold tea from bottles, water, or the luckier ones, milk.

I found lessons boring (who doesn't?) and only enjoyed drawing or composing stories. Like a lot of people I could draw better then than I can now. Many kids have a natural talent for drawing. I was good at drawing wild birds and characters from comics, like Mickey Mouse or Desperate Dan. I fancy my liking for composing stories came from having become an accomplished liar while living with Mrs Bateson and, like many lonely children I was a bit of a dreamer, a romancer. In children, lying, telling tall stories, fantasizing and daydreaming comes naturally and are all related. A very unhappy child might retreat into a world of make-believe. Many writers have an unhappy childhood to thank for their talent and genius (a high price to pay for success in adult life). I believe this is probably my excuse for writing, though I haven't as yet written a masterpiece to prove my point!

Anyhow, back to school.

We were always grateful for a little diversion, and enthusiastically welcomed anything that took the teacher's attention away from us and the lesson in progress, even if it was something serious. A playground accident and a little spilt blood would serve the purpose. Or a bitter fight out in the playground which we all gathered round and cheered the protagonists on to hurt each other even more. Kids can be an unfeeling and cruel lot. Diversions like this could waste the best part of an afternoon. I might add that even teachers get bored with teaching sometimes and while in this mood will do anything rather than teach. It is up to the pupils to cotton on to this and exploit the teacher's weakness and this is what we did. This natural craftiness is also part of a child's education in a world of dog eats dog.

Perhaps this is as good a time as any to remind the reader I am writing, primarily, about War Evacuees. As mentioned, we evacuees had a bit of a reputation (mostly undeserved) at that time. We were regarded with suspicion and not a little apprehension by the local villagers, among whom we had been lodged (and not of our own choosing either). We didn't want to be there and they didn't want us there. Even the teachers in our village school were not free of this prejudice. The reasons for these attitudes are not hard to understand: parochial folk can appear crude and ill-mannered to city folk even if this is not true. And, likewise, us evacuees, many from inner city areas, must have appeared brash, cheeky, mischevious and crafty to the simple country folk. Suspicion was rife on both sides. Many evacuee families scuttled back home as soon as they could, preferring their terraced city slums full of polluted air, to the strange quietness and biting fresh winds of the countryside, and the sidelong glances and mutterings of the locals.

Remember Johnny Locke whom I mentioned in an earlier chapter? He was the evacuee who attacked a teacher and wrestled her to the classroom floor. It was the best math's hour I'd ever had (or rather didn't have). It was people such as Johnny who gave us evacuees a bad name; but I suspect he'd had a very troubled past, as had most of us. Johnny was always in trouble and later his infamy continued to spread the length and breadth of the region, even though he was just a kid. He was the Dennis the Menace' of the evacuee world!

At that time I envied Johnny his daring and contempt for those in authority. I was becoming a frustrated rebel myself, but never daring - 'til much later - to let my feelings of bitterness and of being unwanted and misunderstood, spill out in anger and threatening behaviour. Because of the traumas of my early life I spent many years treading a fine line between being a normal, well-adjusted citizen and a criminal: but I wasn't aware of this danger for a long time. The sooner we are able to release our simmering, pent-up thoughts and feelings, the sooner we begin to get some sort of balance and begin to see other peoples' point of view. My time of trial would, and did, eventually come. A psychiatrist would have said there was no way of avoiding it (apart from a lobotomy!). And, as events would prove, he would have been right.

Two particular incidents, peculiar to my status as an evacuee, occurred about this time, while I was attending

Kingstone School. Both incidents concerned the American Air Force camp situated in the area.

It is pretty well known that the 'Yanks' caused quite a flurry in the districts in which they were stationed during the war, and many anecdotes, amusing and otherwise, can be remembered concerning them. There is indeed, at the moment, fifty years on after the war, a highly coloured television series depicting the Yanks in England era.

To the phlegmatic English the Yanks seemed a strange mixture of flamboyancy, big-headedness, humility and politeness (a contradiction in terms) and they were always well-dressed and well-paid. Their flamboyancy was not intentional. Compared to their British counterparts most of them had had a pretty cushy life in peace-ridden America and came from comfortable middle class backgrounds. A posting, in a fancy uniform, to quaint little old England was merely a fascinating adventure for them. War was just a part of it.

The local lads were jealous of the Yanks success with British girls. But who could blame the girls? They were suffering a grey dreary life because of the austerities and shortages of the war. The British lads seemed surly and undemonstrative and unsophisticated in the words and ways of love. In comparison the Yanks were relaxed and fun-loving, extrovert and outgoing, and brought the be-bop-a-lulah culture and music to our grey British shores. They were mostly taller and dressed in smart uniforms and, above all, had two or three times the spending power of their English rivals. Away from home, parents and responsibility, they seemed to be able to do as they damn well liked (as they would say) and, apart from lectures of restraint from their officers, they damn well did. As G.I. babes (and their resulting babies) would surely testify.

But the Yanks were always generous.

One Christmas time they'd had a whip-round and had purchased some beautiful boxes of American Candies (as they called their sweets) to present to local good causes. In class one day we evacuees were called out one by one and given a box of these candies for Christmas. I could never forget this incident for my memory is deeply shadowed with the different emotions aroused and affected by the presentation that day in the classroom in front of my friends and peers. What should have been a straightforward gift, generously given and received with delight, turned out nothing so simple. Of course, at first, surprised pleasure and delight, and a sense of wonderment and awe at being given the colourful, luxurious and splendidly beautiful box and its contents. The Yanks and their presents are nothing if not colourful. It was a large gaudy box and the American Candies appeared huge, juicy and munificent to our war-weary sweet starved eyes, each one a different brilliant colour and shape and liberally coated with glistening sugar. In reality I suppose they were only extra-large lavish jellied fruits, but to me then it seemed as if they'd come from paradise itself.

In rationed wartime Britain, viewed by a rather sad, timid and deprived evacuee, this was a sight to behold indeed. And what's more, they were all mine!

My classmates crowded round, to peer into the box at the sight of this magnificent array of multi-coloured sweetmeats...

There were gasps, and oohs, and aahs.

The teacher, afraid I suppose that they'd all be grabbed and eaten there and then, snapped "Shut the box, Michael. You must take them home and eat them later. Now you lot, get back to your desks". (I have always been called Michael by the stuffy mob.) The teacher was obviously responsible for making sure only the evacuees got the sweets. The point is, the rest of the class (the 'normal', local children) were to be left out.

Well, from my natural childlike selfish point of view, this was all right.

I could eat them all to myself later, in the privacy of my bedroom (or the shed) which was more of a sanctuary to me than my bedroom.

In actual fact, 'Em, intensely jealous made me share them with her and her son, the fat and spoilt Billy Bunting. And, like any normal kid, I resented this.

But the pain of sharing them was nothing like the pain I felt from the reaction that emanated from the teachers and my school pals. Their jealousy towards Johnny Locke and myself and the other evacuees was almost palpable for weeks afterwards. It was "Those damned evacuees again, getting the best of everything". It was my first real taste of reverse discrimination, and I would gladly have given those candies back to have avoided the unpleasant taste this experience left in my mouth. The experience has affected my giving and receiving of presents for the rest of my life. I cannot give or receive a present without a feeling of uncertainty, guilt and fear of rejection. (Psychologically I suppose I am scared of frightening away my friends, as I thought I'd done all those years ago).

The Yanks featured in another amusing episode left indelibly in my memory of that time. One of my home chores was to fetch paraffin from the village store a mile away, to fuel the household lamps and stoves. One day I was struggling back home to Blythe Bridge lugging the heavy can, stopping every few yards to rest, when a large American jeep passed me going in the opposite direction. On seeing me it stopped with a screech, shot into reverse, spun round in the road, and drew alongside me. Feeling apprehensive and dwarfed by the size of the vehicle (I was small anyway), I placed the can on the road and looked up at the towering jeep and its occupants.

Four giant, gum-chewing black Yanks sat there, highly amused, laughing and grinning broadly. "Look at the poor little Limey." "The kid's a weed. A good meal'd kill him. He can hardly lift that can." "How far ya goin' kid? Want a lift?"

Before I could answer (I was struck dumb anyway) a huge muscular rock hard black arm reached out, grabbed me by the collar, and hoisted me bodily into the jeep as though I were a rag doll, followed by my can of paraffin. In high spirits the jeep spun round again, twice, quite unnecessarily and headed off towards the Blythe - my village. Nestled between these jet-black, clean-smelling, uniformed giants, I felt like a million dollars, albeit a bit awed and scared. Encompassed by friendly and protective iron-strong arms, and being accidentally prodded by belt-bayonets, I was generously showered with packets of gum and even offered (jokingly I hope) extra-large exotic-looking cigarettes. Depositing me like a sack of spuds at the garden gate they breezily waved and chorused to an astonished Mrs Bateson, who had come to the door to see what the hullabaloo was about, "G'day Ma-am. Helpful kid ya'ave there. Have a nice day Y-all" and sped away, tyres screeching. One of them (I suspect) was to return another day, in rather odd circumstances. But that's a later tale.

I began this chapter on my way to Kingstone Village School one snowy winter's morning, and will end it with an anecdote that happened on my way home, one balmy summer's evening.

Our own hens hadn't been laying too well and I'd been instructed by 'Em to call at my Aunt Bessie's farm near the school and collect a dozen eggs, to supplement our own meagre supply. I collected the eggs and ambled off down the lane towards my home at Blythe Bridge. It was high summer and I was in no hurry. It was one of those rare summer days when I felt I hadn't a care in the world. I loitered about exploring the hedgerows looking for bird's nests and whatever else I could find. Country children are an inquisitive mischevious lot. I grouted up a feed of pig-nuts from the warm soil, and picked strawberries, gooseberries, and blackberries that grew wild and abundant then on the wayside verges of country lanes, in those not-so-far-off, pollution-free days of my childhood.

I spotted a browsing buzzing wasp, and carefully watched and tracked him to his nest in the embankment skirting the hedgerow.

What gets into us when we are young? We are full of thoughtless mischief at this innocent age, and beg not to be judged on our boyhood misdeeds, antics and foolishness. If it was left to kids, they would destroy everything in sight, and then wonder at their own foolishness (a bit like grown-ps really, when you think of it). At this age I acted first and thought later...much later, if I ever thought at all. I was a thoughtless doer then, not a thinker. Curiosity killed the cat, and many other innocent creatures as well...

In curiosity I poked a stick into the nest. Was I to know it would enrage the wappies? I'd heard stories but had to find out for myself. To my amazement and fright they started to attack me. Stupidly, instead of running for my life, I fought back... "Damn wappies. Damn wappies" I panted and, swinging my school satchel in all directions, bashed wildly at the nest in the bank. The damn wappies flew up in buzzing swarms and chased me along the lane, some stabbing me with their stings before I managed to outrun them (ever tried to outrun a swarm of wasps? They will follow you for miles). And you can't outrun them either!

'Nuff said. I was sent to bed as a punishment when Mrs Bateson came to unpack the eggs from my satchel only to find them pre-scrambled into a gooey mess. "What the bloody hell have you been doing?" She screamed. "I can't trust you to do the simplest thing. I knew you were a bad lot the minute I clapped eyes on you." She never missed an opportunity to belittle or abuse me, as well as punish me.

The stings of the angry wasps were nothing to the hurt that Mrs Bateson could inflict when she was in full fury. Grateful to escape to an early bed that night I nursed my many painful stings, a belted-sore behind, and a breaking heart, in secret. As many sad creatures know (including my poor wasps) the sanctuary of a secure and secret bolt-hole is sometimes the only place left in the world, when you have no-one or nowhere else to flee to.

CHAPTER 6

The Long School Hols

Looking back, I remember the long school summer holidays as a mixture of magic times interspersed with long periods of absolute boredom. Kids don't realise it, but, like millionaires of leisure, they have loads of time to waste. And it is probably one of the rare times in their lives when they will have all this throwaway luxury of time.

Boredom can be a problem, like everything else. Some time during our life we have to come to grips with it, and each of us will tackle it in our own individual way. Surveying the situation now, I realise I had, at my fingertips, a period in my life when golden opportunities lay before me, like fields of summer buttercups and the deep river pools of limpid water, waiting, like life itself, to be explored, enjoyed, and understood.

I had few friends. There simply weren't any near at hand in our remote and quiet village. Surprisingly, the few I did seek out and mix with soon bored me. It is wrong to assume we all naturally want or need friends, and I suppose when we are young it is just another aspect of life we have to explore, otherwise we think we are missing out on something. The same can be said for almost everything. My mates continual bemoaning of having nothing to do and their aimless wanderings infected me too. A strange feeling of ennui would seep into my soul as we idly wandered the lanes and fields looking for diversions, idly spinning pebbles across the river or catching tiddlers in jam jars. Tom Sawyer knew all about this, that's why he got up to all his mischief. There must be more to life than this I thought, and still do, though procrastination has its charm.

The saying 'The devil finds mischief for idle hands to do' was never more true than during our summer holidays. We sometimes took part in quite serious escapades and damage, all caused by boredom. Just what does one do when one has all the time in the world and is also brimming over with the frustrated burgeoning energy of youth, in an area of nothing but open fields and woods, and most of them private and out of bounds anyway? This is one of the problems of the modern world: youth is bursting with energy and a sense of urgency but doesn't quite know what to do with it all, or what he is supposed to do with it, or what he wants to do with it. At one time in history he wouldn't have had time to stand about and moan. He would have been helping his family to survive. Now, like a caged animal, he feels short of space and opportunity to burn up his energies and to express himself.

But I think, in retrospect, all things considered, I made the best of a bad job. I have a naturally questing and inquisitive mind and a sense of adventure - I also prefer and enjoy my own company. All this I had yet to discover: like most youngsters during the growing and developing age, I had to unravel and understand myself, at the same time as I struggled to understand the complex world I found myself in.

I soon realised I hated being indoors. Mrs Bateson's obsessive houseproudness, her fussy ways and boring company, didn't help. As, with duster and polish she huffily puffed and panted her way around the furniture and floors, I quickly found my boots and beat a hasty retreat outside. She had found her favourite way of passing her time, I was still trying to find mine in escaping to the great outdoors.

If it was cold or raining I went into the shed. Thank God we had plenty of outbuildings otherwise I don't know how I would have passed the long days during bad weather. My favourite was the old Wheelwright's shed (the property had originally belonged to a Wheelwright). This was a huge high-roofed building with planked walls and a corrugated-tin roof. In winter it was very cold, but I still preferred it to being in the house with 'Em.

It used to contain an old derelict car and also a huge pair of bellows used by the Wheelwright for his furnace. To me, the bellows were an antique curiosity (they had been discarded then, but would be a genuine antique now). They were an exact copy of the small house bellows used by cottagers at that time for starting their home fires. They had been left leaning on the side of the shed as though a prehistoric giant had discarded them in a hurry. Us kids often tried to move them but they were too big and heavy, so we used them as a slide. The folding concertina part was made of thick leather that had cracked and hardened like iron. I think they were eventually broken up for firewood. What a waste! We also played in the ancient windowless car and gripped the large old steering wheel and sped through fictitious wonderlands at fantastic speeds. All in the mind of course, but it was great fun. Who needed graphic computer games and virtual reality then? And this was all for free.

The floor of the shed was ankle deep in sawdust and wood chippings built up over years of chopping firewood and sawing logs. In the rafters a brood of fan-tailed pigeons cooed cosily and soothingly as I played alone down below.

While the rain pattered on the tin roof I crouched on the sawdust floor and built roads, houses with gates and fences, and sometimes a whole village complete with a river with real water! When I got cold and stiff with crouching, I climbed high into the roof rafters and disturbed the preening pigeons whilst trying to achieve my goal of swinging hand over hand across the beams that buttressed and traversed the whole length of the shed. It took many years of growing strength and agility to finally swing right across the shed from one side to the other, in one go, and I got many splinters in my hands. I also developed great daring, by dropping the whole way from the rafters to the floor, with only the occasional sprained ankle for my thrills.

Later, like a circus performer on the high wire, I walked and balanced along the beams. I couldn't have had such dangerous and undisciplined fun inside Mrs Bateson's tidy and impeccable abode. The huge old shed was as good as a modern gymnasium: an ideal lonely boy's play-paradise, really. It strikes me today when many youngsters spend a fortune going to step-aerobics and gymnasiums, or even putting expensive exercise equipment into their bedrooms - that I was getting all this practice, privacy and exercise for free. With the added bonus of it being great fun too. Sweet are the uses of adversity. I even realised that this exercise could also keep me warm during the cold winter days.

As I grew older, stronger, and more useful I went on wood-collecting expeditions into the surrounding woods and fields, dragging back tree branches and rotten tree-trunks salvaged from decaying hedgerows. It was just something to do, to pass the time. I brought back driftwood thrown up on the banks of the River Blythe which flooded at least once a year. Eventually I built a hand-truck with planks and old tyreless bicycle wheels and later still, one with inflated tyres which was easier to pull and of which I was very proud: (the march of progress!). Wood gathering was a necessary full-time accepted chore then, when all houses had coal fires which needed endless supplies of combustible material. The countryside was being plundered for wood, and the day would come when there was hardly any left. Farmers later got angry at the constant 'hedge-pulling' which was, technically, trespass and stealing as it left holes in the hedges around the fields that were meant to contain the cattle and lifestock, but at this particular time in history, this hadn't been fully realised: we could wander anyone's fields 'hedge-pulling'. It was an accepted country tradition.

But we had to keep the home fires burning. Once or twice, while tugging at a hefty branch embedded in the muddy river bank, I'd overbalance and fall into the river. Provided it wasn't too deep, it didn't bother me. I was dressed in my old play-clothes anyway. I often walked through the river in my shoes: they dried out later. Once I came across a large old water-logged tree-trunk lying half in and half out of the river. It was too big and heavy to move. Wood was getting so scarce I decided to try and split it and get it home that way. I went back to the house and fetched a sledge-hammer and an old wheelwright's chisel, and hammered it into the log. The squelchy water-sodden wood wouldn't split and it swallowed my chisel like a soft vice and I couldn't get it back out. So I fetched a thicker chisel which also stuck, and then a thicker one and so on. About seven or eight chisels (our whole stock in fact) of varying thicknesses ended up embedded and fixed in the soggy trunk. As it was getting dark I finally abandoned my endeavours and left the chisels stuck in the log. I said nowt to no-one as 'Em would have been none too pleased at losing her entire stock of chisels. This, like many scrapes and secrets we have as kids, has remained on my conscience all these years, and is now only admittable because 'Em has departed this earth. For all I know those chisels might still be stuck in that damn log, all these years later...

Incidentally, we had so many of these chisels, because they had been left in the shed when the old Wheelwright died: he would never had guessed his chisels would have been 'wasted' like this, by a mischevious war evacuee, not so long after he had gone. The passing of time hides many 'sins', forever.

Once I'd got a truck-load of drift-wood home I'd saw it into logs and split some of the logs into sticks in the old shed. Stacked neatly high and kept dry this kindle lasted us right through the winter months, and gave me plenty to do.

Other times, when the weather was wet, I would sit on a log in the shed and fashion catapults, and working models of guns and rifles out of wood and rubber rings cut from bike inner-tubes. It was also possible to make quite bouncy balls from these rubber rings. Kids are nothing if not ingenious, and, like kids from every age, we used new materials as they became available. Even the perspex from war-time planes was fashioned into rings and lockets: it was a novelty. We youngsters then were quite clever at making our own toys (mainly weapons). I made wooden swords and daggers and patiently smoothed them to a fine point with sandpaper and neatly lashed the handles with cord, to give them a good grip. Wooden knives must have been popular as stabbing weapons sometime in history. I also tried my hand at making wooden puppets; and then aeroplanes and boats, but these were more difficult, and took time, patience and skill. It was amazing how far I could flirt a pebble with my home-made catapult, once I had made and modified Mark 1, 2 and 3. I can still remember the thrill of devising a weapon that had such power - probably much like the cave-men did. As kids we were thoughtless and cruel, and shot at birds with our catapults and bows-and-arrows often managing, with a feeling of great pride, to score a hit and a kill.

Catapults are innaccurate weapons and are difficult to aim and fire at random. My pride and joy was my home-made bow and arrow, which was more precise. After discarding many attempts, I finally made a state-of-the-art weapon. Hazelwood was the best wood for the bow. And for the arrows finer points included pen-nib tips and goose-feather flights bound on neatly with waxed cotton. A well-fashioned bow will send an equally good arrow a great distance, straight and true (as Robin Hood and Davy Crocket well knew). And I remember the thrill of killing my first crow with my bow and arrow. The death of the crow was merely incidental (though Grandad Bateson liked his crow pie). It was the skill of the archer and his pride in his home-contructed weapon that gave such pleasure to the kill. The poor old crow just happened to be in the wrong place at the wrong time. Any creature would have done. It was a target we were looking for really, and moving targets are more fun. I have completely changed my attitude to killing animals now of course.

I honestly think early man fashioned his weapons just as much for the pleasure of making them as for the necessity of using them to kill animals for food, otherwise how do we explain modern weapon emporiums in town shopping centres where there isn't an animal in sight, except for the meat that is, in the butcher's windows, that has already been killed and prepared for us on a massive scale and in a much more sophisticated manner.

Our home-made toys and weapons gave us much more pleasure than the high-tech factory made artefacts bought at high prices in the shops today, as much of the satisfaction was in the making of them, as well as in the success in using them. Holidays equalled boredom, and boredom equalled the construction of these clever, ingenious and lethal weapons, and thus many animals had to die. Necessity is the mother of invention. There must be a lesson for the human race here somewhere: we still kill sometimes, because we are bored - well, some people do.

As I grew older and more knowing in country lore, like an Indian tracker I learned how to spot the runs and tracks of rabbits and other wild creatures and I laid wire snares and gin-traps. I tell you these things not because I am proud of the achievement (just the opposite in fact) but to show how many of us are ignorant of the concept of cruelty when we are young. This is why children pull the wings off flies: it is more curiosity than cruelty. But that doesn't justify it and make it right.

Animals can be incredibly brave: braver than most of the humans who torture them, in fact. I remember a rat gnawing his own feet off to escape from one of my gin-traps, and it was not the only time this had happened.

Another time I spotted a young rabbit bolt into a cleft at the base of a tree trunk. I hauled him out by his thrashing protesting back legs and whapped him on the back of the neck with a stick as Grandad Bateson had taught me. Rabbit meat was a welcome addition to the stewpot during the war, and I would sell this rabbit for a couple of bob (shillings) in the village or to the towny spivs.

Being brought up in a family-slaughterhouse atmosphere, I took the killing of all animals as a matter of course. For a few years I was to become the hired and paid killer of all Christmas poultry and other unwanted, sick or injured animals in the village. A task I would one day regret.

Other lone pursuits took me wandering the fields and woods. At one time I could name many of the different wild plants and flowers, trees and birds of hedgerow, field and wood. I must have gained this knowledge in a natural and unconscious way. I even knew what leaves and plants one could eat to cure various ailments, but I can't remember who told me. I have forgotten most of it now.

To stand alone in a hushed and wooded glade white with delicate wood-anemones, and kept cool from the scorching rays of the high summer sun by the canopy of leaves, is one of life's cherished memories that every child should experience, among many, many others. The feeling cannot be expressed in words, though poets have tried. Modern times are mainly brash and urban and scorn such dreamy visions of nature and bring in the bulldozers to squash them out of existence. Personally, I think we do so at our peril.

On my rambles through the fields and woods I took a packet of sandwiches with me so that I need not return 'til nightfall, though I needn't have done. I wouldn't have gone hungry. There was plenty of food available in nature's larder then if you knew where to look for it, but not so much now I fear.

Occasionally - my childhood imagination fancying myself as an intrepid explorer - I carried my bow and arrow, or an axe, and always a knife. This is an illegal practice now, and I was only about ten at the time! Looking back it was amazing the risks we kids took then, and survived.

What did I get up to on those day-long leisurely expeditions on my lonesome? Good question. Well, when I was a lumberjack, I felled small trees and watched them fall with a mighty crash. When I was Davy Crocket the hunter I shot at birds and animals with my bow and arrow, but rarely hit them. I was Al-capone with my wooden gun and elastic-band bullets. I had, after much experimentation, fashioned a throwing-knife with the blade purposefully heavier than the handle that would, hopefully, make me a knife-thrower extraordinaire. But I lost this precious home-made masterpiece whilst trying to hit a rabbit at fifty paces. It is in a bush somewhere in Kingstone Woods, bulldozed into the ground to be found by some future explorer, when the new houses built there are long since gone, and the earth has been reclaimed (if it ever is) by nature once again. A boyhood relic of modern history!

These were gentle, halcyon days. Oftimes I dawdled, looking for birds' nests in the hedgerows, trees, banks and marshy reeds. Egg collecting was a common popular hobby: few people gave a thought to endangered species then (the birds and animals were not under such a sustained attack from man as they are now). Now and again I would attempt to jump wide, fern-camouflaged ditches, fail, and fall deep into the stagnant, frog-spawn filled depths. Or I'd climb the highest tree in the wood and, like a look-out sailor in the crow's nest of a ship's mast, scan the horizon for miles around.

I would invariably end up at my favourite ditch. I had fallen, arms a-flailing, into this ditch one day only to discover it was an Aladdin's cave full of exciting junk. Inadvertently I had stumbled (or tumbled more like) into the village rubbish dump. So henceforth I made this my mecca as I turned homeward bound, the reason being, if I found any treasure worth having, like an old bike or pram, or an old wireless set, I could take it home with me and try to repair it, or canabalise it for other uses. I was good at this sort of thing. I think my present liking for rummaging round car-boot and jumble sales is just an adult version of me as a child, rummaging in that ditch. At heart, when it comes to junk, I am still a child looking for that illusive treasure. They say a Leopard cannot change its spots, neither can a child change his basic nature when he grows into a man.

Another day I discovered a dark, narrow, overgrown path leading through the wood that went all the way from my little hamlet of Blythe Bridge to Kingstone Village over a mile away. This was a real discovery for me at the time for I knew of no other way to Kingstone apart from the main road.

I wondered who had made the path and imagined a secret tribe of pygmies who lived in the wood that us villages knew nothing about. The narrowing path was grassed over in places and criss-crossed by brambles and tree branches; a tunnel of greenery, indicating it was only used now and again.

At points the path was so narrow and canopied with overgrowth I had to crawl on my hands and knees to get through. But my curiosity was aroused and, imagining myself as a jungle explorer trying to find that lost tribe, with my little heart beating ten to the dozen and my knife slicing through the brambles like a parang, I pressed stubbornly on. I eventually emerged at an isolated farmstead, with a shambles of derelict outhouses and a tall and bleak, sinister-looking, curtainless farmhouse. No dogs barked nor chickens clucked. I walked swiftly through the empty farmyard into a part of Kingstone Village I'd never seen before (I was approaching from the 'back'of the village). It was an eerie and a scary experience.

Some months later I explored the path again and got the same awful feeling of foreboding. Later in my life, this path (and my deep rubbish ditch) entered my nightmares and dreams along with other shadowy experiences of my childhood days. It is now part of me, my psyche and my dreams, and I suppose they will last as long as I do. Many of my dreams (and certain daytime experiences) seem inextricably bound up with dark and damp places, feelings of fear and claustrophobia, and of emerging into frightening unknown places. The path gets narrower and narrower and I have the feeling I shall never reach the end...

I suppose writers of horror films get their scary images from similar childhood experiences.

I have a theory about dying, which will cheer you up no end. It is that our worst nightmares, from which we sometimes seem unable to escape, but always do, will one day (or night) go on to their ultimate conclusion and we will know at last the dreaded termination of the dream, or the last scene in our play of life. (Termination being the operative word). We shall fall from that high tower, and finally hit the hard concrete: we shall get stuck in that black chimney, and finally suffocate: we shall finally drown when we fall into the water: in my particular case, I shall reach the end of that narrowing path, and when I emerge, scratched and bleeding and sobbing from the cruel brambles of life, it will be heaven's gate I find myself standing at and not a derelict farm house. Well, I certainly hope so. We can only hope.

I didn't always play alone during my long summer hols. Sometimes, along with village pals, we'd plan a day picnicking and swimming in the River Blythe, miles away from home. My best pal George lived in the Old Mill - and if his Dad was out (he didn't like us playing in the Mill as it was a dangerous place) George would tip me off and we'd spend the day playing in this fascinating building. It was four storeys high and was surmounted by climbing never-ending, unstable, rickety wooden steps to the top storey. Some of the steps had rotted away and were missing, as were the planks on the floors of the different storeys. It was possible to stand on the top floor and see right through the four floors to the bottom. It's a good job I didn't suffer from vertigo. On the fourth storey giant wooden hoppers that used to funnel grain provided hiding places (our dens) where we would never be discovered (a seemingly obligatory necessity for all self-respecting boy-gangs bound on plans and mischief). Here we smoked our first fags: it was an accident waiting to happen as the whole edifice was built of wood.

We also tasted our first whisky here (and became lifelong addicts or not, depending on our natures). We exchanged stories of our latest sexual discoveries and told each other dirty jokes and anecdotes, and no doubt had our first wanks. Boys will be boys. We also shared out loot pinched from home or various other sources (mainly Mouldies' Shop, the village stores). We certainly were no angels.

In the old days when the Mill was working sacks of corn were hauled through double trap-doors on every floor from ground to top storey. Thus is was a thrill for us to open all the trap-doors and drop through them, swinging on the rusty old sack-hauling chain that passed through the doors from the top to the bottom of the building.

Access to the huge old derelict wooden water-wheel could also be gained by climbing through small doors on the outside wall of the Mill. Here a giant's world awaited the child-explorer's inquisitive widening eyes. The thick wooden-paddled wheel rose high, and went deep down in its tower-like brick enclosure. Heavily water-logged now and with rusted axle-shaft, this once mighty beating heart of the Old Mill had been stilled for years, and would never turn again. Deep down in the smelly murky bowels of the cavernous pit of the enclosure, where the river's concentrated turbulent waters still rushed in through the now collapsed sluice gates, logs and branches, old posts and various other pieces of driftwood, and even dead fish and the rotting bloated carcasses of flood-drowned sheep and other animals, had become entangled and jammed the huge wheel which lay like a stilled petrified dinosaur from prehistoric days.

Looking like ants on The Big Wheel of a fair-ground, we kids clambered around the paddles of the colossal wheel, While the frothing rushing waters below struggled noisily to get through the jammed wheel and driftwood, to continue on its course down-river. We climbed...first to the top of the wheel and then, using its paddles as a giant ladder, right round and down to the swirling waters in the hissing bubbling pit of the cauldron at the bottom. Once down below we climbed about on the unstable bobbing driftwood, tumbling and struggling to extricate itself with the help of the rushing waters, from the paddles of the wheel. Its a wonder we were not swallowed up in this maelstrom and drowned, like the poor old bloated sheep that we trod upon. One slip on this bobbing drifting rubbish, and we'd have been under the water!

We also swam in the Mill pond. Within these dark waters were set the upright water-logged shafts of old underwater posts, used for some long past mysterious purpose connected with the Mill. The tops of these blackened posts had been washed to a sharp point, like upright spears standing just below the surface of the water. You could hardly see them. Considering this was our favourite diving place (because it was so deep) it's a miracle we didn't impale ourselves on the posts. But we knew they were there and were extra careful, and dove between them.

With the emphasis on safety today, such boyhood pranks and pastimes would not be allowed now. And indeed, I've no doubt it was all very dangerous. But, like many things in life, great thrills go hand in hand with great risks and, in a way, it's a pity that most of today's youngsters are deprived of these natural adventures we enjoyed years past. Such boyhood escapades, linked to the disturbing emotions and vivid imaginations of the adolescent, albeit dangerous and at times downright frightening, nevertheless can produce a future generation rich in imagery and unafraid of exploring all things, within and with-out oneself.

The ramifications of The Old Mill reached far and wide, up and down the river and its tributaries. A complicated system of dams, ponds, sluice gates, lock gates, weirs and crude bridges and stepping stones had been contructed to stop, narrow, flood, ford and generally manipulate and control the river in various ways. I came onto the scene when modern methods of grinding corn were superceding the old mills. But like many other thinking people I stood and wondered at these complex and wondrous constructions built and operational only a few years before my time. The time, labour and skill, not forgetting the materials, taken to build them must have been immense. Were they built and operated by giants? Did they really once actually work? I would have loved to have seen them.

Another time our gang came across a fisherman's wooden hut by the river, miles from anywhere. These huts, locked and equipped with the bare necessities for survival, belonged to those well-off, licensed-for-fishing, city businessmen, who would use them perhaps two or three times a year, when they felt like a week-end's fishing in the country. My Grandad

CURRANT BREAD

Bateson owned most of the fishing rights, and rented stretches of the river out to these city slickers.

That evening, in our den in the Mill, a conference took place. One pal was ordered to procure milk, sugar and tea. Another had to supply bread and bacon and whatever else he could scrounge. I was designated to raid the local hen-houses for fresh eggs, because I was the smallest and could get in through the holes that the hens used (and because I could run the fastest if I was caught). Yes. We had it all planned.

My job was easy. I'd done it many times before. The worse part was getting my hands, knees and legs covered in yukky hen droppings as I crawled through the tiny door (and there's no muck more yukkier than chicken muck). But I didn't mind this: a dip in the river would soon wash that off.

This time the main problem was, the hens hadn't yet laid any eggs. Three were sitting, but, as any country dweller knows, hens are unpredictable creatures and take twice as long to lay if they are being watched. They are highly-strung and excitable birds, nervous and easily alarmed if you invade their space. I squatted for ages in the corner of the smelly hen-hut waiting and betting on which one of the three nervously clucking hens would oblige first. Evening was drawing nigh and I knew that the farmhand would soon be coming to collect any eggs and to shut up the chicken pens for the night. I might get locked in with the chickens. But I intended to have my self-cooked supper and do my bit for the gang, and I was eventually rewarded for my patience with three large, brown and warm bum fresh eggs which I conveyed proudly back to the hut.

No meal ever tasted quite so delicious (or was it our imaginations?) as that amateur fry-up on that cooling summer's evening in the old fisherman's hut on the banks of the River Blythe. The bacon was fried in rancid fat and burnt to a cinder in the old dirty rusty fry-pan, and the lovely fresh eggs were turned to leather by us inexperienced young hooligan cooks. The tea was made with river water laced with cow's piss and boiled over a candle in an old tin the fisherman had used for his maggots. Our stomachs then were made of iron and could take anything we flung into them. No luxury hotel meal could ever equal that stolen and illicit hotch-potch of a feast we young villains enjoyed that evening, no matter how prettily it was embellished, or how much it cost.

The River Blythe provided us with many pleasures as well as throwing up driftwood for the winter fires. The Old Mill had sprung from the source of the river's energies - a source of natural power. We paddled, swam and fished in its cool deep waters. Many times I have stood with bare feet on its round, hard, cold pebbles, while its twinkling waters tickled my ankles, and the minnows nibbled my toes. A strange delight in itself.

One balmy magic summer's day I stood alone amongst the reeds and waterlilies. Thigh deep in a cooler shaded spot, I watched rapt the iridescent metallic-blue dragonflies hovering and darting in this phantasmagorical Garden of Eden. It was a rare and only boyhood moment in a lifetime, when everything about me seemed to stand still, and I felt as though I didn't exist - as a body. I had become a part of everything around me: I had become a part of nature (which, of course, is what we were before we had debased ourselves by civilisation). I have heard of these out-of-the-body experiences spoken about, and I am not normally a mystical sort of person. But I know this happened to me.

It was not a feeling or an experience that one could create (like being in an artificial fair-ground wonderworld). It had to happen spontaneously. I was neither doing nor thinking anything in particular. I was watching nature, contemplating and dreaming.

Some years later I was to write a poem around this memory. It was printed in our school magazine:

While paddling in the river
On a hot and sunny day,
I saw a dragonfly,
Resting on a Lily leaf.

Its body long and shiny blue
Quivering and gleaming.
Its wings reflect its body hue.
A thing of natural beauty.

The coolness of the water
Soothed my aching feet,
And the beauty of that dragonfly
Made its sting less painful.

The corniness and the metre might upset the pundits, but it was my teenage attempt to recapture that magical moment in the boyhood of my youth.

CHAPTER 7

Helping out

There was a time when most village kids were cajoled into attending Sunday School whether they liked it or not. Maybe they still are for all I know.

It was a tacit, concerted effort by parent and village Vicar. It suited parents to get their off-springs out of the way for the afternoon: after a boozy morning and a large Sunday lunch, the parents liked nothing better than to get their feet up and read the News of the World, then have a well-earned snooze or a sex session (or both)! Their self-awarded reward for completing another long hard working-week. Of course, some of the parents went to church themselves. And it suited the Vicar whose job it was anyway to (try) to turn up-and-coming young rascals into religious pillars of society, if this were at all possible.

Like little Victorian choir-boys we were tarted up in our 'Sunday Best' and sent up the lane a mile away to Kingstone village church clutching our bibles, prayer books and attendance-record cards. As I've stated, ninety-nine per cent of my time was spent wearing 'play-clothes' and rambling the muddy fields and woods and I didn't like this dressing up business one little bit. The whole Sunday performance made me feel ill-at-ease, like a fish out of water. I was becoming a bit of a lone country-ranging Maverick and this smacked too much of control and conformity. The unfamiliar church atmosphere, cold, damp and musty and strangely silent; my friends and school pals turned into stuffy over-dressed mannequins, singing primitive dirges in odd falsetto voices; the robed, hooked-nosed and pale-faced Vicar presiding imperiously over us from his pulpit, sermonising and intoning meaningless quotes and veiled threats from the bible and by default from the mysterious God. It all made me feel uncomfortable and fidgety. Who was this enormous giant called God, who lived up in the sky beyond the clouds? How did the clouds support his weight? If he was so big, why didn't he fall through them and crash to earth like that Giant who fell from Jack's beanstalk? - that Giant made more sense to me. And who asked this God's only begotten Son to get himself crucified for us humans? Why did he do it? How was that supposed to help things? It didn't add up. These were the questions I really wanted answers to. I couldn't understand what it was all about and what I had done to deserve all this lecturing. I began to hate Sundays.

Whilst I pretended to join in this peculiar charade, I was more interested in the architecture of the church, and the huge stained glass windows. Mighty men, like Hercules, must have built these churches with their massive granite stones and high windows I thought (my mind was full of giants then). I studied the solid oak columns and arches and carvings, and wondered at the way the saints' haloes lit up in the coloured glass as the bright sun shone through the windows. Any diversion for this young boy to escape the intoned sermon lectures. I reasoned that as this was God's House, as the Vicar had sternly told us, and that the same God Almighty had also made and controlled the sun, then he must have had these pretty windows installed so that he could shine his sun through them to light up his glass saints and his Son's crucifixion, to create these beautiful illuminated pictures. Thinking along these lines, this God bloke started to earn my respect. Though why his son had to be crucified in order to achieve this effect, I couldn't fathom out (I questioned everything). Was the pain he must have suffered worth it?

I was not, and am still not, being facetious or taking the name of the Lord in vain. I am trying to point out that these things are often incomprehensible to small children, who tend to see things in simple terms which they understand.

To encourage our regular attendance, a brightly coloured religious stamp was merited each time we attended Sunday School, and stuck in our little stamp book. The stamps bore queer-looking pictures of doe-eyed saints in silly odd poses, standing sideways in silhouette. They also stood in kaleidoscopic coloured windows. They all seemed to be gazing in dreamy rhapsody at something in the far distance...were they looking at God? Thus I mused as I stood with my little opened hymn book, my rather weak and unwilling voice being drowned out by my more enthusiastic gustily singing peers.

Though I was becoming an acquisitive little devil, this free book of holy stamps seemed completely useless to me and also failed to inspire in me any feelings of religiousness, pride, or loyalty to the church. In truth, the opposite happened. I was proud of the missed spaces indicating non-attendance and resolved to collect more of these. As the parable of the sower said, the sowers' seed, in my case, was falling on stony ground and I was already becoming a lost cause and would probably bring forth no fruit. I simply didn't belong in church: I was very much a square peg in a round hole.

But, like most experiences, my enforced visits to the church were not entirely wasted. Every cloud has a silver lining and there is a grain of useful stuff to be found in most things. To avoid Sunday School I started 'helping out' at home on our farmstead,in earnest. When 'Em shouted "Michael! Come and get ready for Sunday School," I would make sure I was up to the ears in muck of some sort. I'd be cleaning out the pigs, or the cows, or the chicken pens. Anything rather than go to Church. This was how my crafty psychology developed. When Mrs Bateson called me I would not answer until she got impatient and had to come out and find me. Then I would say helpfully, "I'll just finish cleaning out the pigs" or whatever. My objective was to look useful and busy and waste time and be late, so that I would miss my pals on their way to Kingstone

Village Church. 'Em would see that I was busy (and very mucky) and, after all, I was saving her a hard and dirty job of work. It pays us to know how people think, in advance, and the earlier we cotton on to this, the quicker we can exploit it. It eventually became just too much trouble to find me, wash me, and dress me up in my Sunday Best...I was making myself indispensably useful. So the noble Sunday School idea eventually fizzled out; for me anyway. What's more, I began to almost enjoy work. It not only kept me away from Church, it relieved the boredom and improved my health and muscles, of which I was becoming increasingly more aware and proud of and kept 'testing' for hardness. And there was always plenty of work to do around our small farm.

We had a large variety of animals that had to be fed and watered and cleaned out. Geese, and ducks especially, have to be rounded up and fastened inside for the night as protection against dogs and foxes. Geese will stay near to the property but ducks will wander for miles in search of wide expanses of water, and they are rather stupid birds to bring home, staying out 'till dark and seeming not to know in which direction their home lies. Hens, on the other hand, are little trouble and most of them go naturally and instinctively to roost as the evening light begins to fade.

In the summer there was hay-making which is (or was then) a very hard and laborious process. Also, about this time, old Grandad Bateson, due to the loss of his arm, had passed on the running of the knackeryard to his eldest son Zac. With profits made from the slaughter business Grandad bought the Blythe Inn, which was a couple of hundred yards down the lane from our house.

Grandad also kept animals about the premises and I was required to help out with his goats, cattle, poultry, ferrets and general stock. If the cantankerous old man loved anything at all in life apart from eating all types of fish, meat and wildlife, it was his ferrets, of which he kept many. He went on rabbiting expeditions almost daily, carrying his ferrets in a sack in one hand, and his double-barrelled twelve-bore shot-gun in the crook of his other artificial hooked hand. All his ferrets had names. His favourite was called Smokey Joseph because of his smokey-streaked coarse yellow coat. Smokey Joseph was a tough, wiry writhey specimen that had been around for as long as I can remember: which was not hard for me to do as he had hung on to the end of my finger quite a few times with his needle-sharp teeth. As anyone who knows anything about ferrets is aware, you don't dislodge them easily once they decide to take a grip and sample the quality of your blood. They are used for catching rabbits, and this habit comes naturally to them.

Because of his disabled arm, and because he was always busy serving ale in the pub (and imbibing it himself) Grandad was glad of my unpaid and unsupervised help. In return I was given a toffee each morning before I went to school, and as many windfall apples as I could eat. It suited us both anyway, since I had long since learned to use my own initiative , and helped myself to fresh peas and beans, strawberries, currants and goosegogs from his garden...and later, cash from the pub till.

Grain husks (hops, a by-product from local breweries at Burton - a nearby Brewery Town) were delivered to the pub by the lorry load as winter feed for the cattle. On frosty mornings the large lorries tipped the still steaming hot piles of sweet-smelling grain husks in the pub yard. It was my job to barrow them in to the old pig-sties where they were stored, then shovel them into the building and firm them down hard by 'treading' them with my heavy farm boots. (It was sometimes better to use bare feet). This was an extremely hard, messy and smelly job. The grain was soggy, hot, stinking and gaseous, and very heavy. The ancient wheelbarrow I had to use was made of solid, thick oakwood with a clumsy metal-rimmed wooden wheel that had to be force-pushed through the deep rutted mud to the sties.

The barrow handles were so crude, rough and thick, my small blistered hands could hardly encompass them and I could barely lift and push the heavy, wobbling barrow-load of grain on the tortuous path to the distant sheds.

Despite all this, I slaved willingly, hour after long hour. At the sties the grain was flung inside through the low narrow door with special grain forks, and sometimes shovels. As the loose hops piled higher and yet higher and reached the roof, we went inside and 'trod the grain' with our studded boots. As the place filled up the space between grain and roof got smaller and smaller. It is similar to grape treading. This operation consolidated and compacted the grain, the dual purpose being to squeeze out the air to help preserve it throughout the winter, and to pack more grain in. The atmosphere inside the stuffy, ever-decreasing space was claustrophobic, though the dense steaming and pungent brewery smell was not unpleasant.

If you like the smell of beer, you'd enjoy the job of 'treading the grain'.

It was only later in life that I realised why I always felt light-headed and woozy doing this job: they were supposed to be spent fermented brewery hops, but obviously still had a lot of 'ferment' left in them! I could have been gassed in that small space, by beer fumes! But what a way to go!

As a small and, as yet, unmarinated youngster, I suppose I was getting sloshed on the fumes in that confined space. I was unknowingly getting drunk for free. No wonder I felt light-headed and extremely happy doing this particularly tiring job!

One day when I was barrowing grain-hops my eldest brother (Bob) visited me from Liverpool. This was an important and traumatic event and a milestone in my life the full story of which will emerge later. He took a turn with the barrow and as he wobbled across the yard through the mud, he was amazed. "How do you manage to push this bloody wheelbarrow?" he gasped. "I'm twice your age and I can hardly lift it". He was a soft towny you see, by profession a beach-photographer. He had rarely lifted anything heavier than his camera. He had his crisp gartered shirt sleeves down over white and flabby arms, while my sleeves had never been down in my life (I'd ripped most of them off anyway). My arms were deeply tanned, rock hard and muscular, as most country folks' are, or used to be before machinery did most of the work for them.

"Hugh! 'Seasy" I grunted. In truth, although it was hard work, I did it for six or seven hours a day, every day, I told him. I was used to it.

I had been toughened and forged in an adverse environ-ment in more ways than one. Not only were my muscles hardening, but so was my character. It was tough at the time, as all true life-lessons are, but it did me more good than harm in the long run.

The annual hay-making season was also hard labour. A mixture of crude machines and manual labour now harvested the corn and hay. Sometimes the machines - the mechanical mowers, rakes, and turners were drawn by horses, and sometimes by tractor. The process was in the transition stage. Many areas of grass were still hand-scythed and raked, turned and lifted by hand, a particularly skilled and tiring job that required great strength and physical endurance over long hours. A scythe is a peculiarly awkward tool in the hands of a novice. Farmers and contractors shared expensive equipment and machinery, and often helped out the smaller farmers and smallholdings. Paid labour was not shared as it had been years before, but casual labour could always be bought. The odd itinerate labourer still wandered the lanes and offered his help at various farms. These individuals vacillated between boozing their hard-earned money away at the pub, and offering their part-time services at the local farms, to replenish their booze money.

I spent many a blazing hot summer's day turning the swathes of drying grass with the large wooden hay-rake that was bigger than myself. Or forking the dry hay up into ricks or stacks with an equally large fork. The rough wooden handles rubbed and blistered my hands. It was sweaty and thirsty work. Jugs of lemonade, cold tea, or beer were available most of the time.

After a day in the hayfields, cows still had to be fed and milked, and dairy utensils washed and sterilised. Then the ducks and fowl had to be rounded up and penned for the night. Then finally, late in the evening, everyone sat down to piles of sandwiches of thick slices of home-made bread, filled with home-cured ham or cheese, followed by apple or wild-blackberry pie and fresh farm cream, and all washed down with the seemingly bottomless jug of ale.

About this time the insobrient village Blacksmith, Mr Smith, popped his clogs and disappeared into history along with his forge and anvil...and shortly afterwards most of the village cart-horses went too because there was no Blacksmith to shoe them, and tractors were taking their jobs. Mr and Mrs Mould (the Mouldies, as we cruel kids dubbed them) the village shopkeepers, who, until now had sold all manner of things from their small cottage-cum-shop, were rapidly prospering and needed more room. They bought The Old Smithy, tossed the anvil into a stagnant pond at the rear of the place and converted the Smithy into a proper shop, complete with a large window to display their wares. A little later they extended the place and had built the latest thing in brick bakery ovens at the rear of the building.

The enterprising Moulds, living just across the road from us, were very welcome and transformed the hamlet into a busy meeting place, as villagers came from miles around to buy cigarettes, sweets, fresh bread and cakes and many other things not normally available in the country. It was incidental that they also transformed my life, as I was soon doing jobs for them for pocket money. And they were nice folk, if a bit eccentric.

On baking days, the smell of fresh bread now wafted through the village, and tempted in shoppers to sample their tasty and luxurious fresh baked bread and cream cakes.

I soon discovered that old Harry Mould, a jolly, likeable soul, would actually pay real money for my labour (a thing I had never received from the economical Bateson family). At first, along with a couple of cream cakes, the odd shilling was slipped into my grateful hand. As I made myself more and more useful to them and spent more time on their premises helping out, they started paying me a regular generous weekly sum. From a bob to a florin, from a florin to half-a-crown, and eventually to five bob. In retrospect I think it was very good of them: they were the first people to make me realise a good job of work could equal a good regular income ...which opened many doors to a kid who, previously, had never even received pocket money.

I retain deep and fond memories and feelings for this couple, especially for Old Harry. He was kind and always had a twinkle in his eye, and time for me. I think he was manipulated and urged into being a go-getter by his wife for, as long as he could have a cigarette and a laugh with the village kids, he seemed happy enough as he was.

To my lasting shame - and for which in this narrative I now belatedly confess and ask forgiveness - I later abused their kindness by breaking into their shop.

Like a complicated piece of embroidery, a thread runs through our lives linking certain thoughts, events, and emotions together: the end result is ourselves: how we feel, what we think, what we do and who we are. Hating Sunday School had turned me on to hard work, and hard work turned me into a robust boy with a healthy appetite for fresh air and more hard work: and that brought money. The down-side (in modern parlance) I suppose, is that God missed out on me (or did I miss out on God?). If I'd liked Sunday School I might have stayed a weedy little fellow who couldn't and wouldn't push a barrowload of grain! Still, I never lost my admiration for those beautiful stained glass windows in God's house, so my church experience wasn't totally a waste of time.

CHAPTER 8

Old Harry

A Jam tart in the trousers of Micky,
Just out of sight of Old Tricky,
They're for his lunch,
He could eat a whole bunch,
But they make his Dicky a bit sticky.

If I'd been asked to write an epitaph for the tombstone of Old Harry Mould, our village Baker, the above ditty could not have been bettered. After the Blacksmith had gone, Harry and his money-mad thick-speced myopic wife became our over-the-road neighbours. He wrote this ditty for me when I was about twelve year's old. He must have known I was pinching his jam tarts, and...true, often concealing them in my trousers pockets!

Old Harry used to love joking and talking to us gaggle of kids who gathered outside his village shop window each morning waiting for the school bus. If we had any money it was here we set ourselves up with sweets, cakes and lemonade, to pop into our lunch bags and satchels. If we were skint - which was more usual - and Old Mother Mould 'The Missis' wasn't around to watch him, Harry would hand out free sweets, or 'kahlie' (Lemonade powder) which we either sucked through a straw, or dabbed with our spit-moistened fingers (but, strangely enough, was pretty hopeless for making lemonade). There were also real wood liquorice sticks around at the time, which you chewed like tobacco into a soggy mess, and dipped them in the kahlie too if you liked the taste.

Harry was a larger-than-life tuck shop owner, straight from the cartoon strips of your favourite comic. With jolly, wobbly, fat and unshaven, rosy-cheeked and lumpy potato face, embedded always with a puffing ciggy, his chuckles and coughing intermingled with the ting of the shop-till as he searchd the clinking coins for change. To complete his Desperate Dan appearance, his flour-dusted striped shirt and large overflowing belly was barely contained by his twangy braces, holding up his extra-large flour-grubby flannel trousers. You felt tempted to punch his cartoon-like belly like a sack of flour, just to see the flour-dust fly up.

Although many of us kids pinched things from his shop, in our own cruel kid-like way we loved him because he was always jolly, and he loved us kids.

His wife Molly, known to us kids only as 'Mouldy's Missis' was just the opposite to her old man,in everything but size that is (she was even fatter - was it all the left over cakes they ate?). Her presence was rarely seen, but often felt, through Harry's jumpy behaviour. He had to keep a wary eye open over his shoulder as she frowned on his easy-going generosity and chain-smoking ways, nagging him constantly to refrain from these habits. She was the brains behind the prosperous bakery money-making machine, and therefore very prudent to boot.

This explains why Harry always seemed to be lighting a cigarette on his coughing and bumbling way to answer the shop door bell: he had to snatch this opportunity away from his Missis to light up. He had to sneak the odd cigarette whenever he could. It also explains why he spent hours sitting in the outside loo: he wasn't constipated, he simply wanted a smoke, in peace. Incidentally, he died coughing in a cloud of smoke, sitting on the loo. The local rapscallions robbed Mouldy's shop rotten: to them it seemed a great wheeze. I was always amazed at their brazeness, nerve and cheek, though modern tearaways easily excel in their audacious criminality. Every self-respecting young nicker knew then that old shop doorbells were notoriously unreliable, and it was easy to put them out of action anyway. The distance from Harry's living room, through the kitchen and bakery, to the shop - with a warning splutter and cough on the way as he lit up, and with his enormous belly not helping either, took him so long it was possible to hoist yourself over the counter and to get back again with the loot, before he appeared in the shop proper, still coughing and blinking through his thick specs and a cloud of cigarette smoke. Looking back, life must have been hard at that time for him.

You went in the shop ostensibly for something really cheap like a penny bullseye or even for something you knew they hadn't got. You could hear old Harry coming every inch of the way. Kids are amazingly athletic and quick (and mischievous) at a certain age. If it were sweets you were targeting, whilst listening carefully, you had time to unscrew the toffee-jars that stood on the counter, reach in and take whatever sticky toffees or lollipops you could get, and stuff them into your pocket. Thus came about Harry's rhyme "A jam tart in the trousers of Micky". We'd pinch anything we could lay our hands on. Kids can be such perverse little devils. I'm sure most of the thrill was just getting away with it.

If the shop door-bell had broken down completely, or if the rogues had disabled it, the word soon spread round the village grapevine. "The shop doorbell's gone" we would tell each other surreptitiously. Then the dare-devils among us would walk straight in barefacedly, and take whatever we liked at our leisure. When many of the gang were reaching their teenage years, they went for cigarettes rather than sweets. The cigarettes were kept at the back of the shop and they had to vault the counter and trail among the shelves to find them. But otherwise they took anything they could get. The human species is acquisitive from the day they are born. This is all very reprehensible I know, and moralists may frown; but it has gone on since time began and how do you stop it?

I had good role-models (or bad, depending on what side of the counter you were on!) and joined in the thieving willingly. Indeed, it went on for a number of years, and got quite sophisticated and more ambitious, which roguery is inclined to do. I am neither proud nor particularly ashamed of this confession. This is supposed to be a true account of my growing years. If I leave out the bad bits or falsify, it will be untrue and a waste of time. This mischief seemed fun and clever at the time, and only looks serious in retrospect, from an adult's point of view...or if you were caught!

Of Old Mother Mould I remember very little. As noted, she was the driving force behind the flourishing business and naturally very cash conscious and whispered as a miser by the local populace. She was probably merely a careful business woman and the gossips maybe were jealous. She was fatter even than Harry, half-blind, and bad on her feet - which meant she had to shuffle and took longer to reach the shop than her husband and was therefore easier to hoodwink or rob. That said, she baked the most delicious cakes and pastries I have ever tasted. She had an odd habit of sitting in full view of passers-by and neighbours, in her bedroom window each evening, counting the large pile of silver and copper takings of the day, out on the window-cill. You could set the clock by the glint from her thick-lensed spectacles and the chink and flash of silver coins piled in neat rows on the cill in the low bright evening sunlight. She wouldn't do it today or the villains would soon be in.

I suspect, like many small businesses in those days, she found she was making undreamed of profits hand over fist (despite us thieving rob-dogs) and was making it faster than she could count or spend it. It must have gone to her head. When she counted her money in the window, she didn't realise half the village was watching her. It was probably this silly habit that got her her miser reputation.

It was a shame that for the Moulds (and for many like them, before and since) it was all happening too late. They were getting on in years and Harry was killing himself with his smoking. They were both grossly overweight, overworked, and, yes, over-excited with their burgeoning wealth. They would soon take their first holiday in years but it would be too late to save them. As often happens neither of them lived long enough to enjoy the fruits of their labours.

They had started by selling the usual small confectionary items, like chocolate, sweets and cigarettes. To augment their stock and takings, they began to bake small quantities of cakes, jam-tarts and other delicacies in their small cottage-cum-shop ovens. They were both talented pastry cooks and their products were so delicious and in such demand they bought the Old Blacksmith's shop and had a large custom-made oven installed. It all took off from there. The reputation of their scrumptious bread and cakes spread far and wide. Remember, this was a small village shop, surrounded by widespread farms and villages: many of these people couldn't get to the shops then. So Moulds had a monopoly. They bought a van and hired a driver-salesman. The countryside was their golden oyster.

It is only now, when I review my life, with an experienced mellowing and a more understanding adult's vision, that I realise how desperately hard the Moulds must have worked to achieve what they did. All I can remember thinking, as a kid, was how tasty those fresh hot jam tarts, puff buns, cream-horns and cakes were then!

As pre-told the Moulds were very good to me. I helped them by lighting and stoking the bakery oven fires, and cleaning out the ashes from the flues.

The day before baking commenced I would be asked to light the fires under the large brick ovens, to get them ready heated for the following day's baking. Over the baking period I kept the fires glowing red hot, cleaned out the flues, got in and stacked sticks, logs, coal and coke and did many other small jobs around the place. I suppose I was what is known today as The Oven/come odd-job-man...or boy.

In those days such businesses (like the slaughterhouse) weren't governed by strict health, safety and hygiene rules and regulations like they are now. In any case, regulations where easily flaunted in country cottage industries then. The cleanliness of such establishments left a lot to be desired (and that's an understatement!). For instance, at the rear of the bakery was a seemingly bottomless stagnant pond, or bog, overgrown with weeds and algae, inhabited by rats, frogs, frogspawn and other peculiar denizens of pond life and, in summer, canopied by swarms of flies and gnats.

It was a dangerous magnet for curious youngsters like myself and I slipped into its slimy, murky waters more than once. I was told to throw the ashes from the ovens into this bog. And garbage from the house, bakery and shop was also tossed willy-nilly into its depths. Moulds had an obsession to fill it in. Anything from unsold outdated and blown tinned goods, to mouldy cheese, fruit, bread and cakes, and even flood-damaged cigarettes and sacks of flour were thrown in. (I dried out and tried my first flavoursome cigarettes from this bog, no wonder I didn't take up smoking!). Inevitably the stench, rats and vermin proliferated. They say where there's muck there's money. As the Mould's grew wealthier they could afford to have this cesspit filled in. As it turned out, it was easier said than done.

But it suited me. This job kept me occupied and earning money for many a year. Lorry loads of hardcore and rubble, and years of ashes from the oven-flues, were tipped into this pond and I had to rake and level it out. But that pond seemed bottomless and unfillable so any rubbish that anyone wanted to get rid of was welcomed. It became the local tip. Like an insatiable monster it swallowed up old prams, bikes, tin-baths and what-have-you? Anything that went in sunk immediately to its unfathomable depths. We could not understand where it was all going. Load after load, year after year, and still the filthy waters rose and the stench pervaded the village and vied with the smell of the fresh bread, which wasn't doing the trade any favours either.

For all I know they are still trying to fill it in today!

Those murky soupy waters gave me nightmares that swirl up even in occasional dreams today. It is another strand in the chequered tapestry of my past. And in the dark waters float the faces of dear Old Harry and, lurking behind, the even fainter and ghostlier phantasm of his sad and lesser-known miser Missis, Molly, still counting her money.

The Mould's speciality was cob-loaf, more crust than bread. A chunk of this, baked fresh on the day and spread thick with our own freshly-made home-churned butter and strawberry jam, and eaten outside behind the shed sitting on a log in the sun, was as near to paradise as I got in those days (or since). Except for the excited strawberry-jam seeking wasps of course, who also knew a good thing when they saw it!

The newly employed van-salesman was named Gerald. About ten-o-clock in the morning I helped him load the still warm trays of bread and cakes into his van. I was to accompany him on his long journeys round the highways and byways of the country lanes to isolated farms, cottages and villages. Housewives would come swarming, attracted like followers of the Pied Piper, as we entered and drew up in the village, opened up the van doors, and let the smell of the freshy baked goodies pervade the village street. Gerald liked a good natter, and carried the local gossip from one house and one locality to the next, bringing scandal, gossip and cream cakes all in one go. And he also fancied himself as a bit of a ladies' man. He had a few fancy women dotted about I think. At these houses he discouraged me from helping him carry the large, heavy bread baskets across the fields to distant farms and I wondered why. I surmised he might be getting up to some hanky-panky but I don't blame him. The thing was, he left me sitting bored to tears in the van, in the lane, for ages, with nothing to do but listen to the birds singing in the hedgerows.

I had my revenge though...

Bored and hungry I would raid the back of the van for the best goodies. Many's the time I've seen him returning from across the fields over the brow of a grassy pathless hill, with a satisfied smile on his face. I'd have half a cream-horn sticking out of my mouth and I'd be chewing furiously. My lips would be covered with jam and cream.

It was a race between me stuffing the rest of the cake down my throat and him reaching the van. I'd had plenty of practice at scoffing nicked cakes, so I usually won the race. You can't beat young kids for fast eating. I think he knew I was pinching his cakes, and also that I was aware of his hanky-panky (he was a married man). So, like many situations in life, we both knew what each was up to and it suited us both to maintain a discreet silence about it. A sort of mutual unspoken understood blackmail.

A few months later Harry Mould and his Missis decided to take their one and only holiday, and shut the shop up for a couple of weeks. They had certainly deserved it. I was now in my early teens and I suppose the degree of mischief me and my mates got up to was also getting more ambitious and serious. I blush to admit, to my everlasting shame, that two of us broke into the bakery and took various bits of money, cigarettes and chocolate.

This accounts for my burst of shame and remorse earlier when I was writing of my old pal Harry. The police were called in and we were eventually identified as the culprits...and we ran away from home. But that's another story in itself.

CHAPTER 9

The Slaughterhouse/Animal Belsen

Here I would advise any reader who might be hoping for a romanticised account of my younger days and who may be a bit squeamish, to give this chapter a miss. It will be brutally frank and honest (as, I hope, is the rest of my story) and will contain grphic scenes from the uglier and more unpleasant sides of my early life. Bateson's slaughterhouse, where I spent many days at a very early age, left a deep and lasting impression on me and, like many traumatic experiences, has indelibly imprinted itself into my psyche. It is clearly a part of my story. It is part of me and therefore needs to be included.

As stated earlier, it was founded by my (adoptive?) Grandad, Old Bill (William) Bateson, who had spawned the entire Bateson clan. Widespread and successful both generatively and in business, the frugal Bateson family eventually owned many of the properties in the Village of Blythe Bridge: The Blythe Inn, The Slaughterhouse, The Old Mill, and the old Wheelwright's place that was my home, and various other houses and cottages dotted around the area. The golden spring from whence sprung the wherewithal for all these landed assets, was the slaughterhouse. So it can safely be said that hundreds of animals had paid for this human affluence with their suffering, with their lives, and finally with their bodies. But what's new? And I suppose someone had to do it.

It has to be said, that at this time, animals were merely dispensable commercial commodities. The ethics and questions of animal cruelty or welfare, and indeed, the linking of meat and fat etc to ill health and heart disease in human beings, had scarcely been thought of. It was taken for granted that animals were killed either because they were sick or unwanted, or required for food, or because they were considered pests, or even for fun and entertainment (many people still think like this). The attitude and the feelings of those who killed, towards their victims, was left to the individual: it simply didn't matter, as only the animals suffered, and they couldn't complain. Like now, some people killed in a disinterested, off-hand, professional manner; some with distaste; some killed as kindly as possible under the circumstances, and a few killed, as they always have and always will, with sadistic relish and enjoyment. It is almost impossible to change human nature.

Grandad Bateson, the original slaughterman, was one of that dying breed of old-timers, the macho-patriarch. Deeply respected and revered by the whole family, toughened, wizened and hardened by old-time austerity, he faced life with a bottle of whisky, a chew of twist (chewing tobacco) and a spittoon. And plenty of meat. During his slaughterhouse days he had pierced his wrist with a steel (the pointed tool used by butchers for sharpening their knives). And eventually, after septicaemia had set in, first his hand, then his arm, was amputated. A bitter blow - for an enterprising old man who had spent most his life slaughtering animals and roaming the fields pot-shooting at any sort of wild-life. But, no doubt, a poetic-justice relief to the animals he had abused.

I must remark that, as a newcomer - an interloper so to speak - into this tight-knit and rather inbred and claustrophobic family clique, I obviously neither felt, nor obeyed, or even understood, the unspoken understanding underlying the respect the family had for old Grandad Bateson and his standing as the head of the family. He was a bit like the Dom in the Mafia. Like a pebble, I had been thrown into the middle of this mixture of loyalties, and the ripples I caused must have upset things a bit. Perhaps this lack of respect was why Grandad seemed to dislike me from the start, either that or he was just a naturally grumpy old sod. Many Grandads are grumpy just because they are old, not because they don't like people. I can understand this now I am a grumpy old Grandad myself! (altho I try not to appear as such). It was all new to me then. This is why many kids have no respect for their elders. It isn't that they consciously want to show disrespect, they simply do not understand the concept of respect. It is the old breakdown of communication and lack of understanding between the generations.

Be that as it may: old Grandad Bateson now owned and kept the village pub, The Blythe Inn, and his wayward eldest son Zac ran the knackeryard for him. They were all characters -like characters in a novel - in their own way. Zac was the good-looking, beer-swilling village play-boy type, who was the main topic of salacious gossip in the village. He was notorious for his womanising. He seemed to enjoy being the village scoundrel, and the village obviously enjoyed talking about him, though personally I don't think he got up to half the things 'Em accused him of doing.

My questionable mentor, Mrs Emily Bateson, who was married to Henry, the youngest of the Bateson brothers, obviously hated her husband's amoral maverick brother Zac who brought the family's name into disrepute. Old Grandad Bateson, like many parents, indulged his eldest son like a naughty but spoilt child, and was probably grudgingly proud of his son's aptitude for putting it around (as they say today). It does happen. Perhaps Grandad was the same in his younger days - I wouldn't know: it was before my time. But he had obviously had a stack of offspring himself.

Where did my own thoughts and feelings stand on the subject of this village villain, my Uncle Zac? Kids are strange and unpredictable when it comes to such things and have their own, mostly hidden, feelings about them. I had an odd sneaking respect for my Uncle Zac even though I never really knew him personally, nor him me - we had just heard about each other in incidental gossip, especially from 'Em to me.

Perhaps I felt a kinship for him inasmuch as I felt we were both viewed as baddies by 'Em, and were sort of pariahs, family outcasts. I liked him maybe, because I didn't like 'Em. But there was another, more mercenary reason why I liked him. Read on.

Therefore, when 'Em confided in me about Zac's latest scandalous behaviour I would think "So what? Why don't you mind your own business. The best of luck to him. At least he's enjoying himself and taking no notice of nagger's and nosy gossips like you". I also used to think, well, if it wasn't for 'Em I wouldn't have known this scandalous behaviour was taking place anyway, or even that it was considered scandalous to behave like that. Gossips can educate you. So it's a good job she did confide such carryings on to me, otherwise I'd have known nothing! It is one of life's ironies that gossips, in the very nature of things, know all there is to know of what is going on: while quiet people, who don't interfere and keep themselves to themselves, and are therefore deemed more polite and discreet, often don't get to hear anything.

One Sunday afternoon, Uncle Zac, going home half-sozzled from the Blythe Inn in his large gleaming Alvis car, happened to pass a little boy pushing a heavy wheel-barrow piled high with weighty sacks of grain. It was me. He stopped, leaned out, and pressed two half-crowns into my sweaty palm. He mumbled, almost apologetically "Here" and drove off (none too safely I might add). Half-crowns, at that time, being large and heavy high-demonination coins, felt like pirate's golden doubloons to me, making me feel very rich. It was the most I had ever had then, and I never forgot this spontaneous, inexplicable and generous act of kindness. Or was it some sort of subliminal conscience on his part, a Freudian gesture, to make an effort at atonement for his latest lapse in getting drunk on a Sunday afternoon? Or even a symbolic poke in the eye for 'Em? It didn't really matter to me what it was: I was five bob the richer, and it was also one up on 'Em as, obviously, I wouldn't tell her what had happened. I didn't understand then that well-inebriated insobrients do this sort of thing anyway, whether they're kind, evil, libertines or indifferent or what. It is no doubt that it was this questionable act that earned my sneaking but misplaced respect for my Uncle Zac. Kids are easily won over by generous and especially unexpected surprise gifts of hard cash. Thus are our opinions of people formed when we are very young mercenary little baskets.

No wonder 'Em didn't like Zac. He was enjoying himself with wine, woman and song, and squandering the family fortune, while her docile hubby Henry slaved away at the slaughterhouse to earn it. As mentioned, her husband Henry was a happy-go-lucky, simple type of soul, extremely hardworking and reliable, but under his wife's thumb. She honestly didn't deserve such a man. She often referred to him as "The salt of the earth" whatever that meant.

At an early age I often accompanied Henry on his daily stride to the slaughterhouse. It got me out of 'Em's way while she bull-shitted the house and it kept me occupied. I didn't mind. I say "stride" because Henry (I should really call him Dad but, again, couldn't, and never did) jauntily strode along whistling as I ran alongside trying to keep up with him. Alongside my heels panted Rip, our short-haired, short-legged, bad-tempered terrier. I helped out in the slaughterhouse. At this young age I dispassionately swilled away down the drains the warm steaming blood from the slaughtered beasts, or carried away offal in bucket or barrow to be dumped in a heap at the back of the sheds. Offal was wasted then, but later utilised as a by-product. Here, in the woods at the back of the sheds, massive mounds of rotting flesh and useless smaller carcasses of cats and dogs etc had been dumped over the years...finally congealing into a mountain of sunbaked solid mass, heaving with a subterranean city of huge, tunnelling rats. I warned you it was gruesome.

Today there are, thank God, Animal Rights protesters who are trying to stop this kind of unnecessary cruelty. But what happens today is obviously not a patch on what happened to animals years ago when no-one gave a toss what happened to God's creatures. But, I don't know - animals then usually lived out their lives in open fields and ate healthy natural grass and corn, untreated by artificial fertilizers and chemicals, although their deaths were stark and barbaric. With modern battery and intensive methods, and artificial foods, drugs and suchlike, the cruelty is more refined. And so are their factory-farm deaths. On balance, nothing has changed. It has probably got worse.

Many times, as a kid, I have watched a beast being dragged into a corner, where a man with a pole-axe waited to whop him between the horns. The animal's eyes would be wide and bulging with terror (and cows have big, expressive eyes) as he was dragged with ropes and by his horns to his inevitable death. He would struggle and throw his head from side to side and stiffen his legs trying to find a grip on the blood-slimy floor to stop his slide into the corner of death. Here waited Henry, simple Henry, the strongest and kindest of men, to bring down the blunt side of the axe with all his strength and force between the horns of the petrified cow. It was his job.

I can not recall being aware of any feelings of pity or horror myself at that age as I witnessed this daily slaughter. That would come later. I was merely an interested youngster, or bystander. I was too young to understand and took it all for granted. This was the world I had found myself in, and this is what grown-ups did for a living. At this age kids do not question the world around them. This is why I was later sought out in the village for killing the Christmas goose, or any other unwanted or sick animal, from litters of kittens to ferrets. It never affected me. I could kill then with the cold detachment of a housewife swatting a fly. It was just a pocket-money job.

With the fall of the axe and a dull thud, the cow's legs would buckle under him and down the heavy beast would crash on to the blood-soaked concrete floor. Not dead but merely stunned unconscious. The slaughtermen had to work at speed to cope with the day's workload. There were no electric stunners or humane killing contraptions then. Within minutes the stunned beast was hoisted, swollen rotund belly exposed, and lashed by two legs to a swinging beam hanging on chains. With a sharpening steel hanging in a leather holster at his belt, and with a steel hook in one hand and a constantly sharpened ultra-sharp knife in the other, the slaughterman would slit the beast's throat and the hot streams of thick blood would spurt forth, and spread like a flood over the sloping floor of the shed, oozing its way towards the drain in the corner.

Then the cow's belly would be laid open, and his steaming entrails removed with a deft flick of the hook and slung skidding across the slippery floor to squelch into a steaming wobbly pile in another corner. Meanwhile I was running around with buckets of water and a brush, trying to guide the rivers of fresh-smelling blood towards the drains, while the zing of the knives on the sharpening steels (the very same that took Grandad's arm) keen-edged the blade still further, to expertly strip the cow's hide from his bloodied torso.

The ramshackle zinc and wood-built knackeryard buildings were situated in the middle of a sloping, beautiful blackberry wood. The blood from the open drains emerged from the rear of the buildings and ran down among the bushes, brambles, shrubs and birch trees. Blood is full of nitrogen and the blackberries nearest the place, that soaked up the first flood of blood, gave forth the biggest and juiciest fruits. In high summer a strange incessant buzzing or droning sound caused wandering (and wondering) blackberry pickers to pause, sniff the pungent air, and prick up their ears. No wonder...they were sniffing the nauseous smells of rotting flesh. And the strange humming music was the grateful song of the clouds of millions of abnormally large bluebottles that buzzed excitedly over the bounteous cornucopia of their favourite food, where they also laid their pupae that would later turn into a seething mountain of maggots.

The business' profits were made in various ways. Much of the meat came from diseased cows and was unfit for human consumption (although it was often eaten anyway , but must have been very risky). Most of the meat was simmered in giant copper boilers. I made my way ankle deep through a thick lake of greasy fleshslime and, being small, stood on an old drum to stir this hideous ogre's broth in the cauldrons. I could have fallen in. Then it was sold as dog-food to foxhound kennels and suchlike. Rare, good meat from injured casualties was OK to eat and choice cuts were distributed liberally around the Bateson family. Owners of injured, old or diseased pets often asked for help from the so-called experts. Little did they know the fate that awaited their adored animals. Their pitiful little skeletal corpses could be found weeks later slung unceremoniously among other bits and pieces of indescribable and unwanted material on the heaps behind the sheds. Many of the Bateson's suffered from tuberculosis, which was a common cattle disease at that time. It was supposed to be a hereditary family disease and, as far as I know, no-one had linked it to the fact that all the Batesons had lived among and partaken of large quantities of knacker meat all their lives. Did they get it from eating the waste meat from the slaughterhouse? It makes you wonder. If they did, I would call it Poetic Justice or, The Animals' Revenge.

Animals could meet their deaths in strange ways. Some would swallow barbed wire, and some might get trapped in mud during floods and drown. I went with Henry Bateson late one night when he and the other men were called out this stormy evening in response to a worried farmer's request for assistance with a cow that had been struck by lightning.

The poor beast had been sheltering under a large solitary tree in the middle of a field (the worst place to go in a storm). The lightning had struck and cleft the tree and had partly entombed the cow.

Lightning plays funny tricks. Amazingly the animal's head was jammed deep among the roots of the leaning riven tree, and it was bellowing piteously. Phlegm and saliva and mud bubbled through its nostrils as it tried to avoid being suffocated. The rain was pelting down, the earth was turning to mud, and strong winds were trying to fully flatten the tree. It was a dangerous situation.

After a hurried debate it was decided there was little hope of getting the cow out alive, but they would try. In the pouring rain and scudding thunder clouds a tractor was brought and they tried to pull the animal free, nearly pulling the poor beast's head off in the process. We can avert our eyes and plug our hearing and other senses from such horrific incidents such as these, but how does that help? It is no use pretending such things don't happen. Somebody has to face them and sort them out. And in the same wise all of us should at least acknowledge the frightening levels of horror in this world, which one day might need our help, consideration and compassion. After all, but for the grace of God, there, maybe, go we.

If the slaughterhouse workers were too busy to deal with a live animal immediately it was turned loose in the surrounding scrub and woodland, to be dealt with later. Many of these animals were ill or injured and were deteriorating rapidly. I came across one of these poor sick creatures on a summer ramble through the woods. He had collapsed or fallen into a muddy ditch and had been overlooked or forgotten. Gasping for breath, his rheum and dirt-blocked nose snorted bubbles in the vile ditch water. Little me couldn't get my arms around his broad neck to lift his heavy head clear of the mire and on to dry ground. I did manage to turn his head towards the sky, and unblocked his nose as best I could. At least he could contemplate where he would soon be going (if there is a cow-heaven that is). I would tell the slaughtermen about him as soon as I saw them.

Some days later I passed that way again. He had fallen back into the ditch and was, blessedly, dead. Over the following months I passed his corpse many times. The elements - the wind and sun and rain (and the maggots) had done their natural job - and, as Shakespeare so poetically put it, the corpse had changed into something rich and strange. I felt an affinity with this poor creature, and that night offered up a childlike silent prayer for him. I felt we both had been alone, abandoned and forgotten. His misery at least had ended. I still had a long way to go.

Rip, our stocky and stubborn little terrier, would sometimes leave me and Mr Bateson working at the knackeryard and return home early on his own. Halfway through the morning he could be observed struggling back down Blythe Bridge Bank dragging, maybe, a sheep's head, or a cow's leg, twice his size and weight. Puffing and panting strenuously as only dogs can, he would drag it a few feet, then stop to rest. After glancing warily around to check whether anyone was going to pinch his sheep's head, he would drag it another few feet, then rest again. As I've said, he was a stubborn little tyke. It might take him hours to travel the short distance from the knackeryard to our home at Blythe Bridge, but he wouldn't give up. He'd get there in the end.

Sheep's heads and various kinds of chunks of filthy rotting meat were buried all over our smallholding. Rip would leave them there for months, and seemed to have forgotten where he'd buried them. Sometimes, while riddling coal-waste, I'd unearth one of these gruesome doggy treasures, stinking and covered in coal-slack. If Rip was nearby he'd try to snatch them from me, as if to say "give me that. It's mine", and we'd play tug-of-war with it. I didn't really want him to eat such dirty offal - or bury it again.

And he hadn't forgotten where he'd buried them either. One day, as if his memory was set with a natural time-switch, triggered by hunger pains, he'd home in on them as if by radar and laboriously dig them up. They'd be soft and white with decomposition and covered with a crunchy coal-slack coating and would fall to pieces like an over-cooked turkey, but he seemed to relish them all the better for that. And they never seemed to do him any harm either. It must have been his doggy way of cooking them.

Later, approaching noon and dinner-time, also with hunger pains and bodyclock alarms ringing in the form of a rumbling tummy, I too would appear trundling down the same bank cocking my nose like a Bisto kid trying to catch a whiff of what 'Em was cooking for dinner. I wouldn't be dragging a sheep's head but quite possibly carrying a cow's tongue sent by Henry Bateson for 'Em to process into pressed tongue to put on our tea-time salads or in my school dinner sandwiches.

At last, towards late evening, as the sun was sinking in the West, Henry would appear round the corner, coming down the bank and swinging his arms in his usual energetic, cheery and jaunty fashion. He would be whistling or humming his favourite tune "Don't laugh at me because I'm a fool". He only knew the one line and sang it over and over again. Although dog-tired and worn out by his heavy day at the slaughterhouse, and despite facing yet another long evening's work seeing to the livestock on our little farm, he remained forever cheerful and chirpy: "The salt of the earth" and a tribute to the human race.

Handbags made of calfskin were, at this time, in fashion. Knowing we dealt as knackerers, our city visitors asked if I could provide a clean and cured, nicely patterned skin. This was a challenge. Ever looking for ways of relieving them of the contents of their seemingly bottomless wallets and purses, and of making myself some dosh, I said I'd have a go. Bringing home a slimy raw calfskin from the yard I genned up on the process in a library book, and attempted to 'cure' the skin. I recall it required salt-petre and stretching on a rack to dry in the sun, and hours of tedious scraping to remove residues of fat and flesh.

It was not one of my more impressive successes, and must have ended up as a rather smelly handbag, but you must give me credit for trying...

I was now beginning to look for ways of earning more money, and was willing to try my hand at almost anything...

CHAPTER 10

Making dosh

It occurred me at quite an early age that money could - and indeed must - be obtained in many ways. The worrying war years were responsible for this premature realisation: it was a time of chronic shortages, especially of fresh country products, and meat, and a rampart black market developed throughout the land. Many people were struggling to survive and to make ends meet.

I have already confessed I filched coins from Tommy Bateson's money-box. Also that I joined in the mischievous plundering from Old Harry's village stores. And later, I was to jangle Grandad's pub's till for the odd florin. So you see, I had various sources to winkle cash from (some people would call it enterprise!). But these were petty, dangerous and unsustainable sources of income. It soon became apparent to me that if I wanted a regular supply of dosh, I would have to work for it, and earn my money in as honest a way as I knew how. All this is common sense, and we all realise it sooner or later (or should do).

I had my little job at Mould's Bakery but, like most youngsters I was spending my money quicker than I was earning it. All our lives the vast majority of us seem to be walking a financial tightrope, or treadmill. The more we earn, the more we need. Sharp youngsters soon realise (often with a sudden shock) that they have been born into a vicious dog eat dog society and must buckle to and do something about it, and damned quick.

To fight their own corner in life. To survive. We can tend to think this frightening realisation is peculiar to us only, as an individual. But sooner or later, it happens to all of us, and it is this fear that keeps the wheels of commerce turning, and even on which civilisation is built.

My half-cured calf skin wasn't a total success, but I sold it all the same. I purified it in the sun and fresh air so that for a week or two it wouldn't smell or rot. Appearances are everything in the market place. Spivs, at this time, where cheating other Spivs. It was a matter of who could outspiv who.

Following my failed attempt to cure the skin, I tried various other enterprises, with varying degrees of success and failure.

The posh spivvy folks who visited us at week-ends from Birmingham were a useful source of pocket money. Billy Bunting got his money-box donation each visit, for doing nothing. But Michael, the evacuee boy, had to supply some goods. I suppose this was partly why I robbed his money box. Pure jealousy and spite, really.

These well-dressed and mysterious friends seemed to appear from nowhere at the outset of the war, and disappeared just as quickly at the onset of peace. I didn't mind. They had two cracking, pretty daughters. One was to become my first love, and broke my heart as first loves almost always do - though she wasn't aware of it at the time. It was her seeming innocence, lovely smile, and girlish giggle that got to me. But I caught my friend Brian stroking her feet, and that broke my heart.

As barter these 'Brummies' brought with them ice-cream, large boxes of cigarettes and cigars, rare china ornaments (Royal Doulton figurines) and china roses in bowls that you filled with perfume to make them smell nice (like pomanders). They must have had a cheap source of these things because we ended up with a cupboard full of china roses and crinolene ladies. And they always brought plenty of money with them. In wartime there is often a surprising surplus of 'things' (including money) but a corresponding scarcity of the basics of life, like food.

Primarily they came for the meat that we could provide in abundance from the slaughterhouse: cow's hearts, livers, tongues, tripe, prime cuts of pork and beef, dripping, rabbit, and smelly half-cured calfskins. They'd take anything we could obtain. And they paid well. Very well.

Our own smallholding provided them with eggs, chickens, geese or ducks, cream, home-made butter and cheese, plums, gooseberries, red, white and black currants, apples, pears, and plenty of other garden produce like vegetables and such. We also sold them chutneys and jams and preserved fruits we had made. Because of their money they actually got the best and more of these things, than we kept ourselves.

Each season has its own particular glut of produce and some seasons can be bountiful. Nature has arranged it like that to provide year round food supplies. The Bateson's themselves lived very frugally - most of our best country goodies were sold on to provide extra cash.

My own contributions were gleaned mainly from the surrounding woods and fields. The mushroom and edible toadstool season was a fruitful time, in crop and in pocket money terms. The city folk also liked fresh watercress (another seasonal crop) and I was allowed to keep the money for the half-wild damsons that I picked and sold. I had my own secret blackberrying place (behind the knacker-sheds where the bushes were fed by the copious blood supplies from the slaughtered animals). Here, at the right time, I could pick twenty pounds of berries in an afternoon, which the Birmingham folk made into pies and wine. You couldn't pick such quantities of juicy berries so easily now: most of the blackberry woods have been destroyed, ruined, or poisoned in the path of mans' relentless invasion and rape and pollution of the countryside.

To encourage the supply of rabbits, our visitors bought me my first real gun. Until now, I'd had to snare rabbits in wire 'hangs' or gin-traps, a barbaric way to catch animals. I had fired Grandad's twelve bore shot-gun secretly a few times (and had nearly ripped my shoulder off with the recoil) but now I had my own gun, and I was thrilled. It was a .303 and fired small cartridges. I was a bit disappointed when I realised it had to be shoved almost inside the rabbit's ear to kill it. Also, rabbits killed by shotgun - as opposed to snared rabbits - are full of lead buckshot that gets in the way of your teeth when you're eating them (and has other side effects!). So my kind benefactors got back an inferior product for their gift of a gun (it back-fired on them, so to speak). And it could have back-fired on me too, for real, I realised later. It was a second-hand gun and faulty, and who wants a faulty gun of all things, for heaven's sake.

Of the visitors two beautiful young daughters, I was very shy. By now I was feeling my first adolescent sexual stirrings and didn't know what the hell was happening to me. A few months' later the girls came to our village and camped in the fields for a couple of weeks. The scene was obviously set for the classic teenage summer holiday romance and first love. I fell in love with Angela, the eldest, and, like most first loves, it was unrequited, broke my heart, and tore apart my soul. But I shall never forget that summer, her youthful dark smouldering beauty and my own new and turbulent happy and unhappy emotions as they see-sawed, first to the heights and then to the depths. But I wouldn't have missed it for the world.

I dream and digress. But first love is more important than making dosh, surely.

My mate's Dad ran a couple of lorries and was known as a general dealer, which title covered a multitude of sins. Everyone was on the fiddle. He made a shady living dealing in anything he could lay his hands on, stolen, fishily acquired, or legal. At the time I'm writing about he was trading as a 'sack-merchant'. Unlike the plastic throwaway sacks of today, farmers then used returnable hessian sacks which were quite expensive to produce and were re-used time and time again. The thinner cheaper ones were stamped 2/6 RETURNABLE and the thicker and dearer ones 5/-. (The returnable deposit eventually reached fifteen shillings, half as much as the corn inside the sacks). This was a lot of money to us scavenging young entrepreneurs, and tempted us sorely. We had a meeting in our den and discussed ways of getting a slice of the action. My mate showed me the neat piles of sacks stacked in his Dad's store (The Old Mill). There were hundreds of pounds worth. Although, in retrospect, I suppose this mate of mine was a low-down traitor to his Dad, this obviously never occurred to us then. Young ruffians don't go into the whys and wherefores or bother with a conscience. He assisted his Dad to stack and count the sacks. It was a simple matter to miscount accidentally on purpose, steal the uncounted sacks then sell them back to his Dad. Considering he had confided to me that his Dad purloined a percentage of them when he collected them from the farms anyway, the sacks were truly being recycled and no-one really seemed to be losing out (except the farmers). Is this the system that makes the wheels of commerce go round? Entrepreneurism, recycling, and conservation indeed. We must have been ahead of our time.

Despite this, hessian sacks eventually became too expensive, they were also unhygienic and troublesome. As new materials (especially plastics) became available, they were replaced with these throwaway alternatives. Is this progress? But the changes cut off our crafty little money-spinner, as changes are inclined to do.

For a short while old lead car batteries were recycled and in demand. We also swiped returnable pop bottles from the rear of the village shop, took them round to the front and cashed them in for the deposit. This was a well-known nationwide racket among all budding young racketeers. It was an obvious blatant trick, and I could never understand why the shopkeepers never seemed to cotton on. The quickness of the young outflashing the bumbling old perhaps. Shameful and wrong, but true.

Yes. We got up to some shameful tricks. But compared with today's crimes of burglary, muggings, car theft, ram-raiding, and fraud, we were amateurs. I make no apologies: the kid who hasn't stolen or at least contemplated stealing hasn't yet been born. It is part of growing up, sorting oneself out and learning right from wrong in the University of Life.

My most successful opportunity to hit the jackpot happened like this. Before we went to school, 'Em had a spell of sending Tommy Bateson and myself to Grandad's pub for a toffee and a kiss (not for me thanks. I didn't want to kiss this grumpy old man's ugly, tobacco smelling mouth anyway) - and he wasn't really MY Grandad. We trotted there, got our sweetie and Tommy's kiss, then trotted back to wait for the school bus outside Mouldy's shop.

Grandad was usually sitting on his three-legged milking stool with his head buried in the cow's belly, pulling away at the udders. One morning he squirted a fine stream of warm milk straight from the cow's teat into our mouths splashing our faces and nearly choking us. This is a feat only accomplished milkers can do, and sent him into fits of chuckles. It was one of the rare times I ever saw him laugh and display a sense of humour.

He'd instruct us to go and get ourselves a toffee from the cupboard in his kitchen-cum-living room. His peculiar taste in sweets was as bad as his taste in everything else. Old men eat funny sweets.

I wasn't interested in a lousy-tasting solitary sweet. I was beginning to think big and had got more important treasure to grab, on my mind. I'd generously tell Tommy (who was younger and still innocent) to get my share of sweets and to grab a few extra besides. The idea was to keep him occupied while he fumbled in the cupboard and the toffee bag for a few seconds while I pushed open the door to the pub bar which opened directly onto the till behind the old oak bar-room counter. With one finger on the spring to stop the till bell tinging, I'd grope inside the brimming money-drawer and extract a half-crown or a two-bob-piece. At that time I rarely took more. Sometimes it was a case of getting what I could, like a lucky-dip, before Tommy turned round from his sweet fumbling and spotted what I was up to. It's amazing what you can do in a few seconds when you are a sharp little rascal and as quick as a lightning flash. Half-a-crown would go a long way in those days in the town's sweet shops. From the day of my discovery of this golden cornucopia of a bottomless cash source (drinkers and alcoholics will never let you down) I appeared to be one of the richest lads in the playground. Providing I didn't get greedy, it could go on forever. Grandad lived in a perpetual alcoholic haze anyway, and his sight was getting worse. He never knew how much money he'd got. Kids are much more aware of these things than adults give them credit for, and will cash in on the opportunity while the sun is shining in their favour. Well, I did.

Thieving was also a way of life at school and the notorious pickpockets and shoplifters among us were well known, quite respected and never snitched on or challenged. Our playground was like Fagin's Den. Indeed, these clever-dicks were generally admired by many boys who just didn't have the nerve to steal.

Maggoty Joe was another unusual source of money for me, and paid well. He was a city slicker who originally came to the the village at week-ends to fish (illegally) in the River Blythe. I'd gather him a tin of fat seething maggots from the rotting meat around the slaughter-sheds, poke a few holes in the lid to keep them alive, and he'd pay me good money and use them as fish bait.

This particuar day, on finding the slaughter sheds deserted, Joe went walkabout and discovered the derelect pig-sties in the woods near to the slaughterhouse buildings. As he stood idly watching the swarms of busy, buzzing super-fat bluebottles attracted to and laying their eggs on the rotting meat and carcasses which lay everywhere, he thoughtfully stroked his stubbly chin. He was the double of Popeye, and he never shaved. He had a sudden flash of inspiration.

He confided his plan to me. Did I think I could hang lumps of rotting offal onto those rusty hooks in the roof of the sties during the hot summer months, while the flies were active and, in effect, start a maggot production line?

I secretly thought him batty but willingly agreed. Bemused, but seeing the pound sign in my mind's eye, I would agree to anything.

That very sultry summer the seething mountains of maggots and the bloated germ of Joe's unusual idea proliferated to bursting point. Almost like volunteer suicidal lemmings, the maggots dropped willingly into the old stone pig-troughs below the hooks, ready for me to shovel them into buckets ready for collection by Joe. They say there's money in muck, but Joe had discovered there's money in maggots. Thereafter he was endearingly known around the village as Maggoty Joe.

Joe started selling his maggots to his fellow fishermen back in Brum (Birmingham to you, Sir). On the strength of his rapidly burgeoning profits he later opened a fisherman's store, and sold fishing tackle, necessary and unnecessary. But the underlying core product, his bread and butter line so to speak, of his successful enterprise, remained maggots, supplied by a ragged little urchin (me) back in the Animal Belsen at Blythe Bridge slaughterhouse.

Now, when Joe arrived to collect his maggot supplies he wore a posh suit and tie and drove a new shooting brake. He looked a real country gent, albeit a comical popeye one. He could now afford a shave and a hair-cut and sweet smelling after-shave to mask his maggoty smell.

The maggot trade made us both (relatively) rich. I've no doubt he paid the one who did the work - me - peanuts, compared with what he was paying himself.

But I'm not complaining. It was ever thus and ever will be. It is the way of the world. It was his brilliant idea in the first place and without the idea nothing at all would have happened. In the beginning was the word. Maggots are bigger business than ever today, but he was in at the start. Later he brought me a rather old-fashioned but good quality second-hand fishing rod. It was the first real rod I'd ever owned: such a proud feeling. Until then it had been a bent pin on a stick, refined, as usual in my own ingenious way of improving things. I now owned my own faulty second-hand gun and an antique fishing rod. I could sell rabbits and now river-fish to those Brummy visitors. Things were looking up.

Naturally, making dosh was not so easy during the cold lean winter months when there was no fruit or mushrooms or such to pick and glean from farm, field and hedgerow. But, with leafless bushes and hedges, rabbits have nowhere to hide and are very visible against the snow: so they are easier to hit. And, as any self-respecting money-grubber knows, the onset of Christmas is a great wallet opener, if you have discovered the magic key.

Woolworths ran a grand line in sticks of coloured wax at that time (incidentally, both wax and woolworths is now gone into history). Making things with this hard sealing wax was a popular hobby then. The long boxes of brightly coloured sticks were very eye-catching. I broke frost-covered fancy-looking twigs from the bare trees and bushes and applied my own artificial frost and snow. Softening and forming flower heads with this coloured wax in front of the glowing winter fire, was a pleasant pastime. I became so good at making these artificial flowers and decorations that people around the village started asking, and paying me for them. Along with gold-painted fir-cones they fitted in well with the Christmas tinsel, the mistletoe...and the holly that I gathered from the hedges and sold as well.

As always, nowadays the big boys have caught on, and sophisticated commercially produced plastic flowers are indistinguishable from the real thing. But I was there at the start, making dosh out of them. The trouble is, I got idle and lost my way, and I am not there now, at the end of the rainbow where the real pot of gold lies. I missed the golden boat, as many of us do. I often ask myself, where did I go wrong? It's an easy question but the answer is harder to understand. There is a moral here somewhere!

Christmas is also the traditional time to kill the goose and other fowl and, with my slaughterhouse background, I was your friendly neighbourhood goose-killer. I always took the poor bird out of sight to kill it, feeling a little guilty as I was still practising, so to speak. Well, we have to learn sometime. But it's a bit different when it's murder you have to commit, to earn your dosh. Birds with thick necks, and birds that valiantly fought back and took a long time to die, all gave me messy trouble. But I needed my pocket money to spend on Christmas presents, cards and stamps, to bankrupt myself again...to kill more fowl, to earn yet more pocket money. I was already on that commercial rat-race treadmill, remember? And I still am.

Before I leave this unsavoury period of my boyhood, I recall with not a little pride my last great swindle of that time. I was reaching my zenith in ill-gotten gains and was fast becoming a slick, bare-faced and plausible little rogue and war-time spiv myself. Perhaps my present day contemporary's opinion is that I haven't changed much, even now...who knows? What's more, who cares!

Kingstone Village Church Fete was in the offing and my mate and I had a great wheeze on how to cash in on the good villagers' conscientious desire to financially support their Vicar's efforts at raising funds for repairs to the church roof. Conscience money in many cases, because they hadn't been to church all year. (You have to understand people to get at their cash - even if you are the vicar).

There is a community conscience anyway among village inhabitants: they are very parochial, or like to be seen as such (though not so much nowadays when many villages have lost their individuality). Everyone flocked to the annual fete, and cash, even from notoriously stingy farmers, was expected and squozen. A jolly and pleasant day was always had by all - if it didn't rain that is. Vicars dread rain on fete day. Do they pray to God for a nice day I wonder?

Another pal had recently left school and started work in the local biscuit factory. Already, true to form and with his grounding in Fagin's playground, he was contributing to the gang's loot and was obtaining for us a regular free sampling and supply of biscuits.

He was induced, and succeeded in acquiring (a handy word) a couple of decorative tins of chocolate-assortment biscuits, weighting four-and-a-half pounds per tin.

It is true to say that this time we were not aware of the etiquette of first obtaining permission from the fete organiser, i.e. the local Vicar, to sell raffle tickets or to collect cash for the fete. Teenagers are not normally very strong on things like etiquette, good manners, conventions, politeness, Vicars, church fetes and such-like. I suppose the truth is, we neither cared or even thought about it. Our prime motive was profit gain, which was uppermost in our minds.

We patiently toured the district, bicycling to outlying farms and villages, forgetting no-one in our quest to flog raffle tickets for the tins of biscuits. You're never so conscientious or motivated nor work so hard, as when you're doing it for yourself. Farmers were reputed to be rich, and their buxom wives often held the purse-strings. In this annual drive for church funds, people were very generous. The cash flooded in.

The biggest killing was made on the day of the fete when we touted the pretty tins round the fete-field. We fine-combed the milling crowds who were dipping the bran tub, knocking Aunt Sally's hat off, knocking each other off poles, hoop-la-ing the prizes, or trying to hit an envelope of money with darts. We studiously dodged only the Vicar, easy to spot because of his impeccable white and stiff dog-collar (is this why Vicars always look so uncomfortable?) and his habit of politely shaking hands with everyone he stopped to talk to: "I haven't seen you in church lately? Have you been ill?"

Finally, heavy with coins and fed up at last with flogging tickets (a thankless and off-putting task at the best of times), my mate joked... "We haven't sold any to the Vicar yet."

"You daren't!"

"Who daren't?"

So we tapped the Vicar. He had to smile. It was his big day and he was surrounded by his flock: well-wishers, helpers, heathens and the salt of the earth.

"Oh!" he exclaimed, with exaggerated surprise as we proffered the pile of coins nestling in an old cap (used purely for effect). "Is this for the fete?" A rather superfluous question I thought. But Vicars are like that: always asking questions: "Is God real?" "Is God your friend?" I had observed this at Sunday School.

Well, this bit of money certainly was for the fete Sir, yes. But the other two thirds, that was for ourselves. So we said nothing about that.

"You really should have asked for my permission to sell raffle tickets you know" he intoned, still smiling, though it was beginning to show the strain. "But thank you very much lads, all the same. Every little helps". I've no doubt he knew what we were up to. Vicars are pretty worldly and are not as simple as they're sometimes portrayed. I had long deserted Sunday School and pretended I wasn't up to date with church news. Which was true anyway.

"Oh, sorry about not asking permission. We didn't realise."

"Have you sold many?" He sounded a little suspicious to me, but it could have been my guilty conscience. What little I had.

"Not bad" we lied. (We'd done fabulous in fact). "We'll go into the tent and count it for you if you like." Everyone was being very polite and on their best behaviour today, but tonight at the village pub, and later at the dance in the Village Institue, most of them would be drunk.

Maybe we were being too generous, and hadn't taken enough for ourselves, for our pains, we were thinking.

It would have been nice if I could have told you we donated the whole glittering pile of coins to the church, but being the honest guy that I am, I have sworn to tell the truth, and we didn't. The Vicar seemed quite pleased with the third that we gave him, and that left over a third each for me and my mate.

Today, this little scam would be called business acumen - a euphemism if ever I heard one. so I think we are to be congratulated. After all, it was bloody hard work tramping round those country lanes selling those tickets, and there was plenty of money to satisfy everyone. It was our idea in the first place and the Vicar got a surprise donation he wouldn't have got otherwise. We could have kept the lot and he'd have been none the wiser (but then again, the Master would have known). The Vicar should have been grateful for small mercies, as he was so often fond of telling his congregation. {We can justify anything, if it suits us to do so}.

Funnily enough my partner in crime won one of the tins of biscuits, which was a strange coincidence...but I thought I'd mention it.

Perhaps this shameful little episode, involving the church and therefore, indirectly, God, should at last have stirred any beginnings of a conscience I might have had. But a youth's conscience is yet but a tiny and fragile plant hardly with its head above the surface of its worldly soil. The Vicar hadn't helped by turning me off God with his silly Sunday School stamps and his stern stilted preaching in his bleak and draughty church. It was to be many years before my conscience was hardy enough to stand sturdy and upright, of its own free will, above the battering storms of life, look around and say, "This is not right". And God had precious little to do with it.

CHAPTER 11

Misbehaviour, or what?

The allegation, pertaining to very young children, of "Being a thoroughly bad lot" or "Badly behaved" always puzzled and bemused me as I was growing up, and still does. So, to some extent, does the saying "it was just a temporary lack of concentration". An expression often used by defendant's counsel in court motoring offences.

It is this personal perplexity that prompted the above title. Like most kids, I was often scolded, scoffed at or even beaten for doing something quite innocently: so why, I wondered, was I being beaten? Innocent that is, in my childhood opinion. But obviously not from the point of view of my supposedly better informed elders. My point is, if, in your young life, you are suddeny confronted with a situation you have never come across before, which requires quick, immediate action, what do you do, to do the right thing? You don't really know, do you? You only have your immature wits, speed of reaction, and hardly any previous experience or thoughts on the crisis to guide you through this untracked mine-field.

Most of us would momentarily panic. Then, hopefully, we'd do the best we could, within our capabilities of experience and the speed of our reactions, mentally and physically. But it is a situation full of risk. At best we might do the right thing and at worse we might injure or even kill ourselves (or somebody or something else). More often we just manage to upset our busy mums, who'd give us a quick thwack across the ears for our 'stupidity' in making the wrong decision.

How often have you seen an irate parent yelling at his child "You KNOW you are not supposed to do that. Why did you do it then? Why...why...? How can you be so stupid!?" This is what I mean. The chances are the child didn't know, and therefore is merely puzzled at being called stupid for doing something that was, to him, quite logical. The kid was thinking on his immature feet, so to speak.

I always was a curious little tyke, poking my nose into things, experimenting, taking risks. It's not a bad thing. Again, it is part of growing up, developing and learning - just as long as we don't go down at the first hurdle, and either hurt - or do worse - to ourselves in the process. It's a shame if you drown the first ever time you jump into the deepest part of the river.

Because I was an evacuee (and from a children's home remember) my confidence had already been severely undermined and was shaky. And now 'Em's continual criticism and carping, and the occasional chase around the yard with the copper stick, crushed the new few tender shoots of confidence even before they could stabilise and re-establish themselves (if they had been encouraged and allowed to) within my wobbly psyche. Mind you, that said, I have no doubt I WAS an awkward little sod, a real handful. As 'Em often remarked "You would try the patience of a saint". But, there again, what kid wouldn't? Kids will be kids.

She would criticize my dubious absent father, who could have been dead or alive (as no one seemed to know exactly who or where he was). I felt aggrieved that he was not there to defend himself (or me, for that matter). She also slagged off my mother (who was still alive, but again, neither of us knew that at that time).

"They must have been bad 'uns to have spawned such an evil little bastard like you" she would say viciously. Her coarse and hateful vituperative phrases cut me to the quick. I felt like a beaten, wounded and unwanted cur. The damage she was doing to myself and my confidence at that tender age is probably still apparent in my attitude and behaviour to the world in general, today. It is doubtful that so young a plant crushed underfoot will ever fully recover. A pot cracked in the kiln, so to speak.

Be that as it may. It was a sad and distressing scenario for I stood up for my Mum and Dad against this torrent of abuse, and told myself they loved me, and I loved them, despite everything, even though I didn't know if they were dead or alive. Or that I could even remember them.

And nothing Mrs Bateson said or did could turn me against them. Which, considering I didn't know if they were still existent shows you the natural instinctive love a child has for its parents.

In my darkest moments I did, of course, wonder why they had forsaken me. All deserted children do. But I dreamed and believed that my mother was a rich, beautiful, and loving women who must have had a good reason for leaving me to my fate. She would one day return, I told myself, to take me away from this miserable and fearful existence, and whisk me off to the security, love and warmth of her crystal palace, where we would live happily ever after. But she wasn't a beautiful princess, and she never came to whisk me away. Life is just not like that. You can only escape life for brief moments in dreams and daydreams. I had to make do with fairy tales. It's a good job we can have such escapist dreams in our worse moments, otherwise we'd go mad, and wither away and die.

For my absent Dad's part, again I excused him for deserting me. It could not have been his fault, I told myself. Perhaps he was working and saving up money againt the day he could afford to have me back, and care for me. Or perhaps he had been sent away to the war, fighting those nasty Germans, as most men were at that time. I was probably wrong on all counts. I now believe my Dad didn't give a toss about any of us: he was probably a drunkard and a wastrel as Mrs Bateson had guessed. And I doubt that he ever fought in the war. As it turned out, despite making enquiries, I know very little about my father. He just vanished or even never was, and that's all I know about him.

Mrs Bateson was 'off-colour' one evening and for the first time ever asked me to shut up the goslings for the night. I wasn't very old at the time. "Just shoo them into the tub" she instructed, "then wedge the lid shut with that piece of wood to make sure they can't get out and the foxes can't get in" - (we were having trouble with a fox at that time. He'd already killed a number of fowl). Simple enough instructions for anyone to understand, you would have thought.

The goslings slept in an old empty fifty-gallon wooden beer barrel lying on its side. With difficulty I rounded up the excited squawking six or seven half-grown geese (they can be silly awkward birds, especially at bedtime) and finally got them into the barrel. As instructed I quickly propped up the lid, and braced it firmly shut with the wooden strut.

In the morning when I went to let them out, they were all dead...barring one , who waddled dizzily out like a tipsy Donald Duck, with barely a faint squeaky quack left in him. No, they hadn't perished from beer fumes. Nothing so pleasant. They had suffocated. I had wedged the lid on too tight. It might sound silly now, in the telling of, but no-one had told me that goslings have to breathe to live, just like the rest of us. I had a good whacking from an incredulous Mrs Bateson, who couldn't believe anyone could be so stupid, and I was sent straight to bed in the middle of the day. WAS I stupid, ignorant, thoughtless, naughty, evil - or what? 'Em accused me of being all these things. I honestly hadn't realised at that age, that goslings have to breathe. It is easy for adults to forget how innocent and unknowing children can be. The tight-fitting barrel lid had cut off all air to the baby geese. O.K. it WAS an expensive, serious, cruel and tragic mistake, but so is the burning down of a house by a kid playing with a box of matches, and that's also happened often enough. "I didn't mean to do it" an imp might protest, and why would he? He'd be speaking the simple truth. We've all played with matches when we were kids, haven't we. It was just childish inquisitiveness, curiousity and ignorance.

Incidentally, the tough surviving goose was a character called Rupert (altho Rupert was obviously a girl). She had a twisted deformed lower beak and became a favourite of mine. Because of her beak she couldn't pluck and eat grass as fast as the others. Like kids in a group, they must have sensed she was different and wouldn't have her in the gang and chased her away, so she always grazed on her own ...an outcast. I felt an affinity for all lone and ostracized creature. Rupert will enter (and, sadly, depart) my narrative again, in a little while.

While writing this episode, I remember another 'mistake' concerning fowl that occurred years later (when maybe I should have known better). I had started work on a poultry farm. Mistakes are not the prerogative of the young. I had been told by my impatient and intimidating bossman to get a move on with the daily culling of the day-old chicks. I had never 'culled' before and didn't even know what the word meant. I enquired tentatively what it meant, as one would.

"God" he snapped in exasperation (he was a boozer and always had a blood-red face and a apopolexic temper from the night before), "get on with it Bird! We haven't all day. Just sort out the sick and weedy ones and get bloodly rid of 'em".

On the way to the pens I asked another worker what I had to do. He was busy and preoccupied and just said "you have to wring their necks then throw them into the incinerator."

I went into the pens and stood in my wellington boots amid the seething mass of chirping, panicky yellow chicks, wondering what to do next. I didn't want to show my ignorance of the job, as jobs were hard to come by at that time.

To keep the brood healthy under such humid crowded conditions, sick and diseased or weakling chicks must be scrupulously pruned and weeded out and destroyed.

This far I could understand. But I had never done the job before and hadn't a clue what to do. It wasn't the killing bit that particularly bothered me. Some jobs just have to be done. But

I was used to killing Christmas fowl by wringing their necks (Mr Bateson was a slaughterman by profession, so I had grown up with killing). There were scores of chicks here, but with such scrawny little necks it was difficult to grip them. But it was the only way I knew how, so I tried the same method of neck-pulling as I used on the older birds. I knew no different.

I hadn't realised that, naturally, day-old chicks have frames as soft as salmon bones. Their fragile little necks came off in my hands didn't they.

I threw the twitching bloody results into a bucket, and continued my gory killing spree 'til I had sorted them. Covered in blood from head to toe, and carrying the bucket full of dead chicks to the incinerator, I came across the fellow-worker again.

"What the hell have you been doing?" he asked, horrified at my wild, blood-covered, and white-faced appearance. Then as a jokey afterthought, he said "you haven't by any luck murdered the Boss, have you?"

We all hated our arrogant Boss. It must have been Freudian-thinking on his part. "I wish I bloody-well had" I replied wryly. "I've been culling the chicks".

"I should think you have!" And he roared with laughter as I described the method I had used, and told me the proper way to kill a baby chick. For those technically interested, you place the neck of the chick on any handy sharp corner, and simply crush the neckbone with your thumb. It is as simple as that. Immediate, painless and bloodless. Amazing how tender such life can be snuffed out in a instant. Because I hadn't known, I had made a simple mistake.

November the fifth was nigh and I had no money for fireworks. All my friends had some (they all had loving Mums and Dads!) It would be a good idea to make my own, wouldn't it? Simple and cheap.

One thing I have always been good at is getting and applying any information I need from books from Uttoxeter town library. My 'research' showed me I needed fine iron filings, and sulphor and various other chemicals, which, by hook and by crook and much trouble, I obtained from various sources.

Typically, in my enthusiam and impatience, I mixed far too much: a big round bowlfull - and probably in the wrong proportions. I couldn't wait to light my first giant sparkler.

I filled a trial rolled up newspaper with the mixture, and simply screwed the end for touch-paper.

Trembling with excitement, I lit it. What would happen? Would it work? It smouldered on...

It certainly worked all right! Spitting sparks flew up and out in all directions and the length of the firework disintegrated so quickly, in no time at all it was burning my hand. The iron filings must have been too coarse for when the white-hot sparks landed they glowed for ages.

Worse still, some landed in my clothes and some fell into the bowl of firework mixture. In pain, I dropped the remains of my out-of-control firework and the bowl exploded in a pyrotechnical display of cracking sparks and flame. Some hit me in the face, and some went up my sleeves burning small craters into my skin.

I tried to put out the spitting, sparking conflagration by stamping my hob-nailed boot into the bowl. My boot became jammed and sparks flew up the inside of my trousers, burning my leg.

It might make for funny reading, but it was no joke at the time. Luckily I had the presence of mind to quickly undo the laces and remove my foot from my spark-filled boot, leaving the valuable boot to its fate in the inferno of the bowl. I had no choice: my sock was already smouldering and my boot was badly burnt. Let this little anecdote be a lesson to any aspiring Guy Fawkes out there reading this. Little boys who play with fire will get burnt.

As I said, it was wartime and footwear was a valuable and expensive item then. Burnt feet would heal free of charge and, in my case, pain was considered of little consequence: (I would receive no pity, only anger). But boot, socks, shirts and trousers would take a large slice out of Mrs Bateson's wartime budget. I knew I was in serious trouble.

For this silly piece of 'misbehaviour' 'Em scuffed me across the room and up the stairs shouting "where's your bloody boot you stupid little sod" and locked me in the bedroom. I would get no dinner, tear or supper, that day.

My burnt foot and spark-speckled face, arms, hands, feet and legs were hurting like hell, but I was worried about what 'Em would say when she saw my charred boot jammed in the bowl, in the shed.

Despite all my worries, I still felt pretty pleased with myself and proud of my powerful firework experiment. After all it HAD worked, after a fashion. It was just too crude and strong. In one way it had been a 'sparkling' success. Pity it all went so wrong. I vowed to do better next time...kids never learn.

My 'crime' here, tabbed by 'Em as stupid, in truth was nothing of the sort. 'Em, like many adults, never considered what she was saying and showed great ignorance in comments like these. My mistake had been due to mere inexperience, that's all, with a dash of boyish foolhardiness thrown in. If you haven't taken care to learn to ride your bike properly you will probably fall off and hurt yourself quite badly. You will be more careful next time. You are in the process of learning and gaining in experience the hard way (in the University of Life). The moral is, do your homework and practice well before you consider yourself even half-proficient, at anything.

Talking of bikes, I was sent into town to collect a recharged wireless accumulator. For younger readers this was the power-source (known also as wet batteries) of early valve radios. They were, basically, heavy square glass jars full of lead plates, acid and water. They were quite expensive to buy, but when they went 'flat', for a moderate fee an iron-monger's shop in Uttoxeter woul recharge them. They were fitted with a swinging metal handle for ease of carrying.

The shopkeeper informed me there were two ready in our name waiting for collection - so would I take them both now, or were they too heavy for me? Studying my slight physique and looking a bit concerned he said "Perhaps you can't manage them both today?" He was aware I had come into town from a village about six miles away, but he wouldn't know whether I had come on the bus, or by bike.

I was at a stupid, stubborn, big-headed age. It was that age when young boys are flexing their muscles so to speak. Trying their wings. If I was questioned as to whether I was capable of carrying out a a certain difficult chore which I had never done before, I would shrug my shoulders as if to say "of course I can do it". It is that age when we just can't wait to be accepted as a grown up and feel insulted if we are treated as if we are still little children.

Big-headed clever Dick, I now replied scoffingly, "Naw, they're not too heavy. It's ok. I'll take them both". I set off on the long six-mile journey home, with the heavy batteries swinging one on each handlebar, gripping tight both jars and handlebars. It is awkward to carry anything safely in a bike at the best of times, let alone swinging glass jars full of acid.

I got a bit of a speed-wobble down the hills, but once I got the hang of it, the rhythm, I felt safe enough. It was frosty weather. Holding the swinging batteries tight to the handlebar grips, and manipulating the brakes all at the same time, the meanwhile ringing the bell like hell to warn oncomers a crazy cyclist was on the loose ... doing these things all at once, with frozen blue and stiffening fingers, made me feel like a trick-cyclist doing a circus act. As well as the bike-bell, alarm bells should have been ringing in my head too!

I came to The Bank. This steep bank that led down to Blythe Bridge (where I lived) terminated exactly at our gate. I knew every bend, and almost every pebble. I was always relieved and thrilled to coast at speed down this hill I knew so well, on the last leg of a long and arduous - mostly uphill - journey.

And so I did. In my customary devil-may-care fashion, batteries or no batteries, I sped down brakeless at full speed as fast as I could go, pedalling furiously to try to get even more of a spurt on.

There was deep loose grit on the sides of the road, and the batteries started swaying alarmingly. Needless to say the speed-wobble went totaly out of control and right outside our gate the bike skidded, the batteries locked against the wheel, and bike, batteries and myself went crashing to the ground, grazing my knees and elbows badly. Worse still, both glass batteries shattered, cutting me and splashing acid over my face and clothes.

Most mothers would have rushed with concern to comfort and patch up their shocked, frightened and injured child. Not so Mrs Bateson. "Where's the bloody battery!?" she screeched on seeing me limp into the yard with my buckled bike. "You'd better not have broken it!" (Little did she know then - I had broken TWO!)

I was threatened with having to pay for the batteries out of my hard-earned pocket money, but she must have forgotten or let me off She never mentioned it again. I would like to believe my nasty accident had frightened her, and that she'd felt I had been punished enough already with my cuts, bruises and acid burns, but I doubt it.

The whole of my 'going out' clothes (in those days us kids had 'playing-out' clothes, school clothes and 'Sunday best Clothes) including jacket, trousers, socks, shirt and boots had been sprayed with acid and quickly rotted into holes. I was plunged into a scalding hot tin bath laced with disinfectant and scoured with carbolic soap and a scrubbing brush, then sent to bed feeling unfamiliarly clean and very sore. Sobbing bitterly until I could cry no more, I fell asleep and dreamt of my fairy tale Princess Mum who came to me in her diaphonous flowing dress, to lovingly carry me away to the safety of her lofty palace in her nowhere land.

Of course, the disinfectant bath was absolutely the wrong treatment for aid burns, which are notoriously painful and slow to heal anyway. But this was the standard treatment for all problems in those days. Disinfectant was supposed to cure everything...lice, scurvy and scabies which all kids seemed to get then. It hurt like hell, which it was probably sadistically meant to do as she was a spiteful woman. As this was the punishment for falling off my bike and breaking the batteries.

To be fair, in truth and strange to say, a good whacking (followed by a good cry) and an enforced vigorous bath and an early night, does no lasting harm to a kid at all (though I am not recommending it!). It is a sort of catharsis that seems to purge the body and spirit and emotions - and you feel you have paid your debt. It is probably one of nature's ways of flushing out the body and spirit: she moves in mysterious ways. Next morning you start afresh, on a clean slate so to speak. You've taken your medicine and now it should be all forgotten. But don't let anyone hear me advocating this treatment and opinion: modern thinking is that whacking of kids is no longer to be encouraged.

Altho I was punished, he battery episode must come under the heading of Accident. For the next little anecdote even I dare make no excuses, and I will label my following behaviour as just plain stupid. Even now, I can hardly believe I did this.

I was sent to the nearest country-post box to post an important package. 'Em's last words to me were, "Now, you must make sure the postman gets this package". Meaning of course, don't dawdle and miss the collection time.

(She had often called me a 'Thickie' so why didn't she say that?) But adults often speak to kids the same way they as they speak to other adults, forgetting that kids have to assimilate the message with much less knowledge and experince of life.

Thus I took the instruction literally. On reaching the post box I sat down on the grass verge underneath it, clutching the obviously important package to my body. No one must have it but the postman, I kept repeating to myself.

It was a lovely hot summer's day. The birds were singing and I was surrounded by wild flowers and hovering butterflies. It was very pleasant. I dozed off. The afternoon wore on. When

I woke up (like Rip-Van-Winkle) I heard the cows being called in he distance. It was milking time. A farm labourer walked past and asked "what are you waiting for?"

"I'm waiting for the postman" I replied. "I have to make sure I give him this". I brandeshed the stamped package. He gave me an odd look, but said nothing, and went on his way.

Of course, by then the postman had been and gone! I stood up and noticed the collection times printed on the postbox. It must be way past 6.30 I thought. Then the penny dropped. I should have posted this package and now the postman had been and gone, minus 'Em's valuable package. Of course I hastily posted it, and kept my fingers crossed that 'Em would never know what a stupid boy I had been.

It was just one of those peculiar things that happens sometimes when you are a child. You simply don't know, and therefore can't make out the logic of what should be hitting you between the eyes. It's the child's equivalent of an adult motorist knocking a motor-cyclist off his bike: "I didn't see him. He must have been in my blind spot" you protest, incredulous and full of disbelief that you couldn't see the obvious.

Mrs Bateson was getting agitated and concerned at my long delay and was about to call the police. It was one of the rare times I ever saw her worried about me. And I realised then, that somewhere, deep down, there WAS a vulnerable spot, an Achilles-heel (we all have one at least - no matter how hard we appear on the exterior). And shortly the day would come when I would exploit that weak spot, that chink in Mrs Bateson's cruel armour, to my fullest advantage.

My guess is that she wasn't so concerned about me as she was about being responsible for losing me. These half-glimpsed unintentionally given clues to the vulnerability of human nature, were sign-posts to my gimlet-sharp little eyes. Downtrodden kids especially develop these sensitive antenna. In later years, and verily, all throughout my life, I would learn to spot and exploit these human frailties. We all do this to some extent, unconsciously most of the time. I would not always be the silly little boy who waited for the postman.

I was naughty too one day when I was told to take little Tommy Bateson for a walk "out of Mummy's way for a bit". Country lanes are mostly unverged and dangerous for walkers, especially young children. But there wasn't much traffic about in those days.

Coming to meet us, 'Em caught me walking in the fields, while Tommy waddled along in the lane alongside, alone on the vergeless road. For some reason she quizzed me for hours on end on why I had done this dangerous and silly thing. Like a psychiatrist she kept on and on: "Why? why? why?"

I couldn't understand why she wouldn't just give up and just give me a hefty clout like she usually did. I was used to that and understood it. I would have preferred a straightforward and uncompromising smack around the ears. In any case, I wanted to get out of the house and get on with my playing - alone. {I didn't like looking after Tommy who was much younger than me}. I honestly did not know why I had walked in the fields. I couldn't think of a satisfactory explanation. I was as mystified as she was why I had done it. Does there have to be a reason for everything we do? I tried every trick I knew to shut her up and let me go. I couldn't even think of a plausible lie (unusual for glib little me). I could usually lie or wangle myself out of most of the fixes I'd got myself into, but today it wasn't working. And I couldn't understand why...

I tried "because the fields are full of flowers and I wanted to pick some" , but that didn't seem to wash with her. She was in a strange mood, and so was I. Still she kept on, "but why?" It was a nightmare.

I next tried "Because the ground is softer in the fields". But still the questions came. "But WHY? What difference does that make?"

I was, granted, giving quite silly answers to her silly questions, but silly answers had worked in the past. Silly answers had always sufficed to satisfy her. In desperation and exasperation I declared, "I LIKE walking in the fields".

Finally I fell back on that old favorite of kids who don't know why they did something, "Because I wanted to!" which seemed to enrage her all the more. "Well, don't you think my Billy Bunting might have wanted to as well?" she shrieked.

She was replying to my stupid answers with more stupid questions, and beating me at my own game. My system was failing me. The altercation was getting nowhere. At her next tiresome and boring question I lapsed into my defensive sulky silent mode, as I had so often done before (and answer came there none). This stance usually drove her up the wall, and brought the florid signs of blood pressure rushing into her face. She often went into a near apoplectic ft. Red alert. It meant "watch out, she's going to blow!" There came a time when I could turn her face red on at will, just for amusement.

But now I was beyond caring. I used my silent mode to become unreachable. It was my final refuge from her ravings. To get at me now in any way she would have to resort to violence and even that wouldn't hurt me now. I was becoming too thick-skinned, literally. But my total-silence manoeuvre defensive stance was a powerful shield. Her Archilles heel here was her simple and ignorant nature: she just didn't know how to deal with this strange and silent little monster of a kid that, like a hedgehog, could seem to retreat and shut out the world at will, with a secret switch. It unnerved her. This is what I meant when I said earlier that I had learned to exploit the weaknesses of those I wish to manipulate, or shut out of my life. I practiced on 'Em, because she deserved it. And, at that time, she was all I had.

Many people since then have tried to penetrate my heart and emotions with their metaphorical daggers, hurts and barbs, but - if I so desire - I can shut them out as easily as closing my eyes against the light. It isn't a pleasant or polite tactic, but then, it isn't meant to be. The point is, 'Em taught me this trick and it has stood me in good stead ever since. Thus do nuisance imps learn to shield themselves from the slings and arrows of future life. I retreated into myself then because there was no one else to turn to.

I felt the thick end of the copper stick across my back not a few times. That is why I secretly changed it for a softer, less dangerous weapon. When 'Em ran to get her stick, I ran for my life. The faster I ran the less pain I felt as the stick descended on my back. As I grew older, tougher and more 'hard-faced', and because the hurt became easier to bear, I began to see 'Em's outbursts of angry violence as quite funny, and sometimes hilarious. More of a charade than reality. They were ceasing to hurt me, physically or emotionally. I could sort of stand outside myself and view them almost disapassionately, like a bystander, as if they were happening to someone else. I would over-react my terror, and with arms flailing like a mad thing I would tumble across the yard like a fleeing Dervish. I kept my bonse low so that 'Em couldn't see that I was laughing my head off, or it would have enraged her more. It was he sight of her read face and her clumsy, unseemly and rarely seen frantic stampede after me, that amused me. It was like being chased by a clumsly gorilla. I could also imagine myself fleeing, in pretended fear. As I got older I found I could easily outrun and out manoeuvre her any time I wanted. She was growing stocky, stiff, clumsy and old, while I was growing strong, lean, athletic and into my prime.

Is this another of nature's ways of self-preservation? It makes you wonder. I have noticed that there are many aspects of life that, at the outset, can frighten and traumatise us, and which give us great discomfort and concern. But once we have faced these vicissitudinous monsters, and have come to grips with them, lo and behold they are monsters no more: and we can sometimes even grow to mock and to laugh at them.

Sometimes, if 'Em managed to land a decent whack on me, she gave up chasing me (she was probably worn out). I would flee into the honeycomb of outbuildings around the place, and work off my excited, peculiar wound-up feelings, muck-spreadingm, or digging the garden patch, some other such physically tiring job. It was a small farm so there was always plenty of work to do. Hard physical work can be a type of therapy, and also helps you to forget your troubles. Late in the evening as it was going dark, I would sidle quietly into the kitchen, sneak a catlick wash and a bite of supper, and slink up the narrow stair-case to bed, mumbling "'Night Mmmm". to the dozing hunched figure in the armchair by the fire.

One of Mrs Bateson's prized possessions, that graced the heavy oak three-legged living room dining table, was a deep-piled, heavy, old-fashioned gold-tasselled chenille tablecloth. It was always ornamented with a large cut-glass vase of fresh flowers in the middle of the table. Each mealtime this cloth was covered with a crisp white linen tablecloth which was properly laid for a meal. Oh yes, we did things right in them days. We were very formal genteel and posh folks in our house - well, we aspired to be. Most folk did then.

On day 'Em went out on one of her very rare visits and, as usual, I got up to mischief. While the cat's away the mouse will play.

I was messing about with a lighted candle (kids love to play with fire) experimenting with something. I forget what. It doesn't matter.

What did matter though,m was that while I was messing about, the candle fell over and soft hot wax spilled onto the chenille tablecloth and sunk into the fabric pile of the cloth.

In my panic I fetched a knife and tried to remove the now set and solidified wax. A hopeless task as you might well imagine. Like trying to remove chewing gum that has been trodden into a carpet.

I scraped away furiously. How was I to know this was the worse thing I could have done? Like a moulting dog's fur, the chenile pile came away in clumps. The more I scraped, the more bare patches appeared in the pile. It looked like I had tried to etch a map into the surface of the tablecloth.

To say that I was horrifid at what I had done to Mrs Bateson's most expensive and treasured possession would be an understatement. I was gobsmacked. What was I to do? There wasn't anything I could do but wait for her return and face the consequencies.

I pulled and adjusted the cloth so that the damage overhung the edge of the table, on the dark shaded side of the room. I knew this little trick would not hide it for long. Within a short time Mrs Bateman's sharp houseproud eyes, looking for signs of what I might have been up to, would sweep around the room like radar. She would immediately spot the cloth hanging unevenly and pull it straight. Then all hell would break loose.

Forewarned is forearmed as they say. I went across the fields to do some more muck-spreading. It was either a guilty conscience that made me seek out work, or a weak effort at atonement, or a bit of both. Or simply a desperate attempt to avoid, escape or forget what I had done. Or a mixture of all these things at once, and a few more of less understood ones besides. And simple fear.

Anything to keep myself outside as long and as late as possible. As it turned out, the awful damage came to light the next day with the rising of the sun. I'd had a respite and time to try and compose and to kid myself that it wouldn't be noticed at all, and that it wasn't as serious as it had seemed the day before. This of course was wishful thinking. I'd also had a restless night with a dicky tummy, and rose very early to go mushrooming (to keep out of the way and serve a bit more of atonement...perhaps fresh mushrooms for breakfast would calm her down). But I couldn't avoid going back to the house for ever. I was returning to the farm when the dreaded half-expected loud-shrieked summons came hollering from the house and echoing around the haystacks where I was skulking with my basket of mushrooms. "Michael, are you there! Come into this bloody house this minute!"

The rest is history. 'Em's contorted phizog was at it's most grotesque. Her pursed lips were set straight and cold like waxed stone and her frowning forehead clouded those pig-like angry blue eyes. She stood staring in disbelief and pain at the ruined tablecloth, now unbearably exposed for all to see in the cold light of day. I hung my head, though certainly not in shame. I didn't know the meaning of the word, or so 'Em had told me - so many times that I now believed it. I hung my head because I could not bear to look at the damage I had done. It was like waiting for an earthquake to erupt. Like any of God's creatures that sense danger, it was flight or fight time for me. I got ready to flee - for I hadn't learnt to fight back....yet.

Whether it was the copper stick this time, or the crack around the head, no dinner or supper, or the memorable time she collapsed weeping with her head in her hands (strangely a more sinister punishment and conscience-stirrer than any thrashing) I can't remember. I was beaten that many times. I think this was the time I sustained a lifelong perforated eardrum, from an unusually hefty smack around the ears. Do we learn from punishments like these? It's a good quesion. But of course we do though not what we are expected to learn (the difference between right and wrong). I had learned that chenile tablecloths and wax don't mid. I also learned, later, from a woman's magazine, how to remove substances like wax from such materials as chenile. You use a heated knife. Pretty useless knowledge but you never know. It would have come in handy at the time. I'm hardly likely to do it again, but in years to come my own naughty little boy might. I also learned that a smack around the earhole can burst your eardrums. So the punishment was not totally without value as a learning tool.

And odd thing happened a few months after this disaster. A mysterious occurrence that has puzzled me to this day. I will politely ask the reader (who by now might be ruefully recalling his own childhood misdemeanous - or even frowning at mine) whether he remembers being punished for something he didn't do. If so,don't feel sorry for yourself. You were not alone. Most of us have suffered from this terrible injustice when we were kids, and remember going into a deep and mystified sulk at the unfairness of it all.

One day 'Em discovered the backs of some armchair cushions had been crazily slashed with something like a razor. Naturally she assumed that that little evacuee sod had done it, and I was beaten anyway. But this time I wasn't guilty, and that is the gospel truth. I hadn't done it.

And to this day I remember this 'crime' for that reason. As there was only 'Em, myself, and wee Billy Bunting in the house, it really was a mystery to me who - or what - had carried out this particular and very peculiar piece of mischief. Most of the things I did for a reason, no matter how stupid, illogicalm, or childish it was. I never did damage for damages sake. This was the first time I'd ever seriously considered the possibility of ghosts, or poltergeists (do ghosts exist? A contradiction in terms if ever I've heard one) . I also wondered if I HAD done it and was, at last, going a little mad.

Some days later, when Mrs Bateson grilled me once again about the slashed cushions, I ventured my deep-thought-out theory that maybe ghosts had done it. A quite resonable proposition I thought, under the circumstances. It seemed a particularly silly ghostly sort of trick to me. I was beginning to try reasoning with her over my so-called crimes. To give my view of the story for once.

Ghosts were beginning to feature large in my imagination at this time. I was at that age. They became a handy excuse and took the rap for all sorts of trouble I was getting into. I had realised that ghosts were invisible or easily became so - and could walk through walls, and therefore could escape the consequencies of anything they had done, and would let somebody else take the blame. I was having none of this. They were expected to do crazy things without rhyme or reason, beyond the understanding of mere human adults. A bit like myself at that time actually.

My remark that maybe ghosts were to blame did not go down well with 'Em and met with a blank uncomprehending stare. She was much to down to earth to listen to such nonsense. "Ghosts?" she repeated, as if she had never heard of the word... "Ghosts?" She probably thought I was trying to act stupid on purpose to dodge the issue. I was in danger of getting another clout, so I quickly dropped the subject. But even to this day I truly suspect it was my first ghostly experience, introducing the supernatural world of spirits and odd happenings, as they must, sooner or later, introduce themselves to each and every one of us. Hands up those who think they have experienced some kind of supernatural phenomena when they were young, and more susceptible to such carrying on.

You see, I thought so. Almost everyone.

CHAPTER 12

Running Scared

This chapter, in tune with that period of my life I shall now write about, is mixed up, disconnected, and, like myself at that time I think, a little bit cranky and destabilised.

In a comparatively short space of a few years, at this young age, I had been put into a childrens' home and had lost contact with my Mum and Dad and brothers before I even remembered them. I had then been evacuated from Southern England to the Midlands, and had been dumped with a village family living in an isolated hamlet in the heart of rural Staffordshire. Here I witnessed the slaughter of animals and suffered criticism, abuse and regular beatings from a woman I could not escape from and who was a total stranger to me. No wonder I was growing into a hard, bitter, rebellious and confused child. I had had too many sudden and disturbing changes in my life, too young, too soon.

These traumatic changes, and my resultant misbehaviour and the punishments for such, were leaving their mark. I was becoming an unhappy, mixed-up small boy. Certainly, from 'Em's point of view, I was an unexpected thorn in her side: I was turning into a hard-faced, mischievous, complex, worrying and unfathomable bundle of boy-trouble.

Like fungus, in the minds and hearts of such children particularly, grow these psychosomatic fine mycelia-type threads that weave like convolvulous weeds through the young fertile soil of a child's pain and imagination, blurring their ability to distinguish between fantasy and reality, love and hate, and right and wrong. It is a desperate wish to escape their misery that drives these unhappy kids' introspective habits ever deeper, to try and find some sort of sense and solace within themselves. It's the only place they have to run to. But they will find no peace there, only bad thoughts, bad dreams and...

Nightmares.

Nightmares, and the thought of ghosts, began to trouble me a lot (are they nature's escape valve?). Mainly after serious run-ins with 'Em. I suppose it was anxiety, nerves and worry. I was too young to cope with such feelings.

And my only kind friend Old Harry Mould, the baker from over the road, had recently died. He'd been sitting in the outside loo. Not having a crap but having a crafty ciggy out of sight of his nagging Missis. They'd found him happy but very dead, with his double chins resting peacefully on his chest and a soppy smile on his face. He was sitting in the middle of a scattering of fag-ash and surrounded by a haze of his favourite nicotine smoke, almost frozen to the toilet-seat on a frosty, foggy winter's eve. Not a pretty sight and not a nice way to go. That upset and unsettled me a lot. It was my first taste of the death of a human, and especially one I was fond of.

It was still foggy some days later when, on passing the half-open door of the same toilet, my hair stood on end as I saw him again. Coughing and choking through clouds of smoke, I clearly perceived his old grey floury flannel trousers rucked around his ankles. On seeing me he beckoned in slow motion (as all the best ghosts do) and, smiling childishly, started reciting his Sticky Micky Jam Tart poem. He faded away as quickly as he had materialised. I will always believe he was saying goodbye, as he'd been so surprised by death, he'd missed me the first time.

Many of my nightmares occurred when I'd been sent to bed early after a whacking from 'Em, for it was then that I was at my pits of unhappiness. I was sleeping with Tommy Bateson at one time and this particular night I floated up to the ceiling.

It was weird. In the early hours of the morning when only ghosts and ghoulies should be abroad I felt myself beginning to rise gradually from the bed. It was a frightening yet pleasant feeling at the same time. My body was relaxed. I rose slowly. This isn't really happening I told myself. It's a dream. Another nightmare.

I always have had a pretty analytical mind, even as a kid. Well, I thought, there's only one way of finding out whether this is a dream or not. By now I was bouncing face-forward onto the ceiling. I'll turn myself round I thought, and see if Tommy and myself are still down there sleeping on the pillows. If I was still sleeping then I was either dead and my spirit had left my body on its way to heaven, or it was merely a silly, harmless dream. But if I wasn't there...

So I reached out my arms to the ceiling and attempted to swing myself round.

It wasn't that easy to do. My body seemed weighted, like counter-balanced with lead weights. But then, I analysed, it would be...big heavy bum and all that, at the bottom. A bit like a ship really, bobbing in the water, that won't overturn. So I kept pushing and punching the ceiling with one hand, and bouncing back a bit and trying, like an astronaut in space, to get some thrust from thin air, and to somersault my torso arse-abouts.

Well, it would work eventually, wouldn't it? After all, it was only a dream and in dreams anything is possible. So, after telling myself this, like telepathy, it happened. I spun slowly round and faced downwards with my bum banging on the ceiling. And there, like an inflated rubber doll, I hovered.

Tommy was still there O.K. Curled up, foetus fashion, sleeping soundly with his habitual heavy snoring and breathing. All looked abnormally normal. But I wasn't there. My place was empty.

It is possible, as we all know, to see fine detail in dreams, enhanced beyond anything we see in waking hours. The same as with drugs. I'd eaten some blue-stalks for my supper (a type of toadstool) and I've often wondered if it was these that had caused this nightmare. Anyway, I studied my empty bed space. Yes, the indentation of where my head had been on the pillow was clearly discernible. It looked as though an invisible man's head was still resting there. Likewise the ruckled blankets and sheets. I decided it wasn't a dream after all. I really was floating.

So, with this realisation, I began to feel really scared.

Under some unearthly irresistible force my body swung round again to face the ceiling. I had the feeling that unless I did something quick I would bob about against the ceiling till kingdom come.

So, still pushing my hands across the cold damp plaster of the ceiling and noting its familiar cracks on the way, I propelled myself, still bouncing gently, towards the small open window of the bedroom.

My head went through the window, but I was prevented from floating out into the night by my shoulders jamming against the window frame (thank God, or I don't know what would have happened to me. I'd have floated away). Being physically trapped in the window convinced me I wasn't dead. I was merely floating. With my horizontal body bouncing and wavering about like a straw in the wind, and with my head stuck outside the small window like a man in the stocks, I floated, face up, staring out at the indigo night sky, inset, like diamonds, with twinkling stars.

I felt the cool damp night air on my skin (or was it stone-cold petrified sweat?). A slight breeze ruffled my hair. I thought, this must be real: surely dreams don't have weather. It was a lovely night. If God had called me at that moment, I wouldn't have been at all surprised or scared. I felt it was the right time. I felt calm now, almost happy... prepared. I would have taken his hand and, like Peter Pan, I would have flown willingly with him to heaven.

Then suddenly I was back in bed, jolting upright with a stifled cry that almost woke Tommy Bateson. I was back in the cold land of the livng, and reality. But I had to check. Such experiences as these have a long-lasting effect on us and yet, in the same breath, mean nothing. They either actually happened or they didn't. We are either dying or we are still very much alive. That is my considered opinion anyway.

Another troubled night I awoke to someone calling my name and tapping on the bedroom window-pane, during those awful early hours when nothing earthly or decent should be roaming abroad. I sat up and half-answered the eerie summons with a choked and comic "Uhu?" as the Yankee comics say. Petrified with fear I caught sight of myself in the dressing table mirror, my hair was standing up on end, like frozen stalagmites. What is this thing calling me, so far up from the ground, I remember thinking.

An upside-down face framed in one of the small casement windows leered back at me like the evil dead, the irises of its wild eyes ringed and edged in black like funereal gothic eye-shadow. Its wispy hair hung downwards and blew scarily in the wind. It was a classic horror face, bearing an expression of everlasting pain and terror. Who or what he was I shall never know. Nor why he hung onto the gutters of the house by his toe-nails: for that is what I assumed he (or it) was doing. Otherwise how did he appear upside down outside the window? (me with my practical mind again). For what seemed like an eternity we eyeballed each other, him leering, pulling faces, swivelling his white eye-balls and grinning fiendishly, and me just sitting up straight and stiff in bed wide-eyed and by now wide-awake, and terror-stricken. Perhaps it was a Freudian phantom dredged up from the depths of the mud of my disturbed subconscious: an imagined mental configuration of my missing Dad (a phantasmagorical doppel-ganger) and he was tapping to draw my attention to himself (Look, I'm your father. Let me into your life!). If this was so I later mused, and he looks like that, then he can jolly well stay where he is, be it in Hades or in his grave. I wasn't so much bothered about my missing Pop after this experience. But I still missed my Mom, who appeared in my dreams in a much prettier, gentler, guise.

It was also around this time that Mrs Bateson accused me of neglecting my tame rabbits. "You haven't fed those bloody rabbits again, have you?" she moaned. "Don't think I'm going to feed them for you, I've got enough to do. And when was the last time you cleaned them out, for God's sake. If you don't learn to look after them properly I'll turn them loose in the fields. That'll teach you."

"I thought I'd fed them" I lied.

"You know what thought did?" she mocked, responding to my hackneyed excuses with one of her favourite hackneyed questions. "He shit himself, and thought he did".

She had some silly sayings, some originating from comical Staffordshire wise-cracks and old-fashioned sayings and some from her Granny, from her childhood days. I think she got some of them mixed up - mixed metaphors. I'd often tried to make sense of this one about 'Thought' and what he had done. I mean, if he'd shit himself, then thought he had - how was it that he hadn't known it in the first place, straightaway? I'm sure I would. I wouldn't have to think about it. I was given to trying to analyse conundrums like this. I've never liked vague or silly remarks that don't make sense. That's were a lot of the confusion in life comes from. Vagueness.

Where was I? Oh yes, the rabbits. A few days later, accusing me again of not looking after them properly, she carried out her threat and turned them loose in the fields. It was supposed to hurt and worry me.

But this time it was the wrong thing to do because,in truth, I was not really bothered about my rabbits anyway. I was fed up with looking after them. After a while tame rabbits are boring and messy pets in any case. They do nothing but sit in their pens gawking at you, and jumping about in anticipation of their dandelion leaves and lettuce leaves. And they forever need cleaning out. And they stink.

But, for the purpose of gaining some sympathy, I told my mates (and my mates told their Mums) and everywhere I went they all tut-tutted about that cruel Mrs Bateson ill-treating her

ANNT BREAD

poor little evacuee boy and turning his pet rabbits loose. This suited me as I could do with all the sympathy I could get in those days, and anyway, her 'cruelty' was backfiring on her and spoiling her reputation.

And then rumours spread that wild rabbits had mated with my loose tame rabbits and all sorts of odd coloured piebald monstrosities had been seen jumping around in the surrounding fields, though I never actually came across any myself.

And because of this unpleasant misunderstanding between 'Em and myself I've been haunted by rabbit dreams all my life. And today I can not look a tame rabbit in the face, without a shudder of uneasy conscience. In my dreams I am rushing to my rabbit pens with a feeling of panic that I have forgotten to feed them for months.

Fumbling with the latches, I peer inside the pens. At first they seem empty. I put my head right inside like Alice in nightmare land. Maybe that is where the dream had come from, Alice in Wonderland. I was reading a lot of fantastic fairy-stories at the time. They can make a deep impression on a worried youngster.

Atop and amid the vile rabbit dung and the deep urine-soaked straw, starved rabbits, dead and alive, some already skeletons but still hopping about, stare back at me with their large accusative, buring-bright rabbity eyes. We were dependant on you for food, they seem to be saying. And on cleaning out our hutch. How could you forget us for so long?

And their magnified faces come closer and closer and they grunt and snap at me like dogs with their large, sharp and powerful rabbit teeth. It is quite a nasty nightmare.

We all have scary anecdotes we remember from our childhood years. In the telling some of them might not sound so frightening, but they were at the time. We have a season when indeterminate shadows, and half-formed images cloud our imaginative and impressionable young minds. It is again a necessary part of our development, to help us distinquish fact from fantasy. Who has not seen the nodding seahorses riding the waves on the gently blowing bedroom curtains? Or traced

135

the path of the brightly coloured snake as he wends his way through the lush flowers on the wallpaper? The airborne wraith who taps at your window in the small wee hours (like mine did) and the invisible but unimaginably hideous gargoyle who silently stands and watches you as still and as inscrutable as a statue, in the darkness at the foot of your bed? Who has not heard the half-dead man in the attic, knocking for your attention only when the wind blows? And the giant rat who has been trying to gnaw his way into your bedroom for years, surely he must be nearly through by now?

Messing about one evening I was late coming back from Aunt Bessie's house in Kingstone village about a mile away from The Blythe. I preferred walking the woodland path that bordered two thirds of the road on the way back to Blythe Bridge but tonight it was too dark. I'll take the high-road I thought, and let the devil take the woodland path. I must have been tempting fate and the devil read my thoughts.

This particular journey had never worried me before even as I walked through darkening woods as the evening light faded. I strode confidently on my way without a care in the world.

I suddenly caught sight of a twinkling light dancing among the shadowy black cameo of trees on my left, in the roadside wood.

So what? I told myself... it was simply a star, low in the sky, appearing to bounce along through the trees, winking at me when it found a gap then disappearing again behind a clump. It was playing hide and seek with me, like a firefly woodland sprite wasn't it? A common enough phenomenon.

If, in passing along a snow-covered road, I am hit by a snowball, I will always join in and throw one back. It is my nature. I like a bit of fun. If a star wished to play games with me...great - I will play games back with the star.

So I bobbed low on the unlit country road. But the star was clever and unpredictable. It too bobbed out of sight and I lost it. I straightened up and quickened my pace a little, watching over my shoulder for the reappearance of the mischievous star.

Then suddenly it was there again jumping from tree to tree. Watching closely, it occurred to me that this particular star was not behaving as stars should. Its apparent movement should be following a fixed pattern, but it was not: its course was random and erratic. I should be the only one really moving along I thought, the star is not really alive and playing with me. It is an inanimate thing. It should be fixed in its place in the universe. For some apparent reason, the beginnings of a shiver ran up my spine. You know the feeling: something is not quite right here. For the first time, it occurred to me that someone might be following me, dogging me, in the wood alongside.

Now I felt a bit scared. I tested it out for a star. But when I stooped low and ran the star bobbed up and down in the wood, and when I bobbed up and down on the road, the star sailed smoothly along in a straight line. When I stopped, the star carried on, and when I ran, the star stood still.

I quickened my step still further. The star followed suit. I started to trot, my studded boots echoing on the deserted road. The faster I ran, the faster followed the mysterious flickering light alongside me in the darkness of the trees. With a feeling of growing panic I told myself 'there is someone in the woods with a torch following me. Tormenting me. Trying to reach that path that leads out of the woods before me, so that he can catch me'. My imagination was going haywire.

To this day I don't know what or who it was. It could have been something or nothing. Perhaps a couple of mates having a joke, I don't know. I never make guesses at things I'm not sure about. But was I scared? You bet I was. Spurred on by the wings of fear, I hurtled homewards as fast as I could. I must have looked a comical sight. I was never so glad to see the hated Mrs B and the mellow lamplight from the flickering flame of the ancient oil lamp on the table flooding the old farm kitchen like a misty yellow fog.

Winter evenings were my worst times. With Mrs Bateson always polishing and dusting and nagging and watching every move I made, I found the oppressive atmosphere in the house almost impossible to live with.

I was always trying to find something to do. A favourite boys' hobby at this time, was stamp collecting. I saved my earned (and unearned) money and purchased a superior-quality stamp album. Cheap stamps could be bought in bulk in exciting well-packed envelopes. It was rumoured you might come across a rare expensive stamp among the cheapies, though I never believed this schoolboy myth. Business folk are not that sloppy or, if they seem to be, it is only a sale's gimmick. But single rare stamps were expensive. During these long boring winter evenings, I sat poring over my album. I was developing an avid interest in my collection, studying every single stamp.

Mrs Bateson asked me where I had got the money from to purchase so many stamps and such an expensive-looking album. "You've stolen it, haven't you?" she accused, without waiting for an explanation. As if stating a tiresome fact.

Well, I would hardly have said "Yes" would I? In fact, I'd earned most of it (my sources of stolen money were drying up and I wasn't so keen now on stealing anyway, finding it too much of a hassle, to my conscience and in the act). Well, maybe a little stolen money was in there somewhere. I was getting money, with difficulty, from all sorts of places.

She paced about the room working herself up and getting more and more agitated, nagging and muttering about me stealing money and damn stamp albums. For my part I sat silently with my head bent over my stamps, trying (or pretending) to concentrate on my stamps, but having to listen to this unnecessary vindictive ranting tirade going on in the background.

She must have built herself up into a fury. Suddenly she snatched up the album from under my nose and with the full force of her anger threw it viciously on the fire.

It happened so fast that for a moment I couldn't comprehend what had taken place. I watched in stunned disbelief as it quickly caught fire and the pages slowly blackened, curled, and burned. They turned and burned one by one, as if being turned slowly and deliberately by an invisible spiteful fire-demon.

I can see this burning book in my mind's eye to this very day. Like those graphic detailed nightmares I can even discern the rare and valuable stamps on the pages, scorching and turning black, slowly disappearing into eternity as the encroaching flames took them from me forever. It would not be an exaggeration to say that with them went part of my innocence and youth. From such events are we tempered in the furnace of life. I felt it was the most cruel thing Mrs Bateson had ever done to me ... beside this, beatings were nothing. Boyhood was hardening into stoic manhood. The lesson that treasured possessions,in the last resort, mean nothing at all, was being learnt. The deep as yet unstirrred waters of my soul were being agitated and awakened...into anger, hatred, and...yes, sorrow. I felt tears welling up into my eyes.

There is no point in trying to recall each tremor, each tiny destructive metamorphosis of innocent soul and spirit, into something harder, something more forever implacably unchangeable and unforgiving than anything I'd ever felt before. It was like an emotional earthquake that changed my life forever. The rape and death of innocence cannot be described in any words, not even by Shakespeare. The death of innocence? Yes. Perhaps I WAS an awkward, troublesome, naughty youngster. Perhaps I HAD stolen money to buy stamps. The snuffing out of real innocence is not about mere worldly issues like stealing, lying, or telling fanciful stories. These things are just pin-pricks on the soul of innocence.

It is about the death of childhood and the stark awakening to the reality of the harsh, brutal and thoughtless world of adults. Here, shameless lies and pretence, selfishness, deceit and blinkered ignorance have grown rampant and have free range far beyond anything that any child knows or understands.

For a frozen moment of time my emotions were a cauldron of rapidly swirling, changing and altering feelings. I was under the metaphysical surgeon's knife and my soul was being reformed. Coming into sharp focus were my feelings of aloneness and abandonment. I needed a friend, an ally: I wanted my Mum and Dad. Where were they now in my moment of need? Deeper in the bowels of my soul eddied the recipe that would ultimately make me a man. Sadly it consisted of a good dash of bitterness, a blend of strange intuition and knowledge that would give me a twisted mental smirk at life, and much, much hate - directed, at this moment, mainly at 'Em. We have to direct it at someone.

You might think, well, it was only the burning of a stamp album, so what? Why go on about it so? But I think, in that moment, I mentally murdered her. If my hate had died with the much later death of 'Em, no lasting harm would have been done. But life is not as simple as that. These childhood traumas leave their incised mark. Nay, more than that: they make us what we are. That emotional scalpel leaves a scar. There is no escape. Like Blackpool rock, the imprint permeates right through and is often indelible and indecipherable.

I had a little cry and the salty tears washed out my eyes and dried on my face. But my spirit would cry for a long time yet. I childishly vowed within my heart, once again for the umpteenth time, that I'd hate Mrs Bateson 'till the day I died and, though I'm not dead yet (I hope) I have thought for most of my life that that vow would be kept. But life moves on. There are more pressing things to worry about than to hate forever. But, Writing this, I am a child again, and it is the moment of the burning of my childhood dreams I am reliving. And at that time, hate and sorrow reigned supreme and forever. Although 'Em did not realise it, it was her ultimate punishment on me, or what? Stab the victim enough times and sooner or later you will hit a vital organ. Worse things have happened to me since, but nothing has hurt me quite as much as the burning of my precious stamp album. It was an emotional watershed.

It sounds a lot of fuss over a mere stamp album, I hear you say. If this is your conclusion then you are not hearing what I am saying. You do not understand the links and threads that make the tapestry that form a chequered life. It was not the destruction of the album. It was not my misery and sorrow. It was not even 'Em - though she was the cause and catalyst. At every age we are all fumbling our way through the ups and downs of life, forever trying to make sense of it all and to see a light at the end of the tunnel. This was just my first real struggle, a pivotal event, as they say today, to try and understand my own, personal, pitfall-filled, twisting and tortuous path through that storm.

Neither 'Em nor I could possibly know it at the time, but henceforth and onwards the days of her hold over me were numbered. Our relationship (for what it was worth, which wasn't much) was coming to an end. There was soon to come a point between 'Em and myself when the worm, at last, would turn. The accumulation of hate would so build up, that I would finally pluck up enough nerve to defy, confront and challenge her. I was growing up. With my confidence and courage growing now at every step, I was finding my way through the maelstrom. Modern kids may laugh at this pathetic-sounding story. Let them. For most, in modern-day society, this particular soul-seeking head-ache would just not happen. (But they'll have other different problems to contend with, never fear, and just as painful.) We are living in an unusually - and dangerously undisciplined - tolerant, so-called 'free society'.

But, ultimately, we all have our battles to fight. We all have to find our own path through life, otherwise we cannot grow into maturity. Perhaps this is what is wrong with modern life - there are no longer enough battles?

Aunt Annice
(Oasis of kindness)

The Author, about 19

Blythe Bridge

The Author

*The day of Bob's visit.
Showing niece Erica
the calves*

Olly and me

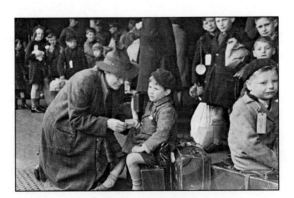

"Where's my Mum?"
(In my case, famous last words)

CHAPTER 13

Oasis of Kindnes

We had few callers at Batesons' smallholding apart from our mysterious week-end spiv visitors from Birmingham who came for their meat and country produce.

They brought their two beautiful teenage daughters with them, and chunky silver coins for Tommy's money box, which later I might extract.

Also there were few other young folk in the village with whom I could make friends. And, it has to be remarked, that if you have little choice of friends at this young age, you pal around with whoever's available whether you like them or not. This is not the case with many adults who, if they cannot find friends they like, will often prefer to keep their own company. But young people need and have to mix with friends of their own age, to keep their sanity and to gain and to give them confidence to feel their way towards adulthood. Young people also learn a lot from having friends of their own age.

So, apart from these few village pals, my life was pretty devoid of sympathetic peer-company. I felt something was missing. There was a gap within me that no one seemed able to fill. We have all experienced this at some point in our lives, mainly in the turbulent wastelands of adolescence. In short, I was lonely.

Loneliness is a funny thing, and like most situations in life has an up and a downside. This is not the moment for an in-depth look and analysis of the joys and pains of aloneness (which is a more appropriate word for what I am trying to explain). Suffice it to say, the up-side of aloneness, oddly and contrary to popular belief, has many joys and advantages and can be very positive; whereas the down-side, if you are the type that lets it get to you, can take many grim roads that, in the extremity, may lead to a withering on the vine, self-destruction, and sometimes, death.

The secret key is resilience, and an self-reliant spirit. But of course as a child you are not developed enough to understand these things. A child is only resilient to the degree that's already inherent in its nature. We are in the position of a young fledgling bird that stands wavering on the edge of its nest ready for its first headlong plunge into God knows what. To say it's a dodgy world out there is an understatement. The young bird might have a resilient nature, but it still has to leap into the unknown, unpredictable and downright dangerous, universe.

The young bird will only survive with a good measure of luck first and much resilience and sharpness later. The storms, dangers, and adversities facing it will either toughen and alert the chick or cause its destruction. It might (and many do) flutter clumsily straight into the open mouth of a marauding moggy who had already spotted the hapless bird teetering on the brink. After all, like most creatures, it was only born to become food for other animals. Or it might splatter itself on the windscreen of a passing car, especially now as (thanks to us humans) there aren't many trees left for the poor creatures to flee to for sanctuary and as a perch - a stepping stone - to his next plunge and foray into life.

Thus it is with all young life. At least young humans are protected from the outset as much as it is possible to protect the young, by the cosseting cloak of civilization.

So, still being here and still slightly sound of mind, I have survived (with a little damage) to tell you my story, and you have survived to read it. And I am forever grateful to the beacons and oases of kindness that helped me survive along the way. In my case they were few and far between and interspersed by many faces of grumps, scoffers, criticisers, bullies and selfish people, most of them with a surprising lack of sympathy, patience and understanding. But to those who always had time for a smile and a gentle word and hand to help me along the way, I say "Thank you". I know there always have and always will be such people, although they are comparatively rare.

Smelly Nothing was one such person. I will devote more to this oddball later. He was an itinerate farm labourer who came to live in our cow shed. His was a tramp's philosophy. He was not clever, nor educated, nor smart. By modern standards he was a no-hoper, an also-ran, a failure and a loser. Battered and bruised by more than his fair share of bad fortune. And he also stank to high heaven. But then again, he had nowhere to wash except the animal's water trough.

But he was kind. We sat on our logs in the cold damp coal-shed and discussed life and its problems over our mashed potatoes, pickled red cabbage, and 'Ems cold gristly beef.

He told me I would be O.K. in life, no more... He seemed wise to me at the time.

And he was right. I turned out O.K. but he did not. More of poor Smelly later.

Aunt Evelyn was another beacon that lit my way: she was not only kind and sympathetic she was young and pretty (and that helps too). One day, out of the blue, Aunt Evelyn came to stay with us. Now Aunt Evelyn was some sort of skeleton in the Batesons' cupboard, and connected with Mrs Bateson's mysterious past. Although I didn't understand these things at the time, I sensed a cloud of shame and some unmentionable scandal hung over the reason for and presence of Evelyn's 'holiday' with us. Don't ask me what was going on. I don't know. For all I know Aunt Evelyn might have had an abortion or something. She might even have been Mrs Bateson's illegitimate daughter from some earlier miss-conception. It's feasible. Such things were often kept hidden then. Something serious was obviously afoot as we never took lodgers. We never took anyone into the house to stay with us. As a mere war-evacuee and not a member of the family clique, I was to be told nothing. Nuff said. Who and from whence came the delectable Evelyn is of no consequence to the point of this particular episode. I have never been interested in family gossip, or the morals of such.

For this obscure reason I think they had kept Aunt Evelyn out of sight during her younger years. She had lived with Granny Bateson way out in another isolated village on the Staffordshire, Derbyshire border.

But now, as my pubescent eyes perceived, in the phraseology of the time, she had grown into a 'fair bit of crumpet'. Dropped into our hamlet of lewd and lusty country lads, she was like a sex-bomb waiting to be detonated and exploded amongst us.

As part of the war effort, a contest encouraging people to save money was launched in the local paper. The war papers were full of contests. There was one called "Kill the Squander Bug". He was a huge hairy horrible monster like a magnified bed-louse. The more money that was saved, the higher went the needle on the squander-bug's cardboard graph, until it tripped the hammer at the top which fell and squashed the Squander Bug to death. It was all about avoiding waste, for the war effort.

Trust me to remember that, over 50 year's later.

"Write a Limerick and win Fifteen Shillings" was this particular contest's challenge. Without telling anyone, Aunt Evelyn - in her early boredom at Bateson's dreary household and feeling sorry for this downtrodden evacuee she found herself living with, wrote and submitted a small simple poem, in my name:

My Brother is a soldier
And many others too,
And by us saving money,
It helps to pull them through.

Just the sort of banal stuff that wins competitions. You don't forget genius like that.

Anyway, it won. Evelyn, in her girly innocence, proudly waved the postal-order under my nose and laughingly announced, "Look Michael. I've won you fifteen shillings!" Emily Bateson was deeply sneaped and jealous. After all, remember, she had a young son of her own - her Billy Bunting. Why hadn't Emily written a verse for him? Especially as she was giving Evelyn a temporary home.

Evelyn bent over me and kissed me. Her sexy perfume and the earthy smell of her drooping breasts were not lost on my developing teenage sensors. We never forget those early stirrings roused by young senses that can tune so finely into love's sweet smelling bouquets, and tantalises us with visions of what (hopefully) is soon to come.

Mrs Bateson's glowering, spiteful and suspicious face hovered in the background.

Jealous Emily peevishly pointed out that my brother was not a soldier, he was an airman, nitpicking that Evelyn was telling lies in her poem. That was just the sort of woman she was. But for the first time in my life, with the help of my new ally, the sympathetic Evelyn, I really had got one up on 'Em (and her spoilt son). I felt it, and I knew it. And I savoured the moment.

Later, Evelyn took me aside, cuddled me and again gave me a shot of her breasts (was it accidentally on purpose? Perhaps she was testing her burgeoning sexuality out on this impressionable young virgin boy). Well, who's complaining? Certainly not me.

"Never mind what she says" Evelyn whispered conspiratorially. "I'm glad we've won".

Later in the week, quite out of the ordinary, Mrs Bateson went out for the day, unwisely stating she would not be back till late. She ought to have kept her mouth shut - for while the cat's away...

For a while now the local lads had been oggling and tittering over young Evelyn every time she made an appearance in the village, usually as she trotted over to the bakery shop (which she seemed to be doing more often than was necessary). If the lads were congregating outside the shop, it was any excuse to display her charms and for them to make ribald comments as lads do. It goes without saying they had all confided in me that they would love to 'shaft' her. Lads at that age are nothing if not crude. It was merely a contest of who would get there first. Teenage bravado talk mainly, for in those days talk was much easier to indulge in than the real thing. Not like today. We only shafted girls then in our imaginations and wet dreams.

Somehow, this day, they found out that Evelyn was alone at home (honestly, I didn't tell them). Like a plague of tom-cats homing in on a she-cat in heat they converged on the house. Shades of Straw Dogs. Probably Evelyn, like most strongly desired and lusted-after young fillies, had unwittingly sent out invitational sexual vibes. C'mon lads, try your luck sort of thing. Strong hot sexual flirting. A hot girl in a girlshort village.

At this age who knows what goes on? Adolescent sexual pulchritude has its own magic way of advertising itself. Like the invisible power of a magnetic compass, without even trying, it can sense the pubescent aromas radiating out from any sweet-smelling fuzz-box.

Like a party of raiding Marines, the village gang surrounded our house.

On spotting them, Evelyn grabbed me and used me as a sort of emotional shield. She whispered breathless excited confidences into my ear as she dragged me from room to room, peeping out through the windows trying to get a glimpse of the boys as they hid behind pig-sty walls and gooseberry bushes. It was quite funny really. "Ooo...ah, Michael! What DO they want? What are they after? (as if she didn't know). "Can you see who they are?" "Who is leading them on?" If I know girls, she was probably looking for her favourite boy among the crowd. Nothing excites a girl more than a pack of lustful boys after her.

I realise now she was probably sexually aroused as well as scared and excited - as these two raw emotions are often linked. "What if they get in the house?" She whispered breathlessly, half-hoping, I suppose, that they would get in. "I hope Aunt Emily doesn't come back early. She'll go mad".

I was being ushered and dragged from room to room, enjoying the unusual excitement. Anything is preferable sometimes, to excruciating long-term boredom. I was still too young to fully comprehend the possibilities of what might happen, though I was already sensing the name of the game.

And this game went on for most of the afternoon. It was getting dark. Soon, Mrs Bateson would be returning.

In the event, she did return early, and there was hell to pay. The marauding boys who had progressed to grimacing and making obscene remarks and gesturing through the windows, vanished like - well, like tom-cats scattered by an alarmed protective she-kitten owner. Someone had informed Mrs Bateson of what what going on, on the village grape-vine, and she had returned post-haste.

Mrs Emily Bateson was not as innocent and as self-righteous as she made herself out to be (are they ever?). But she played the part like an accomplished actress, and both Evelyn and myself received the full fury of her not inconsiderable tongue-lashing. "Good God!" she said. "I can't leave you two for five minutes". I had suspicions that in her youth 'Em had been a bit adventurous herself, in sexual matters. Perhaps that is why she made such a fuss. Hypocrites always complain the loudest.

Later I came upon Aunt Evelyn having sex on a raincoat with Uncle Jim (whom she later married). Wanting to walk with them, I had followed them through the field gate, wondering why they carried the raincoat into the fields on a sunny midsummer's afternoon.

Surely they don't think it's going to rain I remember thinking. Maybe I was slowly beginning to realise what was going on and was curious to find out more. There is an age when we just can't believe what we are hearing about these comical sexual antics that people get up to (well, that is what it was like then). It seems so incredibly private, intimate, personal and athletic, and so removed from everyday life (and so of course it is, for youngsters) and from the nice people we think we know.

Evelyn's head bobbed up out of the ditch they were in and urgently shooed me off. "Go away!" she shouted agitatedly, like you'd shoo away a curious gander. I felt rejected and unwanted again. But, in retrospect and now much older and wiser...I think, good luck to them. Sex in a summer's ditch is not to be sneezed at (unless you have hay-fever and are allergic to it). You don't get the opportunity that often.

Aunt Annice was another woman who seemed to have inexhaustible wells of love and kindness that gushed without strings over all who entered her orbit.

Aunt Annice was the mother of the children with whom I often played in the Old Mill. As children we obviously see people differently from when we are adults. In appearance Aunt Annice looked quite eccentric, and slightly wild and intimidating. She always had a fat red-face and looked rather stressed and hot and bothered.

She would be, I realise now: she had three very naughty kids, a husband who liked his ale too much and who earned erratically and who was always poorly with the inherited family disease of tuberculosis (he was another Bateson brother). There were also serious problems with The Old Mill House, that flooded every time the river rose. Her coarse, wavy grey hair was thick and strong and wiry and always looked unkempt, as though it was too strong to control. She was a large-built woman and, though so disconcerting in appearance, she was in fact very motherly and always wore an apron. She baked wonderful cakes and pastries. Behind myopial glasses glittered gimlet-sharp, piercing, rather angry-looking diamond-blue eyes, with a cast, magnified through the thick lenses of her specs.

We learn a lot about people and human nature as we grow older, and soon realise the saying "Things are not quite what they seem" is never truer than with the outward appearances of the human race. Aunt Annice's angry eyes were true enough.

We kids learned to make ourselves scarce and dived for cover when we saw the lightning flash in those steel-blue glittering eyes. A storm was brewing and would soon break. But her temper was as fast and as furious as any thunderstorm and was over as quickly as it had begun. Providing you didn't catch a punch from her flailing girthy arms, and get yourself mashed, it wasn't long before those same huge pastry-kneading arms were around you, and giving you a bear-hug (and she was as strong as a bear). I wasn't used to cuddles and embraces, and found them embarrassing. But I soon melted and relaxed in those motherly arms, and it brough an inexplicable lump that hurt my throat. So unfamilia and starved was I of motherly love.

I once watched amazed as she chased her two eldest kids half a mile up the field brandishing a pitch-fork like a spear, which, had it hit home, would have skewered them to death. And I knew, in the white-heat of her uncontrollable temper, she was quite capable of doing just that! How she never harmed her offspring I shall never know. But they just screamed and laughed and seemed to enjoy winding their mother up to make a clownish spectacle of herself. She was too big to sprint very fast and they knew they could easily outrun her and that later, in the cosiness of pyjamas and supper-time, Mum would give them a chunk of home-made cherry pie, a large mug of cocoa and a big hug and kiss before sending them up the wooden hill to bed.

As merely a rather lonely outsider, an onlooker observing this homely family scene, my heart would silently break and a suppressed sob would rise in my throat. It was a scene I would never really experience or be a part of.

Looking back, I believe Aunt Annice felt sorry for me. She well knew Emily Bateson (her sister-in-law) was an obsessive house-proud and cold-hearted woman who could never show any love for me. But being 'family', she had to be discreet. There are certain subtle conventions and understandings to be adhered to between even the most fractious of families (which

I well knew about). Blood is thicker than water and outsiders will always be put in their place if they try to take sides during family disputes. I was especially vulnerable in this way: as a very young war evacuee, dependent on Mrs Bateson, I had very little say.

Perhaps, had they not been related, Aunt Annice might have taken me further under the broad spread of her motherly wing (I would have liked to have lived with her). It was just my fate to be evacuated to the wrong one. But, as it was, her kindness to me was limited by these conventions. At the end of the day I was given my piece of pie and a hug, and shown the door. And that is the way of this world. If we don't belong in the first place we are never truly let in and accepted, whether we are loved or not loved.

The knowledge and the feeling of this can blight a rejected soul throughout his life - if he felt unloved and unwanted from the start. It can sometimes mean he will never really feel he belongs anywhere and to anyone, at any time.

Aunt Annice was the nearest I ever came to finding the warmth of a mother, at that time. It was natural to her and I don't suppose she ever realised the effect she had on me. This is how things are: we go through life being naturally nice or spiteful to people in a casual, off-hand manner, but rarely appreciate the life-long effects our actions might have on those people. And even beyond. Ripples on the pond of life.

As I grew older my own family started emerging from the shadows.

Mrs Bateson, unbeknowns to me, had long suspected my real mother was still around. I assume she had certain clues, and knew certain things about my past that I had never been told (kids are the last to be told of anything that concerns them). I presumed my mother was dead or, at the best, was still alive but just didn't want to know me.

In fact my mother was still very much alive and living in Liverpool. Apparently she had 'gone to earth' for reasons best known to herself. Many people lived very hard and troubled lives when my Mum was a girl, worse probably than the worse of scenarios now. Many working class people were desperately poor. Alchoholism was rife, and it was mostly the breadwinner (i.e. the man) who drank, beat and abused his wife and kids, wasted the family dosh, and sometimes ran-out on the whole sorry mess.

My Mum's problems were probably no different than thousands of others each battling along on their own trying to find an answer to their desperate plight. No money to feed the kids; a boozy wastrel of a husband; being hounded by the authorities for not paying their debts - the rent etc, or for not sending their kids to school because they had no shoes. Perhaps eventually evicted and put out on the streets, homeless. It happened ... and worse, on a world-wide scale.

Anyway, apparently she was in some sort of trouble with the authorities and had gone into hiding, dumping us kids in an orphanage for the state to look after. It really doesn't matter to me now, what happened. I'm the result, years later. Nothing will change that.

When I met my mother in later years, I discovered she was a very intelligent, resourceful - and remorseful, woman. Her troubles must have been very serious ones, for these attributes obviously hadn't helped her to solve her difficulties. Meeting her then (she is dead now) I can't believe she dumped us kids in childrens' homes, lightly. Still, it happened. And it led to me telling you this story. It is no use me having a post-mortem on the whys and wherefores of what MIGHT have happened, all these years later.

Anyway, at the time I am writing about, I still believed my mother was dead.

I had, for a long time, been receiving parcels of comics and crayoning books and things ostensibly from my elder brother Bob who lived in Liverpool (but they were really coming from my Mum, I realised much later). Although it isn't of any relevance, most of the crayons and crayoning books, paint-boxes and oil paints came from the firm of George Rowney.

Someone in the family obviously worked for this firm, and had either free or cheap access to these items.

My brother Bob, married now and with proud new wife and car, drove from his home in Liverpool to visit me in this Staffordshire village of Blythe Bridge where I'd been ensconced as an evacuee. This visit was to cause a strained and tense atmosphere in the Bateson household. Although I obviously wanted to meet my brother, I was rather nervous and apprehensive at the prospect of this visit. Nothing like this had ever happened to me before and I felt I was the centre of attention (which I was). Another new feeling. I was now about fifteen. Meeting someone from my family for the first time in over eight years - a family I never knew I had til recently.

When he knocked on our door at Blythe Bridge I sensed a strange, inexplicable and rather frightening crisis arising of which I was the central fly in the ointment ...the main trouble so to speak. When 'Em answered the door her voice had a protesting, angry and indignant sound to it. Tired after their long journey, and longing for a cup of tea, Bob and his wife Thea stood at the door a bit nonplussed. Emily Bateson would not allow them to enter the house. In the background, in the confines of the cold dark kitchen, I cowered, trying to catch snatches of the heated conversation at the door. I didn't really comprehend what was going on though I knew it was about me, and I sensed the growing tension.

"No. You are not seeing Michael. I don't care if you have come all the way from Liverpool to see him. You are not coming into my house!" Mrs Bateson's shrill voice was adamant.

Bob's soft-voiced answer came back quite calm and reasonable: "But why? We only want to see Mick. We're not out to cause any trouble. After coming all this way we don't want to go back without seeing him. We don't have to come in. Just let him come out of the house to see us".

"I know what you're up to" Emily railed on. "You want to turn him against me. He's all right as he is. You'll only upset and unsettle him". (As if I wasn't unsettled enough as it was.)

I couldn't understand why Mrs Bateson seemed so scared that she might lose me or my affections to my family: the trouble I'd given her and the rows we'd had, I'd have thought she'd be glad to see the back of me. She went on: "I know his mother is still alive you know. It's her who sends him comics and parcels isn't it? You pretend they come from you". (This was my first inkling that my mother was alive, and still interested in me.) Like a detective who'd upturned a stone concealing unsavoury details, 'Em continued to truculate. "You thought I didn't know didn't you? I'm not that daft. Why is she so frightened of showing herself? Has she got something to hide? Has she broken the law or something? Is she in trouble with the police?" (These vitriolic suspicions had been growing in her mind for years.)

I heard Bob speak but I couldn't make out his low and measured answer.

Eventually it was decided I could go outside and meet my brother and his wife, but under no circumstances would they be allowed to enter the house to see me. What difference it made where we met, I have no idea. I think she just didn't want to show any sign of friendliness or hospitality to them. Don't ask me why. Perhaps she felt frightened and guilty for some reason. Maybe she thought she'd lose me - now my family was coming to visit me - I don't know.

Bob called my name, and for the first time in my life (that I could remember) I met a member of my own family.

Bob took me for a ride and a talk in his car. Thinking about it, if Mrs Bateson had invited them in, it would have been to her advantage. They couldn't have confided to me anything that they didn't want her to hear. As it was, I was asked if I was all right living with Mrs Bateson, and was I 'happy'. (The subject of my mother was not mentioned.)

The word 'happy' has always made me feel unhappy, and slightly uneasy. Christmas does as well. I wanted to tell them I was very miserable, but, strange to say, I could not, and I mumbled "Yes". I think I was playing safe in this scary situation. I had (and still have) an unfathomable sense of pride and independence, and just plain old-fashioned contrariness, even at that age. I didn't want to admit to anyone that I was unhappy. I felt ashamed of it. It was like having a rare disease: I thought I was the only person in the whole world who could be this unhappy, and if other people found out how unhappy I was they wouldn't want to know me. I know it sounds daft, but that is how I felt. These things are psychologically complex.

Here, I remember one of those odd, silly little things which has no bearing on this episode. It happened as I sat in the car waiting for my brother to return from his talk with Ma Bateson.

He had a flimsy lamp-shade on his back seat and I sat on it and squashed it. You would have thought that that was the least of my worries, wouldn't you? But I worried myself sick about it for months afterwards and I couldn't sleep that night for thinking about it. If you're reading this story brother Bob, sorry I squashed your lamp-shade. Did you ever find out about this guilty clumsiness of mine? I've often wondered. Or don't you even remember it and have I have carried this darkest secret on my conscience all these years for nothing?

Anyway, I owe you the price of a lampshade. I hope it was a second-hand one.

Another thing I remember worrying about was the fact that Thea, his wife, remarked she was dying for a cup of tea. I felt responsible for not being able to offer them one, after all they'd come a long way just to see wee unimportant little me. Remember, I lived in the heart of the country, and there were very few roadside cafes or restaurants around then.

I was about fifteen years old at this time so why was I worrying about cups of tea and squashed lampshades? Shouldn't I have been hugging my brother and asking him about my real Mum and Dad? But again, real life is not like that. That is for the sob-story slush movies. I was too much in reality and well screwed up as I've already made clear. I had no idea of the conventions of behaviour under such circumstances and manifestations of love did not come naturally to me because of my stunted starved emotional upbringing.

Then suddenly I thought of Aunt Annice.

I was not sure whether she would help as she would not want to fall foul of her sister-in-law, 'Em. But I felt sure enough of her friendship to ask anyway, and that is worth a lot. She was the last and only straw I could clutch at. I was hovering in the inexperience and indecision of youth.

"I bet Aunt Annice would like to meet you" I told Bob anxiously. I was assuming she would and also I didn't want him to think I had no friends at all. I felt so embarrassed.

"And who is Aunt Annice?" Bob enquired kindly. He sensed my dilemma and the misery I was in.

"She lives in The Old Mill. Turn the car round and I'll show you the way. She'll make you a cup of tea". I felt desperate and at a loss what to do. I was assuming and taking a risk. I also felt guilty at having to almost beg for a cup of tea. I was dealing with a situation and feelings completely new to me, and I suppose I was too young and immature to cope.

But this is how it is with dependable, loving friends, isn't it? You just know they'll be there to listen and help in your moment of need, and ask no questions and expect no obligation.

And she was, and she did. She was surprised, delighted and even honoured that I'd brought them to meet her. They were ushered into The Old Mill house (an experience in itself for city folk) and plied with as many cups of tea and cream cakes as they could manage. And we all had a happy and a jolly afternoon. Henceforth Aunt Annice always seemed to almost revere my family (and myself). She seemed charmed by them. At the risk of sounding snobbish, I think she considered us 'class'. I don't know why. Nobody could have been classier than Aunt Annice for saving me from a very embarrassing situation and for her natural warmth and hospitality. Real class is not based on learned etiquette, it comes from within. As expected, Mrs Bateson never forgot this traitorous deed on her sister-in-law's part, but as always with such things there was nothing she could do about it but sulk. After all, she was the loser, and - true to her nature - had cut off her own nose to spite her face.

After this occurrence 'Em began to show me a little more respect and kept her distance. I think she was beginning to see the turning of the worm, and the writing on the wall. I was, by degrees, beginning to fight my own corner. Now I had my own family watching over me, albeit from a distance, and she had to be more careful what she said and did. Never again would I feel totally alone and unrepresented. I was slowly (very slowly) gaining ground against her, getting older, understanding my situation better, and feeling more confident. Not quite yet was the worm ready to turn. I was still fumbling my way in the half-light and was still unsure as to what was what. But I was experiencing a new feeling, a feeling of growing power, confidence and independence. And my next stepping stone across the dangerous and turbulent river of life had been pointed out for me by Bob, his wife Thea, and ...above all, my lovely and dependable Aunt Annice.

Much later in life, when I'd left school and had joined, served my term and then left the Royal Air Force, I finally walked out of the Bateson household and went to live with Aunt Annice for a short while. She was getting old now. Her wild grey hair was coarser than ever, and the angry eyes had lost a little of their threatening fire but not their sparkle. People do not change intrinsically as they grow older. She was still the same kind old soul. But, unlike Emily Bateson, I found Aunt Annice anything but house-proud. The beds were never made and the house was always untidy, but it was a pleasure to live like this for a change. These were unimportant trivialities compared with the love I was now surrounded by. Aunt Annice had got her priorities right: Love first, bullshit whenever.

When I left Aunt Annice's abode, I gave her a large edition of The New Imperial Dictionary and she couldn't have been more pleased with my choice of a 'thank you' present. (I had become an inveterate reader and word-nut).

I had a quiet smile. She would never read it. It would be given pride of place at the front of the bookcase. It was esteem and learning that women of Aunt Annice's ilk respected, for they'd never had a chance of acquiring it for themselves. For them it was large families, struggling poverty, and drunken husbands - or worse.

I might as well relate the sequel to this anecdote, though it is out of sequence of the time I write about. Time passed and I lost touch with Aunt Annice. Then, a few years ago, I was belatedly informed that she had died and was being buried in Kingstone Churchyard. In my posh car and my comfortable early thirties, I now hurried back through the old village lanes where once, as a lonesome and unhappy boy I had rode my home-built soapbox go-cart wearing my tatty bus conductor's hat. I hadn't visited the place for many years, and it was a trip into my past, down memory lane. I pulled up at the ancient ivy-covered village church where I had once stood unwillingly earning my Sunday School attendance stamps and had gazed in awe at God's stained glass windows. I had this sense that it was a time for me to pause and forget the bustling world I now inhabited and to reflect on my life - past, present and future (and my own ultimate death) for a moment. We should all do this at crisis or pivotal times in our lives. It is a needful and sobering exercise... Where had I come from? At what point in my life did I now stand? And where was I going to in such a headlong rush, along with the rest of the modern human multitude? Everything in the village seemed to have shrunk, and it had been trimmed neatly into a park-like scenario (a modern trend) and it now appeared to me like one of those toy-town villages where visiters walk around looking like giants.

Where once it had been my life I now felt to be an intruder, a stranger standing in this quaint rural backwater where little had changed but myself. I felt no sentimentality like in the story books: just a feeling of unease and disorientation. A part of me - the ghost of my childhood - must surely still be here, I thought, standing beside me. But nothing felt right. Here I stood in the middle of my comfortable affluent middle years, alone with my thoughts and surrounded by the epitaphs of recent and long-dead villagers (a few years later I stood in the same churchyard surveying the Batesons' family graves - all of them). Graveyards are sobering places, and the ornaments of death tell us a lot about the living if we can but see it. While I stood there I felt insignificent and detached from my present life. The world was too much with me. I wanted no part of this grave and sombre scene. I did not belong here in this place of frozen memories: I belonged to the living present and wanted to hurry back to my bustling real-life normality, to my home, my wife and kids.

But, typically, I was late for my old friend's funeral. The mourners and been and gone and I stood in the deserted churchyard alone and surveyed the flowers on her grave already hanging their heads in the hot sun. A lump in my throat and a solitary tear was all I could offer this dear departed lady who had helped me so many years ago. An Oasis of Kindness indeed. And to be remembered for that alone is the best that anyone can hope for in this desolate world lit only by beacons rare, along the lonely and oft-times desolate paths of life.

People like Aunt Annice will never be forgotten.

Truly kind people,in my childhood, I can count on the fingers of one hand. A few had offered kindness out of pity, sensing my lonely childhood plight. They wanted to help, but didn't know how, and were beset by their own problems anyway. But the few warm gestures they tentatively proffered me did not go unnoticed nor unacknowledged - I hope. My shrewd eyes always showed my gratitude, even though my shyness, timidity and 'training' held me back from any open display of emotion.

Others were naturally kind people: kind to animals, flowers and fauna and other humans...and me. Their type of kindness came almost incidentally. They might be ugly losers or backward oddballs that nobody else could be bothered with, or lazy layabouts too dissolute even to keep themselves clean...but they always had one thing in common: they were kind.

Aunt Ida was another one such. Wife of the scoundrel Zac who ran the slaughterhouse, and mother of my dim-witted pal Olly, she was just the opposite of her house-proud sister-in-law, Emily Bateson. On returning home from a visit to Olly's house I would be quizzed by 'Em if Aunt Ida's place still resembled a pigsty. As was my wont, when I didn't wish to join in any malicious gossip and denigrate my friends (or their families) I would simply mutter a diplomatic and noncommittal "Mm". It was a great conversation killer.

In truth, compared with 'Em's immaculate palace, Aunt Ida's place WAS a pigsty. But it didn't bother me. Indeed, after the discomfort of living in Emily's tidy house, I found it quite funny, and strangely relaxing. It smelled a bit, true, but there was no pressure or tense atmosphere.

Aunt Ida was scruffy, dirty, untidy and lazy. Perhaps this is why Uncle Zac chased other women. I called there on my bike two or three times a week and Oliver and I would cycle into Uttoxeter to the pictures, and later, to the pubs. Coming from an ultra-clean and spotless domicile, Oliver's house was an eye-opener to me.

When I called for him Olly was never ready, and I would have to wait for anything over an hour while he tore around and berated his mother for having no clean or ironed shirt prepared or even laundered and ready for him to wear. He sometimes went out in a still-damp shirt. These problems were unknown to me. Clean, ironed and mothballed-fresh shirts and ready-darned socks came ready out of the bedroom drawers didn't they? I'd never even had cause to question who had put them there. It was as if a unseen good fairy did them for me. It was the same with the crisp white pillow cases and bed linen.

In Aunt Ida's house the old settee legs, springs and padding had collapsed, so you lowered yourself carefully almost to floor level to sit down. It was difficult to find a reasonably comfortable spot, for protruding springs stuck up your backside. While Olly dashed hither and thither, taking odd bites out of his doorstep-thick gooseberry-jam sandwich, while having a shave, while waiting for his shirt to be washed, dried and ironed, I would be offered a doorstep sandwich myself. Although I had just had my tea, I would take it. Young folk always think they're hungry and what other people eat always seems more interesting and more tasty than what they get at home, though this is another illusion of childhood.

The fashion for us young aspiring Don Juans at that time was, believe it or not, to have our hair sleeked down with liquid paraffin. Mrs Bateson used to moan (with some justification for once) how it soaked into her pillowcases. Brylcreem was the usual dressing, but we couldn't afford that.

Olly went one better. He couldn't even afford liquid paraffin. So, dragging his large and obese mother around the room (who was trying to sew on a brace's button, on the move) and eating his jam sandwich with one hand, he'd scoop up a dollop of butter from the dish with the other hand and sleek it over his hair. In the hot weather the melting butter ran down his nose and dripped onto his sandwich. He wiped his nose with his sleeve. I can also vividly recall the residue of the discoloured butter brimming through the comb teeth as he combed his sticky, saturated, butter-filled hair. Not a pretty sight.

I realise now, looking back, it was no wonder we couldn't crack the girls we dogged around the town later in the evening. The hair-laced butter that ran down Olly's forehead and dripped into his beer was going rancid!

Aunt Ida's house was like a tip. Not only untidy and covered in dust, but smelly and really dirty. (Grimed-in-dirt, Ma Bateson called it). But I still found it fascinating after my own overpolished and constantly tidied mausoleum when even a dented cushion was immediately fluffed out the second you rose from the chair. Here, at Olly's, sideboard doors hung off their hinges, dirty washing draped the fire-guard sending up plumes of evil smelling steam. You might trip over the broken and curling lino, or covertly try to remove the unwashed grease from the rim of the mug of your suspicious-looking greyish-coloured teabrew. The cat on the table ate the remains of the dinners and licked clean the plates. I often wondered whether it saved Aunt Ida the trouble of washing them.

The following day Emily Bateson would grill me: "Is the sideboard still thick with dust?" "Are those cupboard doors still hanging off their hinges?" "Has she washed the tablecloth yet, or is it still grey with filth?" "I bet the dirt is grimed in, isn't it Michael?"

Too young to either bother about, or to consider such trivial matters of any interest, I somehow still found these nosy questions offensive, and would yawn with bored distaste. Of what interest was it to me how Aunt Ida and her family chose to live, or to Mrs Bateson for that matter? I would think to myself. Yes: maybe her house is scruffy and dirty, but I prefer it to yours. An illuminating observation from the mind of a young boy, who had never even thought about these things.

Last, but not least, in this chapter of Oasis of Kindness, I will once again take this opportunity to pay tribute to the brightest light in my desert of loneliness. Of all lights...old Harry Mould, the village baker, takes the highest accolade. His kindness also was of the natural kind. He singled me out for special attention and, what's more, he acted and looked the part. He was round and jolly, and patted his belly and chuckled loud with wobbly glee, just like a lovable old kid's comic caricature, or a cuddly toy bear. To a lonely and unsure child like me, he appeared the embodiment of jolly carefree happiness. He was like a year-round Santa Claus. As a bonus he also made delicious cream cakes and jam tarts, and what can compete more for a child's affection than jam-filled cream horns, giant puff-buns and cream-slices? Or is this image of poor old long-departed Harry just a figment of the past in my imagination? Was he really like this? Or is this just a trick played by my fading memories, of those childhood days so long ago...?

I think not. Otherwise why should I remember him so fondly? I've no doubt he was only human, like the rest of us. He probably never intended, nor even enjoyed, being fat.

Nor being robbed by those he befriended. But to the world and to me he radiated a special kind of kindness and I never remember him serious or solemn. And that is all that mattered to me in those days. Rare, kind, happy faces belonging to genuinely kind people. Grown ups, take note. You do not kid kids.

As children we love people for all the wrong reasons: because they are jolly and fat and laugh a lot. But not because they are sensible, thin, serious and honest. Because they make cholesterol-filled cakes and tooth-rotting treacle tarts, not because they feed us healthy pickled red-cabbage and cold beef. Because they have comfortable scruffy houses and don't give a toss what others think, not because they are clean and tidy. It doesn't make sense, and it's not fair, is it? But then, life never was.

CHAPTER 14

Characters ... nice, and nasty

The rare beacons of kindness that helped show me the way were reliable and always there, shining bright and steady, just when I needed them most.

There were other lights, other sign-posts. But these, though offering helpful guidance, burnt not so bright and constant, wavering weakly through no fault of their own, in the muffling winds of convention, or familial or parochial discretion, or with an in-built moral or physical weakness that incapacitated their help and sometimes snuffed them out completely and prematurely.

Smelly Nothing was a case in point. His real name, as far as I could ascertain, was Robert (Bob) Snell. The Smelly Nothing tag sounds cruel I know, but you will only usually earn a comical nickname if you are viewed with a common affection. Kids are naturally cruel anyway. Bob had a friend we kids called George Nothing, supposing him to be Bob's brother. We had just lumped them both together, because they lived similar vagrant lives.

Bob really did smell. And I suppose the Nothing name came from his wandering lifestyle. He seemed to belong nowhere, and appeared to have achieved nothing in his life. I am not being sarcastic, jeering or cynical, just stating it as we kids perceived it at the time. Us kids believed he had no name and no family. There were many 'nothing' people about then, who seemed to be going nowhere, wandering about the country lanes: itinerants, gypsies, ex-prisoners of war, hopeless alcoholics, and generally displaced, dispossessed, and homeless people. Where they came from, and how they lived, and even where they eventually disappeared to, no one seemed to know or care. They lived by whatever means they could, doing odd jobs, selling clothes pegs, begging or taking casual seasonal work like potato-picking, or helping with the corn and hay harvest. They seemed to spend their lives earning just enough money to buy a bit of food, and to spend the rest in the village pubs, where much of their spare time was spent. They had nowhere else to go. They dossed down and lived wherever they could, in barns, in cow-sheds, and the more stable and better off ones in old cold caravans.

Old Bob (as I preferred to call him) had worked at most of the farms in the neighbourhood at one time or another. Through his drunkeness and bad time-keeping he had fallen out with many of the farmers and they would not take him back. When he walked into our yard one morning he was running out of options...and of health. I met him in the last few years of his sad and fateful life.

Why Mrs Bateson took him in, I never quite understood. As you will have gathered by now, she was not a naturally sympathetic type of woman and usually shrank from being associated with anyone who was not living a 'decent, normal and proper life' (whatever that might be). After all, she was the most self-righteous, morally disapproving and conventional housewife I've ever known. Perhaps her motive was nothing more noble than the money. For a couple of pounds a week Bob was offered accommodation in the bing (the narrow space behind the cow-stalls, where the cow's fodder is stored). Here, in a pile of damp musty hay and the overpowering smell of cow-piss and dung, he could live, sleep, and booze his life away to his heart's content - and he did! He would be given one plateful of mashed spuds, red cabbage and knackeryard cold beef and - if he was lucky - a slice of Emily Bateson's left-over stale currant bread. He had to make his own arrangements for any other meals or fare (if he had any) but booze usually sufficed. He washed in the rain-butt and in the winter had to break the ice to get at the water to wash his face.

When he wasn't sleeping, or sitting on a log in he shed puffing a fag, or in the village pub boozing, he chewed the cud with his rubbery mouth like the cows and ruminated to me on the vagaries and misfortunes of his chequered life. He commiserated with my own, perceived, far from happy existence. We were two sad and sorry sights sitting on our logs together.

I suppose my own future was only a stone's throw away from the sort of life he was living, had I but realised it at the time. On such fine axis do the scales of fate swing. At that age I could have taken any road. Perhaps this was the common rapport between us. As far as I knew I had no family myself and Mrs Bateson didn't seem keen on me, nor me on her for that matter. I was fast becoming an unruly rebel and a renegade. Like Bob I spent most of my life out of doors or in the sheds anyway, and had seriously considered running away a few times, but I hadn't got the guts. As it was, I felt a king compared to Smelly. After all, in wintertime when frost and snow covered the fields and hedgerows and even I couldn't stand the freezing cold, I could always go indoors to a roaring fire. I was clean and well-clothed, had three meals a day, and at night always went in to a spotless and sometimes ready-warmed bed; whereas poor old Bob retired drunk and supperless to his damp straw in the unheated and freezing cow-bing.

Old Bob and I often sat on our logs in the coal-shed, eating our mashed spuds and cold beef, discussing local gossip and life in general. He resembled Pop-eye in appearance (but without the muscles: his arms were scrawny). He was always chewing the cud (well, he chewed something) and like a Puffing Billy pursed steam-laden breath and cigarette smoke through his blue rubbery lips on the cold and frosty days of winter. I never saw him without his piece of dirty cloth wiping his runny nose or dabbing his watery eyes, while he coughed, spluttered and snuffled his way through the day. He seemed to be in constant physical discomfort and distress (and probably was).

Being young, I listened to what I thought was his wisdom and his soothsaying. I mean, many wizened old tramps seem to just ooze wisdom and experience, don't they? But this is just another illusion. Many of them were tramps simply because they were ignorant and not capable of being anything else! That might sound sad, critical and judgemental perhaps, but true. As well as telling me I would O.K.in life, Bob hinted darkly that his own fate was already sealed, and that his days on this earth were numbered. "I won't be around much longer" he said. He was a natural pessimist, and obviously had good reason to be. Perhaps he was ill, I don't know: I was too young to understand the hidden currents that cause our miseries. He certainly looked ill. He was, in fact, right on all counts. Was he tempting fate or just tired of living? He hinted that somewhere along the line his family had been quite wealthy, but he had been diddled out of his inheritance. Was this just an old sop's dream? A bit of wishful thinking? It sounded like a nasty fairy tale, and it probably was. A mixture of what we now call faction.

He worked, on and off, between binges, at a farm about a mile away across the swampy soggy fields. He set off in the very early hours in the dirty damp clothes that he'd slept in, with his wellington boots squelching through the dew-soaked grass, each morning about five-thirty, to milk the cows.

Though too young to really understand his peculiar and unorthodox lifestyle, I wondered at and felt sorry for him. He seemed a pitiful sight to me with his wild uncombed wiry and scurfy hair, and his constantly hacking cough. But not quite yet understanding the unwritten rules of modern life, it never occurred to me that he was merely a victim of circumstance, and that his life was really as grim and as hopeless as it looked. He was ill-paid, ill fed, and in ill health, and he was an alone nobody alcoholic on the slippery slope to eternity. And he had no idea how to get himself out of this abyss and the morass he found himself sinking into - even if it had been possible, which often it isn't.

He forsook the village pub and started visiting a pub in Stafford town centre (a ten mile bus ride away). It was rumoured he had met a nice (sic) girl there, and it must have been true for suddenly he was rushing back from the evening's milking to dress up like a dog's dinner.

For the first time ever he attempted to work a bit of overtime and managed to buy a smart new suit through Mrs Bateson's catalogue, paying for it on tick. Mrs Bateson washed and ironed his only going-out shirt. His new suit hung on a civilised coat-hanger in the bing, quite damp and covered with bits of straw (there were no plastic covers then). Poor old Bob was making a valient effort to pull himself up by his bootstraps, as the Americans might say, and to look as smart as he could for his new, uptown lady-love.

I watched in something approaching awe as he hurried across our yard and waved ta-ra to me to catch his bus to Stafford, after the late evening's milking. He had somehow managed to shave in cold rain water with a blunt and rusty razor, and had sleeked down his hair with my liquid paraffin using a near toothless comb. He had dusted down and donned his new (but already mildewed and smelly) suit as best he could in his grotty cow-shed dressing room in the bing, where he'd checked his blurred reflection in a cracked and misty mirror rescued from the dustbin.

His incongruous bright yellow tie with a horse's head on it was a bit awry and knotted wrong, and his crinkly old black shoes had been smartened up with brown floor polish, but he looked as posh as he could under the circumstances, like a seen-better-days country toff. I felt a strange mixture of pride and pity for him and wished him luck as I waved back. For a while he was the epitome of the reformed alcoholic, trying to climb back out of the pit of despond and seeming (and believing) he was succeeding. What a good woman can do for a man! What a shame that most of them soon slide back in, and all the time kidding themselves that they are winning, when really they are losing...losing...losing - their grip on reality and on life.

Anyhow, it did last for awhile, and we felt that there was yet hope for him. But then the rumours were that the unusual couple had had a row. Then they had kissed and made up. But on our dinner time logs Bob told me it was off again. And then on. And then off.

And then of course, she finally packed him up for good. And, not to be outdone and to drown his sorrows, in drink he packed her up too.

Today, with a bit of experience of life, I now realise that they were both probably inveterate alcoholics who had screwed up their lives long before they had ever met, though at the time (I was a budding adolescent, in love with the idea of love) I thought it terribly romantic. Even the falling out bits. But reality is a harsh teacher and this rose-coloured view soon lost its romantic glow as I watched poor old Smelly Nothing's disintegration accelerate over the ensuing weeks. Alcoholics living in damp cowsheds fade fast in the dying stages.

Like a man hell-bent on ending it all, with his life now seeming completely out of control, in kamikaze fashion he went into a flat spin of alcoholic self-destruction. He hadn't much left to destroy, had he? He was already ill with chest trouble, a smoker's cough and alcoholic poisoning. He had bronchitis with living in the unhealthy cowshed. And now, to drown his broken heart he smoked and drank more than ever. It couldn't last. The body can only take so much punishment. It had been a summer love affair, and now winter was approaching again. He had further days off from work, the cows didn't get milked, and he lost his job yet again.

Then suddenly he just wasn't there anymore. I heard whisperings he'd been taken to hospital in the middle of a bitter winter's night. I never saw him again.

It sounds a strange coincidence, but a few month's later I heard that Smelly Nothing's pal, George Nothing (who we thought was Smelly's brother) had been killed. Apparently he'd been bouncing jauntily along a narrow frost-encrusted vergeless country lane in the early hours, rosy-cheeked and red-faced (as he always was - booze and frosty air)) and happily inebriated when he'd been bowled into the ditch by an equally happy, drunk motorist. It was almost Christmas. It was one way to go. There was a time in the good old days when half the world and his missis were drunk: it was a sympton of the hard times they lived in. There was nothing worth living for but drink. With the advance of more civilised times, better wages and living conditions, and more enjoyable ways of entertaining ourselves, itinerants like George and Smelly Nothing became almost a dying breed. And modern conformist society frowns on so-called layabouts and vagrants (though 'cardboard' cities flourish even today). My old friend Bob was one of those weaker 'twinkling lights' I mentioned, quickly snuffed out in the maelstrom life-storms of the harsh times of my youth. His kindness never had a chance to reach full bloom to cast its glow further along my way. He had told me I would be O.K. and I remember and am grateful to him for that. It seemed to give me hope at the time, when I most needed hope. Like many of us, his candle was flawed in the mould, and his fate - as he himself foretold - was already written in the wind. But I remember Old Bob, and hereby write his epitaph. Someone must note his unmarked passing.

Mrs Emily Bateson, whose character I have already well delineated from my child's-eye view-point, belonged to the very nastiest of characters who left their disagreeable, indelible footprint in the desert sands of my impressionable early-childhood years.

It's almost certain that these people were not as nice or as nasty as they appeared to me at the time, and then of course, they may have been! How would I know? I was a child, with a child's eye-view. The truth of what they really were doesn't really matter in the terms of this narrative as it is how I saw them then that formed my everlasting opinion of them. Life is full of convincing distortions. A serious and po-faced school-marm might appear very nasty to the timid and diffident young pupil sitting (as just sternly instructed) bolt upright on his hard bench. But, in truth, the teacher might be of the highest calibre and integrity and have only the best interests of her pupils at heart. In fact, they might very well be quite kind and loving people. Even more so than other teachers who appear warm and sympathetic: so complex are the interrelations between adult and child (and between adults too of course). It is more than likely the child will never realise this eternal truth, and will grow up with nasty memories of that particular blameless and well-intentioned teacher.

Someone recently said to me, "But Mick, Mrs Bateson really did love you, you know". And for the first time in my life I thought, with a sudden small but real feeling of guilt, that they might just be right. That could well be true. But this was many years later and whether she loved me or not I will never know, so it makes no difference to my attitude and my unfond memories of her. The record in my soul has been well and truly inscribed long ago. It is too late to attempt a reprint even if it were possible.

I remember her only as cold-hearted and cruel, extremely unpleasant and unloving, and over-zealous in her obsessional cleanliness and a poor cook to boot (which is as important as anything else to a kid, who places food higher than most things on the scale of things to be loved, desired, and remembered). True or false, nothing can change these ingrained memories of her.

Now her husband, Henry Bateson, was the complete opposite, though with him being away most of the time (in the army) I never really got to know him as well as I knew his wife. He entered the picture after his demob during the latter few years I lived with them. Basically, he was a decent, kind, hard-working and docile man, but completely dominated and guided (or misguided, as the case may be) by his despotic and over-riding wife (though he did have a trick of getting his own way when he wanted to). With Henry, it was anything for a quiet life. He only really knew me through his wife's eyes (and mouth) so to speak. So much for propaganda. I was always much too diffident a person to reveal my true self directly to anyone, and still am. Such natures are often misconstrued as 'devious' by simple unquestioning souls, but in truth are merely psychological, deep and complex. No doubt 'Em always thought of me as 'devious', as I WAS when it came to her. She called me a crafty little sod many times. Call someone names all the time and they will turn out like that.

So even when Mr Bateson returned home, I was still alone and had no ally in the house (Evelyn had gone). I still felt disliked and unwanted by them all; Emily, Henry, and their son, Tommy. As already observed, we are inclined to distance and estrange ourselves even further from people we feel might dislike us, more so when we are kids. Then this withdrawal and antipathy is sensed and a vicious circle begins to develop, with distrust and dislike growing on either side, based often on completely misunderstood assumptions of each other. Thus mutual distrust can arise and can last for many years, even over a lifetime - and all it would have taken in the first place to sort it out was a little bit of honesty, kindness and understanding.

So Mr Bateson at best sat on the fence and didn't interfere in the status quo of the household he found on his return from the war. At worst, in matters of disputes between me and 'Em, he naturally fell behind his wife.

If Mrs Bateson had a reason to castigate or punish me, she now hid behind the male 'protection' of her husband and Henry Bateson was quietly instructed to "Have a word with that young bugger". This state of affairs did succeed in holding me in check for awhile, as Mr Bateson was a very strong man and didn't mess about if he did lose his temper and decide to act. So I buckled under, tried to behave and kept my distance as much as I was able.

Another important milestone in my life occurred round about this time when I suppose I would have been about fourteen or fifteen years of age. There had of late been this spell and series of troubles with 'Em. My pet rabbits had been turned loose, my stamp album had been burnt, and my brother had been turned away when he came to visit me.

My feelings of frustration were bottling up inside me. It came to a head one humid summer's evening, We had all been working hard in the hayfields from early morning 'till late at night, and we were all feeling hot and bothered anyway. Tempers were beginning to fray.

It needed only a catalyst and an emotional eruption, the like I had never felt before, would burst forth and explode from the turmoil inside me. And it did.

Does it matter that I cannot recall the particular remark from 'Em that triggered the explosion? She was always picking on me out of the blue, and making extremely hurtful remarks. It doesn't take much to light the fuse once the firework has been primed. I think she was again abusing my unknown father and nagging again "Like father, like son". It might have been quite a trivial insult. The tension lay within me, not in the barb that would burst and release it.

It is the explosion of anger and frustration I remember. And the climax of the out-pouring of feeling and pent-up emotion and hatred I experienced. This intense level of the powerful feeling of relief was a new experience to me, and quite phenomenal. Stronger perhaps even than the physical and emotional relief one experiences in the sexual climax, or in the cataclysmic explosion of grief on the death of a loved one. But whereas the sexual climax leaves one feeling drained and satisfied (hopefully) this left me with a feeling of increased power and realisation...a different feeling altogether. It was a revelation.

The worm was finally turning.

Until this moment, through fear, I was not in the habit of answering Mrs Bateson back. But I had of late taken to muttering dark protests in defiance to her accusations, abuses and criticisms. At the same time though, I made sure I was either too far away for her to reach out and sock me one, or for her to make out what I was muttering. A rather pointless way to protest I know, but I just hadn't the nerve to confront her head on. I suppose I was practising for the real thing.

The frank and open ways between parents and children today are a much healthier way of going on. Things don't get bottled up and seeth inside one for years on end. Spit your problems and disagreements out immediately, and thrash them out there and then, I say: it can save years of misery and misunderstanding and suspicion on both sides.

Present day children who answer their parents back as matter-of-factly as saying goodnight, will find it hard to understand all this (seemingly unnecessary) palaver and what courage it took then, for an intimidated and cowed child like myself to actually finally rebel. But fear, in certain circumstances, is one of the most difficult emotions to overcome...and justifiably. It has held nations in sway, let alone a single child. And the odd thing is,it takes no more courage to overcome a big fear, than it does to overcome a small one. Fear is fear, and courage is courage, no matter what guise they come along in.

She was berating me over this something and I thought, "I'm going to answer her back". Yes, I actually consciously had this thought.

If a German soldier was prodding you with his rifle on the way to the gas chamber, you might find yourself thinking "I've got nothing to lose. I'm going to grab the barrel, and snatch his gun out of his hand".

At this very point in a nick of time, one of those deep and imponderable hypothetical questions arise: will you or won't you grab his gun? Have you the courage? The nerve? And it is at this juncture, when your courage is being called upon to decide and to act immediately, or within seconds, that your true self, your deep, basic and atavistic nature will be challenged and called to account for itself, or to back away and chicken out. This happens only a few rare times in a lifetime, or never at all. And how you react to this urgent immediate crisis and what decision you make, will change your psyche and your future forever (unless you couldn't get his gun that is, in which case you will have no future!).

So I muttered my seething protest.

"WHAT DID YOU SAY?" Mrs Bateson screamed, her angry florid face pushing itself so close to mine it was magnified out of all proportion and gave me nightmares for years to come. "WHAT DID YOU SAY?"

Perhaps, unknowingly, unconsciously, she was challenging me to defy her. It has been known in the dark recesses of psycho-analysis. I had already made my mind up that this was it. I was going all the way this time. I plunged on. "I said" I continued quietly, threateningly (through trepidation I was really losing my voice) "I said, I'll kill you one of these days!" I hadn't really muttered that at all. Nor did I mean what I was saying. It was just the most threatening and frightening thing I could think of at that moment. In for a penny, in for a pound.

A bit over the top, you might think? Perhaps. But if I was going to defy her I might as well do it properly. Once you have stepped over the boundary, there is no going back: the moving finger writes, etc. If you've grabbed that German's gun, then you might as well press on and try and kill him with it and stop him once and for all at the game he is getting away with. Otherwise, what's the point? The risk and the challenge has been taken in vain and, in a way, you are forever lost. I sensed and at once understood the truth of this hypothesis.

Mrs Bateson recoiled. Her face twitched and grew redder than ever. And then paled. With a tremble in her rather faint and frightened voice she said, "I'll tell your Dad about this, I will. I'll tell him what you said to me. I'll tell him you threatened me...you wait".

She always called Henry Bateson my Dad, though I never did. Perhaps she was trying to instil some respect into me. Anyway, she told him and he chased me around the muck heap with the grain fork that had nobbles on the end of the prongs, and therefore it wouldn't have speared an orange. It's funny the things we remember. But naturally, I would have remembered that, wouldn't I? Otherwise I wouldn't have been here to tell you this story. I knew I was in no real danger from a blunt fork (or from my 'Dad'). And so, presumably, did Henry Bateson, who could be amazingly subtle when he wanted to. 'Em was watching him with venom, spite and glee, chasing me, from the kitchen window, and she didn't know the fork had nobbled tines. Henry had to put on a great pantomime show of anger for her benefit (and for mine) which looked almost funny as he fell across the muck heap in hot pursuit of myself. In fact, he had hardly an angry bone in his body, and had to force himself to look angry. But to satisfy his acrimonious vengeful Missis he had become a great actor and could put on a great show when the occasion warranted it. But having said all that - I WAS scared.

But the real point of this anecdote is that I had, at last, overcome my fear of 'Em. And along with this (to me) momentous achievement, a lot of other fears as well. I trust this little parable will give hope to any readers, young or otherwise, who are at present facing a great fear they are convinced they will never be able to conquer. Most of us have our own peculiar individual fears. One man's fear is another man's joke. If you are in doubt whether you can overcome them or not, but are convinced you are justified in trying, then go ahead. A potential swimmer must first jump into the water; or that timid non-dancer must first take the lady of his dreams into his arms, or he will never get anywhere. I know it is easier said than done. Tell me about it. I've been there. But there is no other way. The secret is to recognise and acknowledge your fear, face it, and ACT.

I was breaking through this prolonged hymen of fear. And with this momentous advance, like a young plant bursting through the ground in a storm, I was seizing the moment and growing in stature the minute. By such lessons do we grow and stretch our searching tendrils towards the light, and maturity. Not gradually, but seeming to stand still and tremulous for ages, sounding out the world around us. Then suddenly experiencing and using a cataclysmic and momentous happening, we recognise the challenge, confront it, and act. If we're lucky and have judged a-right, we move forward and onward. Another advance and another pause. I was growing up, and mine enemies and their shadows were retreating before me.

I perceived and remember my Grandad Bateson (Old Bill who originally began the slaughter business) as perhaps the nastiest person who pervaded my overshadowed childhood. Totally unfairly of course, as I only knew him as an old man and, childlike, thought he had always been like that. The funny thing was, I found no trouble in calling him Grandad, even though I disliked him. Calling someone Grandad, is different that having to say Dad. Any old man can be a Grandad.

Grandad left his imprint in my memory as being particularly nasty and evil, and to me personally, more so. These feelings were based on all sorts of things and feelings. We are hyper-sensitive, impressionable and hypercritical as children. Indeed, it is the time when our mould is being cast and will eventually be the deciding factor on how we think, feel and behave. In essence, the sort of person we become.

Unfortunately Grandad appeared in my life at that age when I was beginning to discriminate between what I thought was ugly and nasty, and what I liked and thought was nice and friendly. He was becoming old, smelly, and ugly, and all round disgusting and cantankerous in his habits. Well, rightly or wrongly, that's how he appeared to me. It didn't help that he was your original slaughterman and that I first observed him killing animals and cutting them up, and cooking and eating them. Also that he was the owner (and therefore to blame) of the horrible and terrifying Animal Belsen in the woods. It was also about this time he had pierced his wrist with his sharpening steel and had lost his hand and arm, and now wore a steel hook. This was quite an alarming sight and sequence of events to us youngsters, shades of Captain Hook and all that (Peter Pan was very much in vogue at the time).

Grandad was an inveterate killer and eater of animals of all kinds, and could still hit a rabbit at twenty paces with his twelve bore shotgun by slinging the gun into his shoulder and pulling the trigger with his gleaming steel hook (he preferred his hook for shooting. His fake clip-on hand was too clumsy). This skill from a one-armed man also mightily impressed us kids. There was no television then, and this dexterous sleight-of-hand (or rather, hook) was the nearest we kids came to seeing the fastest-drawing, one-armed shot-gun-shooter in town.

After the tragedy of losing his arm, Grandad took over the village pub, The Blythe Inn. After all, he could still hold a pint glass. It was here I was required to help him with his grain-treading, or feeding the animals, and often accompanied him on his rabbit-shooting expeditions to carry his ferrets and dead game.

Grandad was a gaunt and blood-flecked rangy sort of man. He dressed in coarse cow-smelling jacket and trousers that retained his nobbly knees and bony elbow shapes even when he wasn't wearing them. I never saw him smile (at me, at any rate) and took this sensitively as a personal rebuff, not understanding why he didn't like me. I assume he didn't like me because he doted on his favourite Grandchild, the cherub-faced Billy Bunting (Tommy Bateson), and this made me more jealous than ever. It was no secret that Tommy would ultimately inherit Grandad's not inconsiderable wealth. I realised this somewhat sophisticated family scheme early on in life - and felt again an outsider deeply rejected and not included in the family plans and fortunes.

I suppose it was for this reason that round about now I started pinching things from Grandad. First merely scrumping his apples from the orchard, then goosegogs, strawberries and peas from his garden. Innocent enough stuff. But later I was to rob the pub till for cash. Clean-living 'Em confided to me (in one of our rare congenial conversations) that Grandad's filthy habits were getting worse. He was now seriously ageing and had recently fallen asleep whilst smoking his pipe and had set fire to the pub living room. An emergency family meeting took place. Someone would have to take the old man in, as it was too dangerous to leave him alone in charge of the pub any longer.

I was sent to clean up the charred living room. It was the first time I had ever seen a fire-ravaged room and found it quite appalling. Having a rest, I pretended I was Grandad, and sat in his deep grubby scorched armchair and sucked his spittle-encrusted stinky pipe, then had a chew of his twist (a thing I had been longing to try for ages, as it looked like liqorice). It was vile and I was almost sick and spit it out. How anyone could chew that muck I couldn't understand, and I mentally gave another black mark against the queer old codger.

Grandad both smoked tobacco and chewed it (tobacco twisted into a 'twist) and expectorated his treacly-coloured spittle across the room in a black stream to land (hopefully) in the fire. If his aim was accurate it would almost extinguish the fire. It would hiss and spit back as if in protest at being bombarded with this vile slimy liquid. If he missed the fire then it would join the pattern of years of dried spittle that had run down the walls and tiles of the old grate.

You can imagine house-proud Mrs Bateson's alarm when it was decided Grandad should come and live with us! As well as his habits of falling asleep while smoking, or chewing twist and spitting, Grandad had numerous other odd,eccentric, dirty and undesirable habits. Not least his taste in food.

Having once owned a slaughterhouse, he was an addicted meat-eater and relished all parts of all animals. He ate heart, liver, tongue, tripe, pig's trotters, and brawn as well as all the better cuts. He had probably eaten many of the cows he had killed, but they had their revenge in the end. Tuberculosis was rife among cattle at that time, and Grandad contracted it, which eventually contributed to his death.

He also ate magpie and crow and, of course, rabbit. Cat and dog I never saw him eat, but I suspected and wouldn't have been surprised. He absolutely adored fish of all kinds, his favourites being conger eel and crab, but any kind of fish would do. Mrs Bateson hated most of these things, and wouldn't have fish in the house because of the smell.

So you see, big problems were in the offing.

The thing was, 'Em could hardly refuse to take Grandad into her house because of the Tommy Bateson inheritance business. Basically, she just wanted Tommy to get Grandad's money when he died. She can't be blamed for that: don't we all want Grandad's money when he's gone?

Nevertheless, it was spelled out loud and clear to Grandad - who didn't really want to come and live at our horribly clean house anyway - that he would have to drastically change his filthy habits if he was to come and live with us. Of course, this would be nigh impossible: he was approaching his seventies and had lived liked a tramp all his life. A large jam tin filled with clean sawdust each day would be placed near his armchair, into which he must direct his spittle...and no missing either.

Cleaning up his staining tobacco spittle would make Emily Bateson vomit and ill (and it did, many times). Fish and magpie and offal meat et-cetera were definitely off the menu, and banned. He must learn to live like we lived, and eat what we ate, at the table, in a civilised manner. This would mean a bland insipid diet of red cabbage, mashed potatoes and cold meat - and lettuce and watercress for tea. Which I knew, for Grandad, would be hard or nigh on impossible to swallow, literally.

And so, eventually, Grandad came to live at our house.

It goes without saying it was a conflict of opposing personalities and lifestyles and was destined not to work from the start. After a few weeks of trying to hit the narrow jam tin through his age-dimmed eyes, and getting the frowned brow and a severe ticking off from the pursed lips of Mrs Bateson, deeply unhappy one-armed Grandad struggled to put on his pre-shaped well-worn jacket earlier each day. To get out of the house he traipsed round the fields rabbiting and mending fences till pub-opening time. Then he toddled off to the sanctuary of his old pub where nothing was expected of him but to down a few jars of ale, and a couple of whisky chasers.

Time passed and somehow our disfunctional household of clashing, unhappy, and eccentric personalities managed to get along without a murder taking place. It was a shame that in the latter years of his life poor Grandad was having such a rough time. But this often happens. It seems that life's dice is intentionally loaded against us as we age: things get harder instead of easier, and I have never understood why. God works in mysterious ways. Like the lengthening shadow of the Hawk of Death over the scurrying mouse below, the final onslaught of the Grim Reaper is often sensed in advance by its intended victim, who bows still lower his frightened head as he hurries along to find what solace and shelter he can from the coming holocaust. But he knows he is running up a shortening, narrowing one-way tunnel and there will be no escape in the final reckoning. It seems to me as if God (or nature) is saying, "Sorry, you're long passed your sell-by date mate and should have given up the ghost ages ago, but you can't escape from me and I can destroy you any time I want". A different version of life and death than the bible gives to be sure, but I suspect a truer one.

It was about this time that Grandad and I passed close, like bristling ships in the night, and displayed our rival flags and bared our teeth. Believe you me, the feeling was totally mutual.

You see, while he would soon be facing the worry of dying, I was growing into my prime. The instinctive realisation of this serious age gulf, with its attendant problems (on both sides, but especially for the old) is known to all creatures, and each creature will react in its own way. These sound cruel observations in the civil and polite world we have built around us but, in reality, it is still a cruel world, and will always remain so. My own time will come and my enemies will think, just like I did about Grandad, thank God, the nasty silly old basket will soon be gone. With a bit of luck (sic) others might mourn my passing. I am not writing the scriptures, therefore

I'm not giving the Christian view. I am telling it like it was, and often is. Sensitive souls might blanch, but I can't help that.

Now he lived with us, Grandad exploited me more than ever, and right to the end. I had to accompany him on his ferreting and fencing expeditions. We sat in hiding behind fallen tree-trunks for hours, waiting for the rabbits to put in an appearance, so that we could shoot them. I put the ferrets down the holes, and he shot the rabbits when they bolted in terror. And I carried the dead rabbits and the sack of squirming ferrets back home. He could no longer wield a sledgehammer, so while he gave me surly instructions I hammered his fence posts in and stretched his barbed wire for him. At the end of a long arduous day, as he sat on a log puffing and grunting and worn-out, I even struggled to pull off his mud-caked, sweaty wellington boots.

And all the time this feeling of hate persisted and grew between us. I didn't want to hate him, but his uncompromising surliness and taciturnity and a barely perceptible and indefinable sense of evilness seemed to radiate towards me personally whenever I was with him. I didn't like it, which meant I didn't like him. So, like an annoyed skunk, I began to radiate my own vibes of distaste back at him and it became mutual. I would think, you grumpy miserable old sod, hurry up and die, and I don't care because you are old and ugly and I am young. And the thing was, I really honestly didn't care, and even now do not regret the fact that I didn't care. Absolutely unforgiving and unchristian I know, but absolutely true. I had sensed that he cared not one jot for me, so I returned the favour. If a youngster cannot voice their distaste for someone, they will show it in other ways.

I was recently shown an old fading sepia picture of Grandad standing with his drinking cronies in the yard outside the Blythe Inn (a rare photograph). Like an evil ghost from the past he seemed to be staring back at me, and I, now an ageing man myself, glared back at him. And, mutual still, I imagined I felt the old hate flooding back, even from his fading photograph.

But, before we move to and beyond the death of Grandad Bateson, a classic nasty, I must tell you about the death of Smokey Joseph.

Above and beyond all humans, Grandad loved his ferrets. Probably because he respected them, as, like himself, they were tough, cold and inveterate killers. And none so much as a sturdy, wiry, smoke-coloured beauty called Smokey Joseph (they all had names).

But now, in wiliness and years, along with his master, Smokey was getting old. A disease was crippling him and his back legs started to collapse and drag.

Now, by their very nature, like rugged old Indian chiefs, ferrets should never know nor show the indignity of old age. In nature, they are one of the toughest of God's creatures.

Remember, Grandad was a lifelong killer of animals: I had never seen him bat an eyelid at the killing of any sort of animal no matter how pitiful. He had even slit the throat of my own favourite, Rupert the goose with the twisted beak, to provide for our Christmas dinner. I had watched in horror as Rupert had slowly bled to death in a bucket, while hanging upside down by her legs on a rusty nail on the cowshed wall. Poor Rupert had seemed shocked and puzzled at the cruelty and pain, and had tried to raise her head and with glazing eyes had looked at me as if to say 'why?' and 'goodbye'. I can still see her, with the unearthly expression of death in her perplexed eyes.

But now Grandad could not bring himself to kill the crippled Smokey Joseph himself. He must have had some sort of perverted love in his evil body. Surprisingly, he asked 'Em to ask me if I would do the dastardly deed. Why didn't he ask me himself? It was things like this that turned me against him. Is it conceivable the old man was too ashamed to ask me? He offered me half-a-crown, and 'Em said I should take up the offer. Smokey should have been honoured: it was the first time Grandad had ever offered to pay for a job.

Sure, I'd do the unpleasant chore I said. I needed the money. Now I was getting older, I was thinking and feeling differently about killing. I was beginning to find it unpleasant and distasteful, and now felt sorry for the animals. But this job had to be done, though I had never killed a ferret. And when I came to do it, I was more than a little nonplussed.

Ferrets are one of nature's success stories. They are tough, wiry survivors. A young and fit ferret is as near as any of God's creatures come to being almost indestructible. Most life can be snuffed out surprisingly easily. A rabbit for instance, can die of fright and shock, or the most it takes is a blow on the back of the head. Chickens are killed by a pull of the neck. But how do you kill a ferret? It will turn its sinewy neck and grab you with its needle like teeth if you interfere with it.

Certainly, a sharp axe can be the sure answer to almost any killing. But many would-be amateur slaughterers baulk at the messy blood-spattering this method entails. Keep the blood in the body, I say. A bloodless killing, that protects your hands from direct contact of the victim's body by the inanimate handle of the mysterious blunt instrument is a popular choice. Also, if your instrument is blunt enough, you don't feel so guilty because of blood-defiled hands. Done in this certain way, killing can be almost polite, and slightly impersonal. You can even pretend you are bashing a sack of spuds, if you need to.

So I battered Smokey's skull with a heavy gate hinge and buried him in the muck heap and claimed my blood-money of half-a-crown from the mean (but by now sad and half-inebriated) old Grandad.

And there the grim story should have ended.

But it didn't.

Nasty things happen down in the woodshed and, believe you me, nasty things also happen in the beautiful countryside.

The next day Mrs Bateson said to me "I thought you'd killed Grandad's ferret?"

"I did" I protested, puzzled.

"You'd better go and check" she said (half kindly, for her). "There's something like a ferret crawling around in the hedge-bottom in the field".

Still puzzled, I went to investigate. Perhaps another ferret had gotten loose from the pen. They are clever, ingenious little devils.

But, sure enough, my darkest suspicions and worse fears were true: it was Smokey Joseph. He was still alive! He came out of the hedge-bank with his inquisitive hazy pink beady eyes and looked at me as if to say "well, what's new then? What do you want?" as only a ghost, back from-the-dead ferret, could.

I was worse than horrified - I was dumbfounded. It was a nightmare. I was sickened. Murder should be quick and final. I had never failed before. I might be many things, but I was never purposefully cruel. If I had to kill, I always tried to make sure it was quick and guaranteed. It's the least you can do for the victim. I had bashed his head as hard as I could at least six times with the gate hinge.

Obviously, Smokey was in a poor way...and though still behaving in the curiously nosy and suspicious way ferrets do, he was, understandably, really half-dead. And it didn't take long to finish him off (properly, this time). I won't go into further details. You (and I) have heard enough.

Whether 'Em told Grandad about my abortive murder of Smokey, I never knew. Grandad hated me already, he could not have hated me more. I was rather ashamed (and somewhat appalled) at this messy killing as I had always considered myself a professional and efficient animal killer. From this day forth my views on animal slaughter began to change completely. And soon, I would never kill anything again. Not for love or money.

Smokey returned yet once more to haunt me in my dreams years later, along with my freed rabbits, and Rupert with the twisted beak. He was digging his way up out of the muck heap, and looking around piteously, questioningly, with his bright little pink eyes as if saying, "Who did this to me?" For such vile deeds are we poetically punished, in our worst nightmares, as in our sleep the evil dead rise up from our past to haunt us, and to remind us of our own mortality.

Now Grandad was getting seriously old, and ill. He was passing through the last winter of his life, in vicissitude and in actual season. In a perverse way, now I am ageing myself, I realise we had similar natures when it came to facing the bleak periods that we all must experience at odd times in our lives, especially the twilight years.

Imagine a tough old man out in one of the worst storms of his life. The wind and bitty frozen sleet pepper and blast away at his veiny bony cheeks and watery eyes. He bends his beaked Roman nose into the storm and pushes on grimly trying to disregard the awful weather that is trying to beat him into the ground. In his misery he ignores swifter, shadowy figures of other younger people, caught also in their own personal times of trial. The pain in his chest is getting worse, and his bent and bony old legs are shaking and weakening. He pauses in the lee to take a shot of the old Johnny Walker. It's surprising how a sip of the hard stuff can refuel and warm the cockles of the heart and pump some life back into the ancient shrinking veins, if only for a spell. The old man battles on ...

Desperately trying to escape from the antiseptic environs of Emily's palace and her nagging and 'long face' as we called it, Grandad purchased an old double-decker bus and put it on his Island Field. It became a local landmark and a curiosity known by the country folk for miles around as 'Grandad's bus'. The Island Field was totally surrounded by the river Blythe. Occasionally the river flooded and the old bus sank and tilted sideways in the resulting mud. Grandad would be marooned, drunk as a wayward lord and fast asleep on the upstairs deck of his decaying, topply bus.

Yet this was his own private sanctuary. His latter years, and then months, fell into a pattern.

He would arise late from bed and struggle for ages trying to strap on his artificial arm with his one good arm, which was also now getting weak and scrawny. Not an easy task. If any of us attempted to help we were brusquely knocked aside with a stubborn but proud disgusted snort. He was so cantankerous and independent. Then he would have a one-armed shave (another miracle independent achievement). Maybe he would clean his gun in the shed outside, then trammel the fields for a rabbit for dinner.

It's doubtful whether he would be seen again until two or three-o-clock in the afternoon, when he would be observed (and commented on) by the ever watchful Emily Bateson as he virtually floated back along the narrow lane from the pub. (He drank neat whisky almost exclusively in his final years - liquid food really).

It was a toss-up whether he would call in for some rabbit-stew or make a bee-line across the river to sleep off the booze in his old bus (rabbit stew and whisky doesn't mix well at that age!) 'Em would curse and ask me if I could eat Grandad's dinner if he hadn't called in. Grandad had to negotiate the stepping stones he had placed across the river to reach his bus. If floods were out the stones were almost submerged and he often slipped and fell into the river, making me laugh as I watched from our living room window.

He flaked out on smelly old hessian corn sacks on the dusty upper deck as the rotting lower deck was either part flooded or covered in chicken muck (or both), for here chickens lived, clucked, roosted and laid their eggs.

Gloaming evening would see him emerge from his Disney shack, and rubbing the sleep from those fading watery-blue eyes set in his blood-flecked alcoholic and tubercular face, he would once again traverse the stones over the babbling river, heading for 'home'. Looking pale, tired and forlorn, and wiping his nose with his sleeve as he coughed and spit globules of slimy phlegm in the roadside grit, he would return unwillingly to the pristine brightly-lit cleanliness of Emily's no-nonsense abode and regime. After a fish-paste sandwhich and a good splash of cold water, he'd amble off to the pub again to join the local farm labourer's, feeling he'd earned a couple of late pints along with the best of them. It's no wonder the poor old bugger died soon afterwards.

Cantankerous, perverse, independent, pitiful, wicked, dirty, awkward and evil to the end, all these words and some unprintables describe my Grandad Bateson as I perceived him then, as a child. Now, I am probably viewed as a grumpy old Grandad myself. And in the light of my new experience of old age, maybe I should review this childhood vision and impression of this ghost from my past. As already noted, we are rarely what we appear to be, to others. After all the ugly frog is always a prince in disguise, and the ugly duckling grew up to be beautiful. Perhaps he was just a normal old Grandad after all, and it was my child's vision of him that was distorted. Life is full of illusions if we are looking the wrong way through emotional, prismatic rose-glasses.

And so, like the grimacing cheshire cat, Grandad finally fades from view as do we all, into the mists of time, perceived by this once lonely evacuee child as nothing but a hateful grumpy old man. So what? ...He probably perceived me as an awkward defiant thieving little bastard. I've no doubt we were both wrong. But, of course, this is only how I saw him, and it is too simple. Like an ice-berg, I saw only the tip. Sorry, the damage was done. And these images, recorded forever and carved deep into the soul of my impressionable childhood, can never really be erased or altered, even by the godly.

CHAPTER 15

Wasting time

What did we do with those long leisure years of our youth? Have you ever wondered? Where did all that time go? It has gone, and what have we got to show for it? At this once-only childhood period of our lives we had abundance of youth and energy and time, and a blank sheet to write upon, that awaited the impressions of future shocks, adventures and experiences. We had manifold things to learn, and many mistakes to make. And also, if we were lucky, we would collect a few friends and learn a bit about human nature, along the way.

Unburdened with such obligations as a wife (or a husband) and the resulting family, mortgages and bills, and that most urgent, pressing and over-riding necessity of all, the need to earn a living...life still seemed to have its problems. Had we but known it, life would never be as free and as unfettered ever again. We needn't have had a care in the world and I suppose that is why the earth then, at times, looked like one big playground specially made just for kids and their games and mischiefs, that we could go on playing in for ever and ever.

I wandered through my boyhood like I was taking a leisurely stroll through the fascinating supermarket of life - which was the world around me. I paused, or stopped on my way, to observe the frenetic activity of the ants, or to wonder at the frantic buzzing of the bees. Why was everything and everybody so busy and preoccupied, I wondered, while I alone seemed to have time to stand and stare? The existent world around me was interesting enough, but the turmoil of the emotional world that seethed within me was not so easy to explain, or understand. I can never remember being in a hurry (except to escape from Sunday School) and I was rarely bored (except on a sunny day when I was trapped in the classroom room doing my maths). Boredom came later, when I was older and had started to put away childish things. Along the way I had plenty of time to make my bows-and-arrows and my soap-box trucks. I grubbed up the cool green grass for pig-nuts and ate them coated still with healthy brown earth. I went bird-nesting or fished with a jam-jar or a bent pin. I paddled in the River Blythe and watched the shimmering iridescent dragon-flies hovering over the water-lilies. They were also in the short summer of their lives, but didn't realise it. Compared with many creatures, us humans are lucky to be able to enjoy and savour a much longer life. Still too soon gone though.

High summer would find me drinking in the winey smell and taste of over-ripe blackberries, or contemplating the buzzing of the blow-flies over the cattle corpses in the knacker wood. In between these lazy, seemingly endless halcyon solitary meanderings I often earned the anger of 'Em and took my punishments in lonely tears. My lessons of death and its awful sorrow took a long time to learn as I innocently killed rabbits and birds, or watched the agonised and puzzled face of Rupert the Goose as Grandad slit his throat for Christmas. Why did he look so sad I wondered. And why did the kittens that I drowned in a sack in the River Blythe mew so piteously as they sunk in the murky depths under the shadows of the river's bridge? Their farewell to the world was written with their last breath in hieroglyphic bubbles upon the surface of the swirling waters. Their murder, not least, deserves a mention and a meaningless apology now I am older and wiser. But all life can not be allowed to continue, as I was to learn, no matter how much it complains or struggles to hold on: something must prune. There just isn't enough room on the planet for all of us to go on living forever. So in nature's great mysterious plan the oldies and other unfortunates must be pruned out to make way for the new. Those wee kittens went before their time, that is all. All of us go in our various ways, under fear, protest and pain,in the last resort.

I was known in the village as "That lonely pale-faced evacuee who lives with Mrs Bateson. You know, the one who always looks so sad. Who always wears clogs and that old bus conducter's hat....You know who I mean...?" My rare smiles and moments of laughter could only be drawn forth by the kindness of people like Old Harry Mould the baker, or by watching the antics of our Cade lamb 'Baarely' as he galloped madly around the field towing his milk churn behind him. Animals can be very funny and there is something refreshing in their style of enjoying themselves, which is completely natural, uncontrived and spontaneous. It is nature's true enthusiasm: the pure joy of simply being alive. There was not much humour to be found within the Bateson household, that was for sure.

The atmosphere improved a little after the war, when Mr Bateson returned home. He had a sense of humour and was more easy going than his dour, sour-faced missis, but he had to be careful how he used it, because she always thought he was laughing at her (which he may have been: I was never sure). Many couples have peculiar subtle rituals going on between them that outsiders are never let into, and these two were no exception. One of the oddest took place most evenings when we sat down to have our tea. It was like a pre-meal foreplay. The table had been laid with a white linen tablecloth, complete with our individual places set out with plates and cutlery etc. The cups and saucers were always laid in a row at the side of the table, each with its relevant teaspoon. Only Henry Bateson was allowed to pour the tea - don't ask me why, it was this ritual. It was probably something to do with being master of the household. A hangover from the patriarchical era which was fading then. A relic of the Victorian age no doubt. We were not allowed to begin tea until Henry B had given a secret signal (which I never actually observed, although I tried to many times). The ceremony started with the pouring of the teas. Henry would look at his wife with a sort of comical secret look, as if seeking permission, then suddenly, with an exaggerated elaborate jerk, he would lift the striped highly-coloured knitted tea-cosy by its large wobbly bobble from the red-hot brown ceramic teapot.

Another mysterious glance at the face of his pursing wife would sometimes bring forth a "Oh...you, Henry" as he proceeded to start pouring a drop of tea into each cup. He would first pour low down, near the cups, and then, keeping the liquid flowing in varying degrees of stream, he would raise the pot as high as he could until the liquid dribbled down in a very thin brown cascade occasionally missing the cups altogether.

All this time the performance would be interspersed with "Oh, Henry" and, "You...Henry" from the frowning brow and pursing lips of the bemused Mrs Bateson. He was obviously teasing her. Henry would giggle maniacally, the cups would eventually get filled, and as they were handed round we could start our meal proper. At least it was more interesting than saying grace, though personally (not being in on the joke) I found it all a bit puzzling and childish.

Whatever was going on here, your guess is as good as mine. I never did understand. Was Henry Bateson asking his wife if the tea was ready and was strong enough to pour? Or was he having fun at being temporarily the officiating master of ceremonies, the boss? He seemed to be asking - at every stage - her permission to carry on. He could even have been insinuating to her that the pouring spout resembled a pissing penis. That would have explained the peculiar glances they gave each other (I presume they had a sex life). Whatever it was, I missed the joke and sat there like a prat with a silly grin on my face, simply wanting to get on with my tea. I had mates waiting outside: we were going fishing.

I had a few friends dotted around the area. There was Oliver with the buttered hair (Uncle Zac's lad) and the Mill children.

I had also made friends with the two sons of a wealthy local farmer, whose sprawling place was a handy fifteen minutes walk from our place.

Harry Fellows was the older of the brothers, and Jeff the younger. For quite a while Harry became my best mate. Jeffery was a quiet, weakly-built, timorous and thoughtful grown-up sort of lad, a worrier and too serious for us two tearaways. He was the wet blanket and was an encumbrance to us, cramping our style and lacking our flair for daring and getting into mischief. He had no sense of adventure. We were miffed because Mrs Fellows made us take him along with us, and he seemed to disapprove of the things we got up to.

I was soon to realise there were certain 'restrictions' on playing with the sons of landowners. When I had gone adventuring on my own, rabbit hunting or 'lumber-jacking', or building dams across rivers - it had never occurred to me I was damaging other people's property. Kids rarely think of this. Also, people at that time never seemed to bother so much: perhaps the war was taking all their attention, or perhaps the country was just a freer and more abundant place. Us kids roamed the woods and fields freely, climbing over and damaging fences, digging up the fields for pig-nuts, chopping down trees, damming up rivers, and generally plundering and vandalising the countryside as if it didn't belong to anyone (we didn't think it did). I never understood the word Trespass until I was much older.

But I remember the beginning of the end, when farmer's began to chase us off their land with guns and dogs. A whole new era and outlook was coming in.

This is the sadness of modern life, where everything in nature seems controlled and tamed, and every inch of space has an owner. Wherever modern humans make their habitat, there is no more wilderness. And owners of land and property are more aware, and more protective of their precious heritage. But it was not always like that. When I was a kid there was always plenty of space and somewhere to roam and play and explore.

We never thought in terms of boundaries. The world around us seemed endless. It is all tied in with the population explosion.

Harry, Jeff and myself played around the farm premises and in the fields surrounding their farm. We made slides down the sides of field ricks and barns bringing avalanches of hay crashing down upon ourselves as we screamed in delight at this madness. We built secret hide-outs deep within the bale-filled barns. If they'd collapsed inwards they would have buried us alive. We pulled wood from the hedges and sheds to build rafts, bridges and dams, or to strengthen our 'Den' in the tree-house. We plagued and enraged the frothing-nosed snorting and stamping bull, fastened by a short chain in his 'Bull pen'. Harry even showed me how to start the old giant Fordson tractor that stood in the tractor shed.

It was all great fun...for us. But I noticed serious-faced young Jeff Fellows would often stand by critically watching us, frowning and biting his nails. I think maybe he was wise beyond his years, and realised we were damaging his Dad's property (and therefore, indirectly, his own inheritance).

Old Farmer Fellows liked his whisky and Harry told me, when in drink, his dad could be really nasty and sometime hit them, and his Mum. So I tried to keep out of the way of Mr Fellows. I was still one of those 'bloody evacuees' remember.

Mrs Fellows seemed a kind, placid and motherly lady. Well, that's how she appeared to me, but her sons told a different story (which I found hard to believe). Most late afternoons, before I ambled back along the narrow lane home to Blythe Bridge, she welcomed me into the house to have tea with my pals. They lived well, as most farm families do. During the week I sat with the lads and the farm labourers at the large, scrubbed-white, planked kitchen table and tucked into huge wedges of home-made bread, cheese and ham, followed by cream cakes and strawberries from the farm garden. Occasionally - on a Sunday - I was invited into the expensively furnished dining room and sat together with the whole family at a posh and formally laid-out table, complete with linen tablecloth, napkins and silverware. A awesome and uneasy treat, for me.

As the etiquette of the time seemed to demand, if it was Sunday lunch, we all sat silently waiting for the patriarchal stern-faced Mr Fellows to start carving the roast beef. Every family had its meal time ritual. Mr Fellows was usually in a pretty ragged mood. He would have been drunk at twelve or one-o-clock after a morning in the local pub, and would have slept the afternoon away, and now, after lunch, he had the milking to face. Then it was back to the pub to spend the rest of the evening boozing. Thus, after grace was said, the delicious meal was eaten in total silence, and woe betide anyone who tried to make conversation while Mr Fellows was in this dodgy filthy mood.

Mr Fellows once blasted a gang of lads with his shot-gun as they were fleeing his orchard after scrumping his fruit. It was said one of the gang was amazed when he removed his cap to find the button had been shot off the top. I can't vouch whether this really happened or not, but it was a good story nevertheless and was told many times along with other hair-raising anecdotes late at night in the gang's den in the middle of the haybarn.

My long summer's friendship with the Fellows brothers came to an abrupt end one Sunday afternoon when Harry Fellows senior, on his way home from the Blythe pub and not a little tipsy, came suddenly round the corner to find us lads smashing tiles on his cowshed roof. He naturally went berserk, as, no doubt, I would have done had it been my cowshed. New rooves don't come cheap but I didn't know that. To me then, as thick as it sounds, a roof was just a roof and they had always been there! Like trees I must have thought they were organic and had always been there as there were hundreds of them everywhere, and I never questioned how they got there, or how much they cost . Kids never value anything until they grow up and have to pay for things themselves.

Mr Fellows and my Grandad Bateson were drinking buddies. Nothing happens in a village that is not sooner or later discussed in the village local. Pub tittle-tattle is better than the local gossip grape-vine for finding out what little tricks the local naughties have been up to. I suppose Mr Fellows told Grandad what I'd been up to, and Grandad told Mrs Bateson, and I was not allowed to visit the Fellow's farm again. Mischevious kids themselves cause kindly doors to slam on them.

It was always so conveniently easy to blame "Those damned Evacuees" for any damge, theft, or vandalism occurring in the village environs. We were also blamed for being a bad influence and for leading the local lads astray (as if they needed leading!). Believe me, they taught us evacuees a thing or two. I suppose we taught each other - swopped 'mischiefs' so to speak.

Because of this, for awhile afterwards I spent a lot of time on my own. I wasn't bothered. I had plenty to do and was quite able to entertain myself. In any case, for various reasons, most friendships fizzle out eventually. This is another bitter truth we all have to learn.

I went back to gathering firewood from the river banks round Grandad's island field, sawing it into logs and splitting it into sticks and stacking it high and neat in our sheds as fuel for the coming winter months. I was so busy I got carried away and filled every available nook and cranny in the sheds, going right up into the roof-spaces. I've always enjoyed doing anything that feels useful or gainful (even if it's not - it's the feeling that matters) and even now will labour patiently for hours if I think I'm achieving something.

I also carried on doing chores around our smallholding or at Grandad's pub. Most of the time I laboured willingly and, in a perverse way, even enjoyed doing the many hard tasks. I was never paid, though it did occur to me that I ought to be getting something for my labours. I was a hard grafter for my age. You are never short of work on a farm. Most genuine country folk work hard (or did then) and I was living proof that hard work hurt no man. At that time I was a hard-muscled, sun-scorched and weather-beaten little urchin who was never seen wearing a jacket, but with open shirt, rolled-up sleeves, short trousers and sockless studded boots, summer and winter. I can't ever remember feeling the cold at all. Wearing a jacket, or having my shirt sleeves rolled down, was unknown to me until I was about sixteen ... when I began to get interested in girls and Saturday night's dogging of such.

It's different now: due to our softer, modern way of life, like most people, I molly-coddle myself to death. Face me now with the work and the conditions I used to take for granted when I was around twelve years of age and even the thought of it would kill me!

When I wasn't working, you'd find me meandering around the fields and woods. Townies would see little of interest in these explorations: fields look empty and boring to the unknowing eye. But, like an Indian tracker on the trail, a country lad knows where and what to look for. That mass of frogspawn in the deep-sided ditches has to be watched carefully each day, for soon, on a sunny day, it will turn into swarms of tadpoles veering this way and that as they try to escape your shadow that is blotting out their sun, as you lean over watching them intently. Farther on, in the swampy low-lying reeds, you will check that peewit's nest to see whether the eggs have hatched - this is an exciting development. Then, on to your wire snares to see whether you have caught a rabbit: another exciting find. Have the primroses, or the cowslips, or the harebells bloomed prolifically this year? and are they in their usual spot, and if not, why?

You check all these things with a satisfied feeling of innocent pleasure, yet know not why. Unlike and despite the cultivated civilised tastes of art in city galleries and statues in city centres, or even the present-day beautifully shot pictures of the latest nature-watch programme on television ... true pleasure in really natural things is more enjoyable and comes naturally to country folk.

For my part, you can keep all these artificial reproduced attempts at depicting nature for the magical sight of one real natural pleasure or incident: A hovering kingfisher waiting to strike for a fish; the Eden-like silence of a bluebell wood; or the shriek of a disturbed shrike fleeing through the marshes from its endangered nest, as you walk home through the fields as twilight falls.

There is a season to check the catkins and try to estimate the future hazlenut crop. The same goes for blackberries, chestnut trees, and bilberries on the heath. The mushrooms will have their day, followed soon by the edible morels. Damson and crab-apples and sugar-plums, each has it own in-built clock. And so, being part of the same process, have we - us humans.

We are another year older, and bigger, and stronger, and can we jump that ditch this year that we fell into last? Who has not looked deep into the clear water of the pond that is fed from the mysterious source of a natural spring, and watched the strange antics of the lively denizens in their own little world in its depths, scudding and exploding the fine mud as they dash hither and thither about their busy ways? Yes...there was always plenty to do, observe and learn, in a country boyhood.

We also kept many pets, but I remember with special affection Baarely, the cade lamb, most of all. We reared him from a spindly, wobbly-legged little weakling, to a dangerous strong giant - and it was my job to feed him warm cow's milk through a baby's rubber-teated bottle.

Later we had to buy a special heavy-duty proper lamb's rubber teat as his strong sharp teeth would now rip the previous ones to shreds in seconds. When he was small I could handle Baarely easily. My superior strength could tussle him physically into his shed for the night, or through a gate into another field. I first noticed his growing strength when he started head-butting me as I was feeding him his bottle. In his eagernesss to get a better grip on the slipping teat, he'd suddenly buttjerk his head violently, almost breaking my arm which was encircling his neck trying to hold him steady. I found I couldn't hold him fast any longer, and he'd break loose.

Then came the day when, on calling him at feed time, he came galloping down the field like a charging Rhino and hit me wham-bang fair and square with his hard skull, in my stomach, up against the cow-shed wall. I was desperately winded and almost collapsed. From then on I started to feed him through the five-barred gate so he couldn't get at me to head-butt me again.

Baarely began to crash and trespass his way into neighbouring farmers' fields. 'Em told me to get a rope and tether him to an old heavy milk churn. This held him for a couple of weeks, then sheep and milk churn disappeared through the hedge again!

Trying to discover the balance of strength I sat astride the churn, but he merrily dragged me around the field without even seeming to notice the extra weight. My next ploy was to fill the churn with bricks.

Again, this held him for a short while. But not for long. His strength now was such that I could ride him like a horse, gripping his thick wool coat for dear life as he galloped me around the field. Great fun.

We had a rapport.

I think he enjoyed it as much as I did!

Next, I nailed his rope to a fallen tree-trunk - and that held him for quite a while. But in his curious search for pastures new, his overpowering strength and enthusiasm soon overcame this little obstacle. It was a hilarious sight to see Baarely bounding around the field while the tree-trunk bumped and tossed in all directions behind him. This, in turn, would alarm and excite the flock of grazing geese and they'd chase after him, screeching and flapping their wings as only geese will.

But all things have their day, and their hour of glory and full fruition. Surprisingly soon, Baarely was over his youthful exuberance, and the springtime of his youth settled into balmy summer...and then winter. Now, when I tried to ride him, he was soon winded and weakened. And it was back to the empty churn for him. Then, later, in his approaching old age, when he could no longer vandalise the hedges and trespass, or even torment the geese, he was given total freedom once again. We humans, with our four-score years and ten, don't realise how lucky we are: while his accelerated animal years sped by and he grew frailer, my more moderate human pace meant I was growing stronger, and into my zenith.

Somewhere we passed and Baarely, being unfortunately born into a frugal knackering family that wasted nothing, least of all meat, soon found his way to the Animal Belsen in the woods; and no doubt onto my plate of mashed potato, pickled cabbage and cold mutton. It was his final trespass.

Though I was never told, or I wouldn't have eaten him.

One summer holiday it was arranged for me to go potato picking at a village called Somersal Herbert about a twenty mile cycle ride away from Blythe Bridge. Here lived my other Granny and Grandad (on Mrs Bateson's side) in a small roadside cottage. It was arranged I should stay with them for a week, while I did my spud-picking at a local farm. This would be my first serious hourly paid job of work. Maybe it was a seen as a chance to give me a taste of the world of work, which was just around the corner, and to keep me out of mischief during the long school hols.

Granny Bloor looked a typical comic-book Granny, complete with kind eyes and motherly ways, but, like most of us, she could be strict if she wanted to (I was also beginning to learn the childhood vision of things are not always as comic-booky as they seem to be!). She was of the old school, and baked a mean meat-and-potato pie. If anyone upset this Granny, she had a way of letting them know, without actually saying anything. This was done with a mixture of flashing glances and disturbing, conscience-pricking, pregnant silences. You were made to feel shut out and in disgrace. Grandad Bloor was quite taciturn and uncommunicative to me, though not as bad as the previously described Grandad Bateson. They both looked as though they had stepped straight out of the pages of an Elizabethan photo-album.

Surprisingly (to me at any rate) despite the fact I had always worked hard at home and was a toughened country lad, I found the potato-picking really hard going (a taste of 'real' work). For the benefit of those who have never indulged in this particular form of torture, it consists of following a moving wagon while tossing the already unearthed and dried spuds into the back of it. A simple enough job. But of course, it is bend, straighten, throw, bend, straighten, throw, ceaselessly, all day long, for a solid nine hours. And your boots get caked with mud until you can scarely propel yourself through the muddy ruts of the lorry. I was to be paid the going adult rate, and worked alongside grown-ups for the full nine-hour day. At lunch time we sat in the hedge-bottom for half an hour and ate our sandwiches. Thinking about it, it was the first time I had been forced to work a full day, for a full day's pay, and alongside adults, with their extra stamina. Previous to this, I had always worked on my own, set my own hours and worked at my own pace (which I preferred). I assume this is why I found it such hard going: I was under obligation to complete the hours set. It was 'welcome to the world of the working man'! Real physical labour can be really hard, as anyone who has done it will testify.

On the Friday, the final day of my 'working week', feeling worn out, I staggered the one and a half miles back through the fields to Gran's cottage. Gran had baked me one of her famous 'Desperate Dan cow-pies', a massive meat-and-potato very thick-crusted pie in a deep-bottomed enamel dish, the way Grannies used to do. "Here lad" she gruffly but kindly proffered, as only the old folk could. "Get this little lot down you. It'll give you your energy back and set you up for your journey back to Blythe Bridge". (The colloquial phrase today is, "Get yourself around this" which, in respect to the size of Gran's meat pie, would have been a more appropriate expression!).

That's how they thought about food then. None of your piddling about with expensive and fiddly small-portioned faddy healthy stuff like they do now. All the old folk used to think they had to 'fill you up' to make you big and strong. Well, at first glance, to simple minds, I suppose it sounds logical. With Mrs Bateson it was her massive bowls of porridge before I went to school. It's different today, when half the world seems obsessed with diets and slimming, and the real content of food. Even meat is becoming a dirty word.

I looked up at Gran questioningly. "What? Is Grandad having his?" I asked (hoping to God, he was). I honestly thought the pie was for all of us.

"No. It's for you. Get it down you" insisted the generous Gran. "Eat it all up. You're a growing lad". She smiled, "You can manage that, can't you?" she continued in a jocular, humorously scoffing tone. All the old Grannies thought and spoke like that then. They all believed in stuffing you rotten, with anything that was going. In their eyes, a young 'growing lad' could tackle anything.

I think, at least just once in everyone's lifetime, as regards food, one meal will never be forgotten, when you reach your acme in eating so to speak. It is that meal, that tastes so delicious right through to the end that you cannot stop eating it, and is so huge that you come as near to bursting as feels downright dangerous. And somehow it becomes a challenge to eat the lot, and leave not a scrap behind. You will never forget this meal: the pleasure, the taste...and the later uncomfortable bloatedness.

After all, as Gran had said, I was a strapping growing lad and in my prime. And I had just burnt up all my reserves of energy after nine hours in the potato fields. Surely I could eat a mere meat and potato pie all to myself?

Well, I ate it all right, after an almightly struggle. I think it was the inch thick pastry crust that got to me. I washed it down with three mugs of strong dark tea and, thanking and waving goodbye to Gran and Grandad, I set off on my twenty plus miles journey back home to Blythe Bridge.

I shall never forget that bike ride either. I felt like a pregnant duck with severe belly-ache. The hills seemed twice as steep and the distance twice as long, and I was dripping with sweat, even in the cool of the evening. Was I relieved to coast down the steep hill that lead to our house? You bet I was! 'Em offered me some mashed spuds and meat, but I declined with a voiceless wave, said "G'night" and went straight off to bed to sleep off my total weariness and belly-ache, and to let that half-ton of pastry digest. The sooner it went through me and I got rid of it down the outside bog, the happier I would feel.

Why should the end of our lives always tell such a sad story (well, obviously, nobody dies happy). What I mean is, why do most of us go in such a seemingly messy and bewildering way?

Grandad Bloor was a Vergeman most of his life. He was employed by the council to keep the verges of the country roads tidy. He set off in the morning with sickle or scythe and sharpening stone and his lunch bag, and spent the whole long-day cutting the overgrown grass, thistles and nettles and generally tidying up the roadsides (better than herbicides, but it cost more). It was a good healthy job. He was a weather-beaten, tough old-timer, a grafter. He looked as though he'd stepped out of a painting of Old England with his bearded face and black homburg hat. The job might sound pleasantly rural, but it wasn't. His work was constantly checked by a travelling foreman, and Grandad was responsible for keeping the whole village and its surrounding lanes and environs tidy. There was little time for respite: he had to keep going. But, like many old men, he was perhaps not so much devoted to his wife (well, he might have been) as he was dependent on her.

She died before him, which is always awkward in such cases. It took away his main reason for living and appeared to disorientate him, and his whole life seemed to collapse in on him. He pined and could not cope with life on his own. I heard all this on the grapevine some years later, when I was married and working all hours to pay off the mortgage and raise my kids. One day a short column in the local paper caught my eye: A Homburg hat had been spotted floating on the water by a local fisherman as he stood in his waders fishing under the bridge that spans the River Dove. Grandad was the only man I'd ever known in the area who wore an old fashioned Homburg Hat. I read on...

It was just another drowning. A suicide they thought. It happens all the time. Only this time I knew the man. And as we all know, we sit up when it's happening closer to home. My memory was stirred and I felt intensely shocked and saddened. As I've said before, there is a time in all our lives when we are forced to stop dead in our tracks. Then, feeling strangely disturbed, for a while we survey the world around us, and try to perceive our present standing in the scheme of things and count our own time left, and wonder once again what it is all about. It is always a sobering moment as it is one of the few times when reality tries to reveal itself to us in all its shattering truth. But this particular view of reality takes some facing, and we soon turn away and can't wait to get back to the illusion of our 'normal' life, where we feel secure surrounded by our own particular friends and props, and in our own - as we perceive it - rock solid, real, and comfortable scenario.

Like the ticking of the historical clock, with Gran and Grandad Bloor's passing went my own particular glimpse of the generation and the world that existed before I came upon the scene. And so it goes on. For me at least there will be no more meat-and-potato pies on the scale of that one Gran baked for me. Today's pies are factory made, they're too small and are also suspect: they might have mad cow disease thingy hiding inside them. Anyway, along with almost everything else we enjoy, we are told they are bad for us.

So why was Desperate Dan the strongest man in the world when he ate a cow-pie every day for his dinner? Had he secretly got CJD? Had he got it all wrong? It is a strange world we live in...was then, and will be ever.

CHAPTER 16

The Bank

Blythe Bridge Bank, as it was known, was an extremely steep hill that terminated right outside the five-barred gate that led into our yard, and it's surprising what memories even this hill holds for me as I recall my growing years. People have fond and peculiar memories of the places where they grew up, and things and places that adults take for granted leave a much deeper and different impression in young peoples' minds and memories. Kids often know the nooks and crannies of their district much better than their parents as they spend more time exploring the surrounding areas. At that age, they have the time to spare, and everything is new and seems to lead to new adventures at each turn.

It was down this hill which Henry Bateson strode on his way home from work each evening, humming "Don't laugh at me because I'm a fool". If his dog had not come home earlier, then he would be accompanied by our bad-tempered wire-haired terrier Rip, who'd be proudly carrying his piece of knacker offal in his mouth, to bury in the slack heap.

It is also down this hill which I tested my home-built Mark 1, 2, and 3 wooden soap-box go-carts, and scraped my knees off as the poorly designed early models overturned and sent me sprawling across the gritty surface of the road. And the very same where I skidded off my bike with the glass accumulators and spattered myself with glass and acid. You might also have observed me bowling along a clattering tyreless bike wheel and guiding it skilfully with a wooden stick. Our games were simple then. Later, as times got better and bikes were discarded and replaced with new models more often, it was a bike wheel complete with tyre and inflated inner tube, which bowled along smoother and quieter. This felt like the last word in luxury to me! I tried bowling car tyres down the hill for a while, but these were heavy and dangerous and I found I could not control them with a stick. They went down the hill faster than I could run and I was concerned they might hit someone. Soon, as more and more people became better-off and bought cars, the country roads became busier. If a car or a cyclist had suddenly appeared round the corner, the careering car tyre could have caused a nasty accident. Kids would no longer have the country lanes and roads as their own private playgrounds.

I remember when the high verges that bordered Blythe Bridge Bank produced quite good crops of wild strawberries, raspberries, and sometimes gooseberries. This is where I learned my first natural lessons of nature, which has helped me as a keen gardener ever since. Each season, I realised, suited a different species of plant. Perhaps this is nature's way of sharing out the nutrients etc present in the soil. One year there'd be loads of strawberries and no pig-nuts, then the following year perhaps loads of violets, but not a strawberry anywhere. I remember one year when there was a heavy crop of wild sugar-plums, and the following year the crab-apple tree was loaded. No one but me bothered much with these wild crops, which suited me for when they were ripe I climbed the trees and scoffed the lot. You won't get fresher or more natural fruit than that! I was motoring through my old village recently (in a sad vain bid to recapture the magic of my youth). I stopped my car on The Bank and walked along the hedgerows hoping to taste once again those wild strawberries, and to locate the sugar-plum tree of my boyhood memories. I should have been so lucky. Due to the council spraying the verges with chemical poisons, and what with tractors cutting into the banks, and drifting agricultural herbicides and insecticides, the once flourishing and verdant bank-sides were now damaged and degraded to such an extent that even the hedges and the grass looked blighted and seemed to be struggling for survival, let alone the insect and bird life that had once flourished there.

Our hill was so steep that passing cyclists got carried away (literally) and found themselves going faster down it than they'd anticipated. At the bottom of the hill they'd suddenly find themselves going too fast to take the sharp bend that lead off from the village. A quick decision had to be made whether to go straight on into the river, or to attempt to take the corner. Deep loose grit gathered on the bend and many a cyclist came a nasty cropper there. They would have been much better going straight on into the river, it might have been cold and wet, but at least it was a soft landing.

This was a favourite game with us lads. We'd pedal furiously down the bank, then coast straight through the village square steering our bikes by our feet on the handlebars, and go headlong into the river on purpose. The challenge was to try and get from one side of the river to the other without coming off our bikes, which was easier said than done as the current was strong and the bed of the river consisted of deep loose stones that the bike wheels sank into. We came off in the water many times, but it was just a laugh. We were young rough-and-tumble tearaways then and a good soaking was the least of our worries.

Old Man Pitchfork (Mr Pitchford...an appropriate name now I think about it in view of the following anecdote), an aged Mr-Punch-faced farm labourer who worked at Fellows' farm came down the hill at speed every night on his way to the milking at Fellows' place. I suppose because he'd done the trip every day of his life he'd got used to the sharp corner at the bottom of the hill and had developed his own technique for turning the corner without using his brakes or slowing up. Blythe Bridge lies in a valley and, after heavy rain, the river Blythe often rose and flooded the roads, occasionally going into the houses. This particular darkening September evening the river had flooded suddenly (a flash flood) and as I stood looking out through our living room window at the rising water, Mrs Bateson suddenly remembered Mr Pitchford.

"Run outside quick Michael" she told me, "And try and catch Mr Pitchford. Tell him the floods are out, otherwise he'll go straight into the water!"

It was too late. As I ran outside I saw the old man hurtle past our gate. I flew into the road and was just in time to see him go head over heels over his handlebars as he hit the flood water at full speed. He was a frail, lightweight bony old geezer. He loved speeding down the steep hill but he should have known better. Still, it was a comical sight and I laughed out loud, although it really wasn't funny. Mrs Bateson came out and said, "what are you laughing at?" I turned and remarked, "Old man Pitchfork's just gone straight over his handlebars into the floods!"

We both ran down the road to help him. His arms and legs were floundering in the deep water, but he eventually managed to drag his sopping-wet self up, along with his rusty old-fashioned sit-up-and-beg bike.

We offered to take him in the house for a warm and a cup of tea but he was more concerned that his bike-light had been extinguished and he might be late for the milking. He continued on his way, dripping wet and wobbling precariously along the flooded lane on his way to the farm. The aged fogies were tough old boots in those days. They don't make them like that anymore.

Another time, some years later, two young girls came speeding and squealing down the bank dressed to the nines on their way to a village dance. On hearing the commotion our dog Rip ran out to investigate and have a bark at them. He got tangled up in the bike wheels and fetched them both off with a crash onto the gritty road, which really gave them something to squeal about. Rip wasn't hurt, and ran away yelping quite pleased with himself. But the girls had nasty grazes on their hands and knees.

They limped into our kitchen pale-faced, shaking and dripping blood. Mrs Bateson bathed their wounds, made them a cup of tea and tried to console them, while I looked on fascinated at this rare vision of red-flecked smooth white female thigh, and damaged beauty. They were more concerned at their ruined silk stockings (a precious and pricey luxury commodity at that time) than they were by the grit embedded in their bloodied knees and they certainly weren't going to miss the dance. Youth is surprisingly resilient. We repaired and refreshed them as best we could, and with a cursory check over their bikes they went on their way. They had a date with the American airmen stationed nearby, and that they would not miss for anything. They depended on the Yanks for their silk stockings!

On the subject of flooding, one memorable year the River Blythe went into the worst flood in the living memory of the village. Obviously, as a child, I had never seen anything like it, and couldn't believe my eyes. I stood gaping in disbelief at the unfamiliar floodscape of marooned animals standing forlornly on small hillocks of islands of grass, surrounded by acres of swirling water. We couldn't reach or help them. Drowned sheep and cattle floated down the river, later trade for our knacker yard or some to get caught in the old mill water-wheel.

During the night the water crept higher and higher, watched and monitored by the anxious eyes of the villagers. I couldn't understand where all the water was coming from. The Old Mill down the lane, built at the lowest point to catch the river water, was the worst affected and could only be reached by long legs in wader wellingtons, and then dangerous. Landmarks disappeared under water and you could not tell which was river, and which was land.

The Mill House and The Mill itself was submerged in over five feet of water and totally flood-locked. We tried to get to them by wading where we guessed the lane should be, but this was particularly treacherous as a deep part of the river ran alongside the lane and you couldn't tell where lane ended and river began. Furniture and carpets floated about inside the house and were ruined. The porous crumbling old walls of the Mill soaked up the water like blotting paper and the place was damp for months afterwards. The ducks and geese loved it though and swam about the village lanes and fields quacking excitedly. It was certainly lovely weather for ducks, as they say.

For the first time ever the water even reached Moulds', the village shop, but stopped just short of our house which, fortunately, lay a little higher up the road. It's a good job it did or it would have broken poor old 'Em's houseproud heart.. floods are no respecters of pretty houses. Goods from the shop floated out of the door and deposited themselves like driftwood yards away. When the floods finally receded (after what seemed like weeks to me) sodden packets of Blanc-mange and custard powder, tins of soggy mustard, and even packets of spoilt cigarettes lay dotted around the verges of the village square. We kids had a field day collecting them and making up messy 'dinner-mixes' in our playhouse, while we tried to light damp cigarettes with damp unstrikable matches.

American airmen were stationed in the area, and entered my life at odd times and occasionally in odd circumstances. There was that time they gave me a lift in their jeep, and then there was the box of candy that had caused so much jealousy at school. But perhaps the strangest event happened one bright sunny afternoon whilst Mrs Bateson was humming "There'll be blue birds over, the white cliffs of Dover" as she contentedly dusted the furniture. I was playing outside when suddenly she came running and calling me.

"Michael. Michael", she whispered urgently, excited and breathless. "Come into the house quick will you, and stay with me. There's a black man coming down the bank!"

Now this was an extremely unusual thing to see in an isolated village such as ours. Very few people walked past our house anyway, let alone black men. It was almost an event to see anybody and if we did it was usually someone we knew. I was half-dragged into the house and posted like a sentinel look-out at the kitchen window, and instructed to give a running commentary on the man's progress as he nonchalantly came strolling down the hill towards our house. It was a black American airman - a 'Yank'. 'Em, hovering in the background, kept whispering, "What's he doing now Michael? How near is he? Is he past yet...is he? is he?"

I couldn't see what the Yank was doing other than walking, as I could just about see his head bobbing along behind the hedge. "He's still walking down the hill" I informed her, feeling rather silly and apologetic that I couldn't offer anything more interesting than this rather obvious observation.

I sensed immediately that there was something fishy about Mrs Bateson's behaviour. But, being so young and not realising what sometimes goes on between consenting adults, I didn't try and put two and two together to make five. Why 'Em should take fright at a seemingly innocent Yank out for a summer stroll through our English country lanes, I shall never know but I'll hazard a guess. I suspect she had met him somewhere or sometime earlier, albeit inadvertently, which would be strange because she hardly ever went anywhere. American airforce lorry drivers often waved to us as they passed through the village taking ammunition to a local underground storage dump, - perhaps she had eye-balled one of these, I wouldn't know.

Anyhow, the black American reached the bottom of the bank and stood whistling and pacing about outside our gate, in a rather nervous and undecided manner. Then, as if suddenly making up his mind, we heard the gate squeak as he pushed it open and came into our yard.

"He's coming in!" Mrs Bateson shrieked as she retreated into the safety of the darker confines of the living room, dragging me with her.

"Michael...whatever happens, stay with me" she begged. Like a little girl she could act vulnerable when it suited her. At these times, I became confused. I've always been a soft touch in the face of innocent vulnerability and her confiding in me and seeming to need me aroused these feelings of grown-up protectiveness in me - and yet, I didn't like the woman. I hardly knew how to behave.

This unaccustomed intimacy was embarrassing. I was totally bemused. What the hell was going on? (as this intruding black airman might have remarked, had be seen the confusion he was causing).

In retrospect, I realise now that Mrs Bateson was probably merely using me to protect herself. The whole thing had happened so suddenly she hadn't had time to shut the door. The huge ink-black Yank stood politely tapping the house door now and again. He was still whistling...a completely tuneless tune.

"Halloo there. Anybody in? Are you there Missis" he shouted, poking his bulbous eyes around the kitchen door as though he was playing hide-and-seek.

Eventually he walked in; just like that. Apparently uninvited, yet, in a strange way, as though he knew he was welcome and expected.

"Why, Halloo Missis" he drawled politely on seeing us cringing in the living room. "A've just called in to see ya. How are ya?" He had obviously been brushing up on the time honoured English manner of greeting. He spoke with a odd mixture of American drawl and formal English.

Mrs Bateson, hiding behind me and using me as a shield, gave an unaccustomed nervous smile and a disconcerting silly girlish giggle and replied, "I'm quite all right, thank you. And how are you?" This was hardly the reaction of a woman whose house had just been virtually invaded, which is why I wondered whether something had been pre-arranged between them.

Sorry to have to report such a banal conversation, but that is exactly how it went. The American might have genned up on the preliminaries, but he hadn't conquered the discreet and subtle art of English conversation completely. "O.K. then Missis?" he continued, trying to quell his own nervousness as well as hers (though he was surprisingly calm, under the circumstances). "It's a lovely day, ain't it?" He'd almost got the opener...the weather bit right. Perhaps he'd been reading "How to get on with the natives" back at camp. Many servicemen are issued with comical booklets telling them how to behave and converse with the local folk, in foreign climes, full of banal stilted phrases in most cases, that no native would ever use.

It was mid-summer and there was no fire in the grate. Yet this Black American stood like a typical English Lord of the manor with his back to the fireplace and his hands clasped behind him, rocking backwards and forwards on his heels as only an Englishman knows how (had he learnt that in his booklet too?). He looked comfortable and quite at home. He was not overly nervous and seemed quite laid-back and relaxed, as Yanks are prone to be.

Then a strange and strained silence fell. Perhaps he didn't know what to say next or perhaps he was waiting for me to get out of the way, so he could get to grips with whatever it was he wanted to get to grips with, I don't know. Like a tableau vivant we remained like this for some time. Him rocking backwards and forwards on his heels, and occasionally humming or whistling, and 'Em keeping behind me and holding on to my shirt with a grip like iron, using me as a sort of shield in case I decided to dart outside to play. I felt like a useless trapped mouse- yet feeling protective while at the same time knowing I couldn't have done anything, had anything untoward happened! Like most kids, I was unpredictable, and I was beginning to get bored with this odd adult game of charades.

The Yank finally broke the silence. "Ah decided ta come out for a walk" he informed us. "Lovely village you have here". As we didn't answer, the one-sided conversation petered out again. You know how it is. Emily Bateson obviously wasn't going to encourage him to stay, or help him in his attempts at having a conversation, I'll give her that.

After what seemed another lifetime of silence, interspersed with his humming, whistling and rocking, and weak attempts at conversation, he suddenly bade us farewell.

"It's been nice seeing ya Missis" he drawled, as though he was in the habit of calling regular, "and your lovely house and cute little boy." He handed me a couple of packets of gum and went on his way, waving and grinning in a familiar manner as if he was an old friend.

Mrs Bateson breathed a sigh of relief and yet, at the same time, looked rather disappointed. In a way it had been quite an exciting happening as we rarely had visitors, and certainly never a black American.

What had been going on here? Your guess is as good as mine. I have often wondered.

It could be that the cheeky Yank was merely lonely. In a foreign country, almost trapped in the confines of their barrack life-styles, many foreign servicemen have a great curiosity to see inside the houses of, and to talk directly to, the local inhabitants of their host country, and to see how they live. This is well known, and quite healthy and natural - and, in my opinion, should be better understood, welcomed and encouraged, especially by us rather reserved English people. I was a serving-overseas serviceman myself once and I know the feeling. There is a great loneliness in barrack-life, especially in a foreign country. And servicemen get homesick and yearn occasionally to feel like 'normal' civilians again, even though they realise it can only be a temporary feeling they enjoy.

And I've often wondered whether my self-righteous and God-fearing house-proud 'Em had a darker - or a lighter and more adventurous side to her nature (depending what your morals are and how you view these things). War has a nasty way of distorting the behaviour of normally quite moral and decent people. It concentrates the mind like nothing else. Like thousands of others, Mrs Bateson's husband had been away a long time at the war, and like most war-wives she must have felt terribly lonely at times. Nice or nasty, we are all human. Loneliness and sexual frustration are a potent broth. Perhaps she had given this American Airman the impression he would be welcome to call anytime, and then, on reflection, she may have realised (like many women do) he had taken the message too seriously and she had now changed her mind. Discovered she had bitten off more than she could chew.

Whatever had taken place, it was a very odd occurrence. Like most events in my young life, I tried to make sense out of it and to piece it together in later years as I grew to understand more the complexities of human nature, and the urgent drives of sex, loneliness, excitement, and risk.

But do you know what I remembered most of all about this episode?

Guess?

It was the remarkable and staggering politeness of that American Airman. He had after all gate-crashed our house and privacy, and had tried to engage us in conversation (as well as he knew how) and had left in a pleasant and friendly manner. I'm sure he meant, and caused, no harm. And the outstanding and lasting lesson he imparted, to a small wide-eyed and wondering evacuee boy, on the peculiarities of the human race, was that most Americans are among the friendliest and most polite people on earth. And knowing more about people now, I believe this is true.

For many years during the war, large military lorries trundled through our village day and night. I would lie awake listening to them as they changed gear in readiness to climb the steep bank outside our house.

They were carrying amunition, shells and suchlike, to store at a massive underground 'dump' near the village of Fauld, some miles away.

Millions of pounds worth of ammo must have been stored as these trucks seemed never ending. They passed through our village at least once every hour. We got to know the drivers (English and American) and would wave to them as the heavy trucks rumbled ceaselessly by. It was supposed to be a war secret, a hush-hush operation, but everyone knew what was going on.

This little bit of info would hardly be worthy of note, as this sort of thing was taking place all over the country, but for one thing.

On November the 27th, 1944, this huge underground ammunition dump blew up. The explosion was heard and windows rattled for miles around. Houses and farms, and tractors with their drivers, were blown up or overturned. I believe some twenty-six people died, some of them simply disappeared in the explosion cloud. The crater the explosion left is still there to this day. They were never sure what caused it. One rumour was that a worker had accidentally hammered at a detonater on a shell - but how would they know? You can blow up many things, but don't blow up an armament's dump or it'll cause the biggest bang you've ever seen.

I mention this because it brought home to me the futility and terrible waste of war. As a little kiddie I had watched and taken for granted these lorries that continually passed our house, knowing they carried bombs but too young to understand the full significance of this (despite me being evacuated because of the bombing of Southern England). How innocent we are as kids. To me the lorries were fun and part of our everyday life, and a distraction from my boring village existence and because I could wave merrily to the drivers. I thought these lorries had always passed through our village, and would continue to do so for ever!

But now, older and wiser, I see this episode for what it was: a shocking waste of time, money, raw materials, and manpower...and, eventually, when they were finally used to kill...lives. While I waved cheerily to the drivers and thought what a jolly jape it all was, on the other side of the world kids of my own age were fleeing from these same bombs as they rained down from the skies, to terrify, to cause unimaginable pain, sorrow and horror, and to maim and kill. And here is a link in the chain that forms my life and of which I am trying to join to make sense. I am evacuated because of bombs: in my now safe environment I wave merrily to the lorries that carry bombs destined for the bombing of Germany: and over there kids like myself flee as the bombs burst around them. And in my ignorance, I am just an unhappy little English evacuee child, who doesn't like the woman he has been billeted with.

I thought myself hard done by. Tell that to the jewish kids on their way to the gas chambers, or the foreign kids who ran for their lives as the bombs rained down, as I bemoaned my own petty lot: I didn't know when I was well off! Here endeth another lesson.

CHAPTER 17

Moving on

Suddenly, it seemed, my days of aimless childhood wanderings were coming to an end (do you remember when life suddenly began to look serious?). It was time to move on. No one told me or gave me a written warning to this effect. It was always in the scheme of things. Life - and time, never stands still. We might think that God is in his heaven and all is well with the world...but, disconcertingly, all thinking people know it can never really be like this. Our lives are in a state of perpetual flux, and we are growing older by the minute, although we would like to think our lives will go on as they are at present for ever. There can never be a state so cosy.

I moved on to the Secondary Modern Boys' school in Uttoxeter town, about six miles away from my village of Blythe Bridge.

We travelled by school bus. In theory, according to sociologists, this change, this challenge and push into a more adult world, should have done me good. After all, I was moving away from my lonely village life and into the wider world of the main stream of my own age group. And I agree, you would have thought this could do me nothing but good. In fact, as in most major changes in life, things seemed to get more puzzling, worrying and more complicated than ever.

Now, three things seemed to dominate my life and cause me great bewilderment and anxiety. The harder lessons I faced - and the learning of them (the main reason for going to school) came well down my scale of worries and priorities, as they do with most youngsters. As should be very obvious by now, I was, in many ways, quite emotionally disturbed. The original mixed up kid. And I was, once again, floundering to find my way through a miserable tangle of turbulent, complex and inexplicable emotions and the unpredictable behaviour resulting from this floundering. Being an adolescent didn't help either.

Contrary to what teachers and our betters seem to think, many kids are not so concerned at learning what makes the world go round, as to what their mates might think of them. Get the sign-posts turned round the right way first I say, before you start teaching the three R's.

I ought to have had the opportunity to sort my emotional problems out first before I could even begin to imbibe the stodge of learning. But modern life has this impersonal way of pushing you into a situation and letting you sink or swim. I'm sure it doesn't have to be like this. A few simple directions from sensible adults (our mentors) could clear a lot of things up for us at the start. But the need to get us through school stuffed with as much knowledge as possible in the few short years of school-life allotted for this purpose, and to get us out into the work-place to earn our own living, seemed then to over-ride everything else. Everything seemed so urgent, and there seemed so little time.

To sort myself out emotionally first was easier said than done, as at that time I didn't even realise I had a problem. This is how I thought life was - just one long worry and anxiety. These days computers are brilliant at solving a problem in seconds, but adjustments and solutions to complex disturbed people are far from simple. Anyway, we didn't have computers then, so everything was in a mix-up. (Many would argue that it still is!).

In the relatively isolated village of Blythe Bridge I had only a few simple country friends. Now, at this secondary school, I was suddenly surrounded by hundreds of boys of my own age group, and of every sophisticated type imaginable. Thrown in at the deep end, so to speak, I had no idea how to mix. In the playground of this senior school I found myself surrounded by comparatively worldly and street-wise teenagers from all walks of life, from city, town, and country. Here were gangs, bullies, cowards, creeps, swots and even a few nice guys. I had never come up against people like these before. I would have to jostle and compete hard to find myself a respectable niche in the pecking order. We have to cotton on to things pretty quick at this particular stage in our lives. I had to liven myself up.

As well as quickly being rudely awakened to the fact that I felt an emotionally crippled cuckoo-in-the-nest at my new school, my second headache was a more mundane and immediate one and and concerned the problem of not being allowed to wear 'long trousers' (i.e. going into 'longs' as it was known). "When are you going into longs Mick?" my mates would ask, and I would cringe. Now this might seem an unimportant and trivial matter to you, but to me, at that time, it was the most important thing in my life. Who cared that I couldn't do my sums, and that practical drawing and history drove me screwball, I certainly didn't. It was not being allowed to wear long trousers that mainly occupied my thoughts as I sat in class looking so studious and thoughtful. At least I was normal in this respect: I had my teenage priorities right.

Going into 'longs' marked an important milestone in a male adolescent's life then, as the 'short-trouser' period had been a well-established tradition for a long time. Kids were considered kids then, up to a certain age - not young adults like they are today. Like a girl's first make-up marks the day she proudly feels she has become a young woman, the same could be said that a boy's first pair of long trousers makes him feel a man - well, that's how it was then. If his voice broke at about the same time, so much the better. It's all to do with feeling grown up.

Mrs Bateson was very old-fashioned. "Plenty of time yet for that nonsense" she scoffed when I falteringly broached the subject of long trousers, discreetly mentioning that most of the lads at school were wearing them now. "Never you mind what the others are wearing. Let some fresh air get to your legs, it'll do you good". (This was another of her stupid, senseless remarks- she must have thought my legs were plants!) My heart sank. It was obvious I was not going to be allowed to wear long trousers for a long time yet. Though it could have been the expense.

Over the next few months I watched with growing alarm as first one, then the other of the few remaining short-trousered lads went into longs. This was serious: I was in danger of ending up the only lad in short trousers in a playground of over two hundred boys. But that is just what did happen. To my horror, the frightening prospect dawned slowly, finally, into reality. Soon I was the only one in the school not wearing long trousers. To say I felt stupid is an understatement. I felt sick, the odd-one-out and embarrassed all at once. It gave me a headache and made me feel physically ill. I was so aware of this sense of 'inferiority' that I could concentrate on nothing else all day but this feeling of being different, and I was constantly blushing with embarrassent.

If a boy, or a gang of boys, pointed in my direction and laughed, I assumed they were laughing because of my short trousers. Well, they might have been for all I know. Now, if they had been laughing at something I liked and believed in (like a certain shirt or jacket for example) it wouldn't have bothered me. But I didn't believe in short trousers or the fact that I should still have to wear them, and so I was bothered. Very bothered.

Eventually my sulks and apparent desperate unhappiness (over-acted and put on for effect, a little) even penetrated 'Em's hard heart and thick skull, who said I was going around with a face "as long as Litherum's Dog" these days, whatever that might mean. I'm sure she made these queer sayings up. She insisted on knowing what the bloody hell was up with me.

I mumbled once again that most of my mates were wearing long trousers, and that I was the only one at school who was not allowed to wear them, and that they were laughing at me.

I thought perhaps she would feel ashamed to be the 'parent' who hadn't moved with the times and the fashion, and sorry for me being laughed at. I was really seeking sympathy.

I needn't have bothered, and should have known her better. You can't 'blackmail' thick-skinned people like Mrs Bateson. I would go into long trousers when she decided it was time, and not before.

But I must have disturbed a chord somewhere. After a decent time had elapsed, when she thought I thought it was her decision, she conceded. "But you look after them" she warned. "Otherwise...or else...and you change them every night when you come home from school remember. And put them under your mattress so as they keep their shape!" I received this news with a quiet thrill. I would want to keep them nice anyway. I didn't need telling.

But I ought to have known: my joy (which I remember to this day) was short-lived, when she continued, "I'll ask Mould's to order you some".

Now Mould's, if you remember, was the village bakery-cum-general store that had recently gone into clothing to try and diversify and to increase their profits. They knew nothing about clothing or fashion and got their supplies from cheap warehouses. As long as it was cheap and nasty, with a big profit margin, that is all that mattered. Certainly not the sort of stuff a teenage boy would want to be seen in. Most of the lads got their trousers from a certain shop in the town (smart grey flannels at the time) who knew what they were about, and therefore they were more expensive. Mrs Bateson had no time for this stuff and nonsense: my heart sank still further as she said "I'll ask Mrs Mould to get you a good hard wearing pair". So they were to be cheap, unfashionable and hard-wearing. I could have cried, and almost did.

I was given no say in the style, material, or colour...and, worst of all, in the all important width of the 'Bottoms'. (Always absolutely crucial to teenage fashion at that time - and at most times I suspect).

After an interminable wait, or so it seemed (things moved slowly in those days. There were no overnight White Arrows then) 'Em, expecting me to join in her enthusiasm, jubilantly informed me my trousers had come. With mixed feelings and some trepidation, I went over the road to the shop to collect them.

On unwrapping them, my worse fears were realised. I shall never forget those hideous trousers. The nearest I ever came to seeing a pair like them was when I once tried to make a pair myself on our new sewing machine - (have you ever tried to make trousers?) and I'm no tailor, so you can imagine. I think I'd have rather stayed in shorts, and that's saying something. They were made with a coarse cloth and were thick and baggy. They soaked up water like blotting paper and lost their crease and shape forever the first time they got wet. They were a light-blue hairy check, more like a circus clown's trousers, that chafed and made my legs itch, with thick-hemmed fumbly flies that fastened with the wrong sized buttons, or buttonholes, or both. The vital girth of the leg bottoms were ridiculously wide, with thick turn-ups that had to be turned up yet again as they were too long. Throughout the school day I was forever re-turning up these loose turn-ups because they kept coming down, and Mrs Bateson didn't know how to sew them up. Although it was probably my imagination, the whispers and the giggles in the playground seemed to get worse.

The trousers were certainly 'hard-wearing'. It was years before they showed signs of wear and I can also remember my feelings of relief when, finally, with a little crafty help from myself, they did. I did everything possible to encourage them to wear out, like crawling across the playground and fidgeting my bum in class.

At last the knees went threadbare and Mrs Bateson couldn't find the material to match and patch them up - thank God. By now I was allowed a little more say in my own affairs, and chose my own new pair of long trousers. They cost a lot more because they were the standard smart-looking, narrow-legged fine grey flannels with seventeen inch bottoms (which went out of date about twelve months later, but I still had to wear them out) with so-called semi-permanent creases. I can even rememember the fresh 'new' smell of them to this day. I thought they were smack up to date and I felt grown up at last and ten feet tall as my mates crowded round in admiration - or so I would like to think. I was told by a friend of a friend of a friend, that someone had remarked how grown up and smart I looked now, and this compliment was all I needed to satiate my natural teenage longing for admiration. It was long overdue. My morale had been given a boost at last. If you feel grown up, you are grown up. Confidence in yourself works wonders.

The third bugbear that followed me into secondary school, and one that I was never able to shed throughout my school life, was the irritating and embarrassing chore of still having to fetch Mrs Bateson's currant bread. Unfortunately for me 'Em had decided she preferred the currant bread from town to that of the village baker, it was also cheaper, so at least twice a week I had to fetch it during my dinner hour, keep it in the cloak room during the afternoon, then carry it home on the school bus when school ended.

For a while now I had been identified by other school kids as "You know, the one in short trousers who fetches his Mum's currant bread". A rather ignominious description for an apprentice schoolboy who is trying to establish his pecking order and carve his niche in the playground hierarchy and trying to maintain his dignity. When I went into 'longs', at least the "one in short trousers" tag was dropped to "you know, the one who fetches his Mum's currant bread", but even this disparaging teasing title hurt.

How I hated that question, usually shot at me just as I was about to escape to catch my school bus... "Michael, will you fetch me four loaves of currant bread from Elkes' shop in town, at dinner time? The money is in the bag". 'The bag' was a large stiff fawn leather 'old woman's' type shopping bag, bought again because of its hard-wearing qualities, very common at the time and so stiff and clumsy it was not easy to either carry or accomodate on the crowded bus. Nor, I might add, when it was loaded with four loaves of bread - either in the cloakroom, or in the classroom (where it finally ended up).

The trip into town during my dinner hour meant I had to forgo my school canteen dinner and grab a bag of chips in town. This was no hardship as school canteen dinners were notoriously yukky , or so we thought. If there was a queue at the currant bread shop, it was all such a rush. Not only that, my mates didn't really want to be seen accompanying a lad struggling with a large leather shopping bag, so I mostly went on my own. Young folk are a proud and selfish lot, and they very much know what they like and don't like when it comes to street cred. This side of young folk has never changed through the years, and never will.

For the first few weeks I hung the bag of bread on a hook with my coat in the school cloakroom, although it stuck out and got in the way, and bumped people's heads as they jostled by and I often got complained at.

Then someone started pinching the bread. They must have been hungry (or were they just taking the Mick?) as they tore chunks out of the loaves, which wasn't discovered until Mrs Bateson came to unpack them later. A note was sent to Mr Burford, my form teacher, who advised me to bring the bag into class so that I could keep an eye on it as it stood in the corner...as if I wanted to!

So now, right throughout the day, this bleedin' bag stood in the corner mocking me, and reminding me of what an embarrasment it and its contents were, and what a prick I felt as I lugged it around everywhere I went. It's no wonder I was a poor scholar: I couldn't concentrate on my lessons because of that damned bag in the corner of the classroom.

Otherwise, apart from these normal growing-up pin-prick problems (appearing out of all proportion to me because of my age) I suppose I was happy enough at my new school. We all experience problems throughout our lives no-matter how the way is paved for us: it is part of life. Along with the embarrassments and self-searching introspection, I struggled to learn my lessons and to come to terms with unfamiliar aggressive bully types, and friends. And, just over the horizon, I began to take an interest in...girls. A strong new feeling and a mysterious promise of something delicious to come was pending.

Due to my evacuee experience, I've no doubt I had deep emotional wounds and problems. As well as being the only boy in the playground not wearing long trousers for so long, as far as I was aware I was the only one without any parents. Here, at secondary school, along with the well-known problems of all developing adolescents anyway, my extra problems would surely manifest themselves more clearly than ever.

I was passing through another of those early crucibles of life. Would I crack up in the firing kiln. Or would I emerge a stronger and more stable character? The problem was (and always is) that while I was being tested in the tempering furnace of life, I was unaware of what was happening to me. While in the centre of the boiling swirling maelstrom, I felt only that it was very uncomfortable and worrying, sometimes traumatic, and often downright frightening and painful. We can very often not see the wood for the trees, at that age. We feel every day has its crisis.

At this school I made plenty of new friends, and some enemies. I had fights. In lessons I was a moderate to poor scholar, nothing special. I hated Maths, History, Practical drawing, and P.T., but I liked Art, English, Woodwork and Gardening. I hated some of the teachers, some left me cold, while others I liked, and some puzzled and intrigued me. I found many other lads who pinched things, the same as me. And I found 'The Playground' was just as much another separate world of the young (that totally excluded adults and teachers) as was life in the classroom. Apart from the odd blip, I suppose I sound like your average schoolboy type, although I didn't feel average. And it is the odd blips anyway, that make us different and the individuals we become.

I soon realised that something extra daring and dangerous was needed if I was to grab the attention. admiration and respect of those peers I wanted to attract, and to establish and maintain my popularity and standing. Before an incredulous crowd I chewed up razor blades and put lighted matches in my mouth (yes, I really did). It's a wonder I didn't harm myself, but so strong was my desire to impress and 'make my mark'.

Somehow I felt I had to look big. I suppose I had what was known then in psychology terms as an inferiority complex. At this time I was a strange mixture of timidity and arrogance. I latched onto the school bully and gang leader, a threatening, swarthy, good-looking Spanish-featured, but slightly built character nicknamed Spikey Ball.

I suppose I hid behind his macho image, and bolstered my confidence through the mysterious threatening aura and sense of authority he seemed to exert over ninety-per-cent of the other lads at the school. He was like a playground mafia boss. And he, no doubt (like all crooks do) felt flattered at his power over us hangers-on who would without question immediately carry out his slightest request

It was Spikey who got me involved in my first fight. He had this spiteful habit of pushing his cronies hard into someone he didn't like, or had it in for, and egging "Go on, hit him. He's looking for a fight. He's pushing you. Go on, give him one. You're not scared of him are you? You can fight him". It was a crude malicious form of brain-washing: a classic bully's tactic. I suppose he wanted someone to do his fighting for him: why keep a dog if you have to bite yourself? And we fell for it, hook, line and sinker, though these subtleties were not obvious to me at the time, and even if they had been, it would not have been schoolboy ethos to refuse and would have made no difference.

The lad I was forced to fight in this way one day was called Webster. I had nothing against him except that he had red hair and freckles on his face. I gave him a bleeding nose and he gave me a black eye: game set and match. Luckily, as it was getting nasty, the teacher came out and blew the end-of-playtime whistle, which saved us both from further damage and from losing face in front of the gathering playground audience, that had been drawn like a magnet as the 'A fight! A fight!' shout had gone up. Boys love a playground scrap. Spikey seemed quite surprised and impressed at how I'd performed. The experience also taught me a valuable lesson: if you are challenged, don't be scared, and ALWAYS fight back. You might lose the battle but you will definitely gain respect, and in future people will not be so keen to challenge you.

Meanwhile, Spikey and our gang prowled the playground looking for victims to bully, torture and torment. Like all true crooks and bullies Spikey got his obedient and willing henchmen (like myself) to do his dirty work and to harass the ones he would not tackle himself, and picked on those for personal attention he knew would not fight back. Like all henchmen, I was aware that one day Spikey might turn on me, but I had a subtle indefinable power myself that seemed to hold him at bay. Though I never understood what it was myself!

Such a victim was poor Stan Green. Stan would just not speak, or very, very rarely. We didn't know (or care) what his problem was: he was just a curiosity to be taken apart, like a malfunctioning clock. Bullies don't stop to ask questions. Being different is crime enough. Maybe he was extraordinarily shy, or timid, or there could even have been something wrong with his speaking apparatus, who knows? kids rarely understand such things anyway, and even if they did they wouldn't care. He never spoke to us lads in the playground nor to the teachers in the classroom. Playtimes must have been an ordeal for him as he just cringed and huddled in a corner, and watched the boisterous horse-play and battles of the other lads through clenched frightened eyes.

He obviously had a real problem and was natural bully material. It was only a matter of time before Spikey and our gang hove his way.

When we did, Stan saw us coming and screwed bimself up even smaller, probably hoping, like an ostrich, he would become invisible and wouldn't be noticed.

But Spikey had clocked him days earlier and, like all true predators, was merely biding his time and waiting for the right moment to pounce.

Spikey, accompanied by his entourage (including me) stopped in front of the frightened cringing Stan. "Hello Stanley" he said, in a quite pleasant, matey, and surprised way, like boss-crooks do.

Naturally Stanley didn't answer, but tried to give a sickly ingratiating smile, not quite knowing what to expect, and wrapped himself into a smaller ball than ever.

"Aren't you going to speak to Uncle Arthur, Stanley?" taunted Spikey (whose real name was Arthur Ball). As if no one, but no one, dared to refuse to speak to the notorious Spikey Ball. Again, no answer was the stern reply.

A lad, smaller and more spindly than Stanley, whose cruel knickname was Embryo, was dragged forward by Spikey: "Here, speak to Embryo if you don't want to speak to me". Then it was Donkey Dick's turn. Then Shortarse's. (Yes, we all had our special comical nicknames. I was Fishtank).

"What's up Stanley?" continued his limpet-like tormentor. Like a ferret, once Spikey had gotten his teeth into you, there was no getting away. "Have you lost your tongue or something? Why won't you speak? Has someone cut your tongue out Stanley? Can't you speak. Look lads, Stanley's got no tongue, he can't speak". Spikey was forcing Stanley's mouth open to show us he'd got no tongue. We were really interested in why he wouldn't speak. Perhaps he HASN'T got a tongue, we thought. There was a boy in the playground with four thumbs, and another with an extra lip, so it was feasable Stanely might not have a tongue. And if we could be entertained at the same time, so much the better.

Stanley wouldn't even shake or nod his head in acknowledgement to our questions. This only served to aggravate Spikey's progressive exasperation and impatience with the seemingly stupid Stanley. Perhaps Stanley was thinking "Why should I speak to you. You're all just a load of thugs". Thugs maybe: but thugs are dangerous people and can hurt you, so, in a way, it's best to play along.

If Stanley had only nodded his head in agreement, perhaps Spikey would have laid off and let him alone, though I doubt it. You don't usually appease bullies. They need to have their fun and Spikey wanted acknowledgement of his own importance and power. Hoodlums are unpredictable creatures and, like a cat playing with a mouse, will just as soon kill you as let you go. Your fate is merely incidental to their amusement and games.

Spikey would take Stanley's continuing silence as a personal insult, a defiance of his importance. And now, to save face in front of his gang, he would have to continue to try and make Stan speak. Standing at the back of the crowd that had gathered, I was silently willing Stanley to say something. I knew something unpleasant was in store for him if he didn't and, believe it or not, I didn't want to see him hurt. This is an admittance of my own cowardice at the time, and the reason why I remember this occurrence of so long ago so vividly today. I ought to have tried to persuade Spikey to move on to some other less potentially dangerous diversion, he might have welcomed the excuse as well. Human nature is a funny thing. In retrospect, I could have tried.

But this time I really did not want to be involved at all. Stan seemed harmless enough to me, so why torment him? I preferred boys who attempted to fight back. It gave an element of fairness, was more fun, and gave the tormented a chance to earn some respect. So I moved further back and away from Spikey's vicinity. With a bit of luck I'd be forgotten and could take a back seat. It was simple cowardice really.

I needn't have bothered. Stubborn Stanley was just what Spikey wanted: a cringing, silent, willing victim. It was just about Spikey's measure.

The gang leader took Stan's arm and began twisting it up his back. "Speak to me Stanley" he implored in a sinister mocking tone, sounding gentle as all professional torturers do.

But...still nothing. A passive stare back from Stanley of...what? Fear? Hatred? Sick cowardice? Who knows?

His arm was twisted further up his back. "Go on, speak to Spikey please Stanley". Spikey's voice got even quieter, and sounded more ominous for that. I'm sure he was a budding psychopath.

He's going to break his bloody arm I thought.

Eventually Stanley gave a strangled squawk. That's the only word that describes the sound that came out through his clenched and anguished mouth.

We were all dutifully amazed, and cheered and clapped loudly for the benefit of Spikey's success at literally squeezing some sound out of him, not for Stanley's noble effort for holding out so long. It was the first and last utterance I ever heard Stanley make, although people told me he could speak. Personally, I felt rather ashamed at the incident

Once again the whistle sounded and saved Stanley's bacon from further torture. That was one thing about being in a playground - if you got yourself into a scrape, a corner - if you could stall things a bit, sooner or later a teacher would appear to save you. It was about the only time you were glad to see a teacher make an appearance.

This was one of the nastiest pieces of bullying that I had ever witnessed (I've seen worse since). Shortly after this, following a respectable premeditated pause, I distanced myself from Spikey's gang. If he carried on like this I told myself, he was heading for serious trouble, and I didn't want to be around or involved when it happened. I was a little worried that Spikey might now home in on me but, although he noticed me keeping my distance, he kept well clear. He had pushed me into that fight with one of the large bruisers in the playground, and I had given a respectable account of myself although I lost the fight, so Spikey had seen me in action and knew I didn't lack courage to stand up for myself. I had proved myself and had earned my place in the pecking order of things and I no longer needed him to hide behind.

I bumped into the grown up Spikey many years later at a flea sale. He was scarcely recognisable. He was meekly following a rather dominant and self-assured looking wife, taller and younger than himself (and funnily enough, she was a swarthy Spanish-looking type too). I don't think he recognised me.

While he hovered in the background like a coward, on his behalf his assertive and self-assured wife purchased a camera from my stall. It was broken, but they didn't know that, and I got a good price. Serve you right I thought, poetic-justice at last for bullying poor old Stanley when we were at school.

The characteristics that had first attracted me to Spikey years ago were what made me notice him now: the sulky threatening face, and the hunched shoulders. But that was all. When we are young our salient physical features seem to give out vibes which largely determine what sort of friends we attract, and how we are perceived, and how we react to these perceptions.

Up to a point, other people (our friends) make us what we become. When we are older those same characteristics which once might have seemed to emanate power, vibrancy and magnetism or whatever, can now look odd and almost comical. This is what had happened to Spikey Ball. His whole gangster image had been built around his body language and aura, and a naturally threatenintg facial expression. He was simply born looking like that, and was probably no more inherently vicious than anyone else. Us lads had attributed him with viciousness and he had recognised this power and had exploited it. Many bullies evolve this way. I always think Hitler did.

His once dark wiry hair - what was left of it - was now greying and wispy and blowing pathetically in the slight breeze. He seemed to be smaller and looked weaker and more slight in frame than when he was fourteen and the school bully. Then he had looked strong and tough. Now he was pacing and dithering about nervously as though he was frightened of his own shadow. How have the mighty fallen, I thought. I felt almost sorry for him.

No writer's recollections of their school days would be complete without the recall of emotionally-tinged memories of certain teachers...liked and disliked...popular and unpopular.

I say emotionally-tinged because our teachers have a deeper effect on us than we realise. After our parents, and sometimes despite our parents, teachers are our role-models whom we may or may not decide to emulate, albeit often unconsciously. In my case, I had no parents to look to for guidance, only Mrs Bateson, and I had no wish at all to base my life's behaviour on her's.

Teachers appear to us, at that young age, as larger than life. Their behaviour, opinions and moods possibly influence us more than their teachings, although they shouldn't. Well, they used to. I don't know about modern youth, who seem to have the freedom and the confidence to make up their own minds about everything. Whether this is a good or a bad thing, and whether they make the right choices, I have no idea. This is another one of those separate, imponderable questions.

In truth, and now in retrospect, I realise teachers are only human beings and vulnerable like the rest of us. But then we really believed they knew best and something about life (as different from academic knowledge) that we did not, and turned to them for guidance and wisdom. But just like adults everywhere, some would listen, while others could not be bothered. Some could help, while others were just as confused as we were ourselves. Some were easy going, happy and likeable, while others were taciturn, bad-tempered and moody. Some were conscientious and energetic, while yet others were lazy and couldn't care less. To sum up, some were good teachers and some were bad. As I say, a pretty average bunch of people. You find all sorts, in all walks of life.

Like most of us, teachers turn up for work in a good, bad, or filthy mood: feeling well or off-colour. The big difference is they have a classroom full of energetic, boisterous and unruly kids to face, whereas we ordinary mortals have either maybe a machine, or a computer, or merely a desk full off paperwork facing us that doesn't continually fidget, complain, or play tricks on us, and answer back. If we feel ill or in a bad mood, most of us (hopefully) can turn ourselves off, or inward for a while, while we recuperate and regain some sanguinity.

Somehow, despite being a dunce, I wangled my way through school, and found myself in the "A" stream and went through secondary school trying to kid myself (and others) that I was cleverer than I actually was. I have quite a receptive brain, but an awful memory. I can usually understand what is being taught, but I have forgotten most of it ten minutes later. This has always been my great failing. As an example of my denseness, I learnt to tell the time years after my contemporaries, and even used to spell gril for girl. I was once asked to write my name on the blackboard in front of the class, and wrote Michael Brid instead of Michael Bird, and got a whack on the back of the head as well as an embarrassing titter from the rest of the class. I can sympathise with dyslexics. A teacher once asked me what the hell I was on about when I wrote in a composition "the two grils stopped to watch the brids hopping about among the fris". So I changed it in front of him and wrote "The two gorillas stopped to watch the brides hopping about among the furze". I was so embarrassed at the i r business. But I suppose the rephrased version shows a twisted intelligence of a sort. What I lacked in the knowledge absorption department I made up for in quick-thinking cunningness! The fact that I got another sneer for writing such a silly sentence didn't bother me, as I knew at least the spelling was correct.

There is an up-side and a down-side in being graded into a higher stream than one really merits. The up-side is it boosts your morale and you can feel superior (when it suits you) to your lower graded, supposedly, dimmer-witted pals (where you secretly suspect you belong). Also, being streamed with the bright ones, with a bit of luck and a lot of hard work, some of it might actually rub off on you and into your obtuse brain. This is the position I found myself in. I was rated cleverer than I actually was.

Again, at that age you do not understand the truism that being cleverer or brighter than your peers does not necessarily make you a better or even a more successful person. The two things are completely different. That sort of knowledge comes with wisdom, much, much later. It is this confusion that can give one a lifelong inferiority complex, and in a way wastes your life. And this was part of my problem.

So it was, I really struggled to get through my lessons and tests at this school. I'm sure no one ever realised just how thick I was. Although I wasn't aware I was doing it I suppose I sort of conned my way through school (and thus, probably, on through life!) learning more the arts of craft, guile and cunning, than anything academic, erudite or educational. But you also need guile and cunning in life to survive, so it wasn't a complete waste of time.

My class fell lucky in having Mr Burford, the most popular teacher in the school, as our form master. Physically burly with an outward full and placid-looking face, under stress he was capable of suddenly erupting into a ferocious (and dangerous) temper. We pupils played on this and when we got bored we could wind him up and trigger his breaking point with absolute precision. Sorry Mr. Burford, but you really should have seen through us!

This mischief was never spoken or planned premeditatedly. It just seemed to happen, springing from a spontaneous mass gut feeling: a classroom mood. An unpopular math's lesson, an oppressively hot summer's Friday afternoon, and the time seeming to drag interminably on...and on...

We would sense Mr. Burford was bored too and beginning to get ratty, looking for a diversion - or a distraction. Well, we could certainly give him that. Someone or something would - almost unconsciously - act as a catalyst. A loud fart was a popular and effective trigger, or perhaps ruler-flicking a paper pellet at the back of someone's head on the front row. It might miss and would scud across the floor into the corner of Burford's eye as he chalked dronishly on the squeaky blackboard.

"Who did that?" he would snap, turning sharply round.

He had a discernible way of trying to sound angry and serious, when he wasn't. It was not his nature to get angry straight away but it didn't take him long, he had to wind himself up to make himself angry, and then he was unstoppable. Like many teachers (and indeed, many people) he had probably chosen the wrong profession and found himself trapped in a situation he hated. Once locked in there is not always an easy way out. Us lads could all sense his discomfort, his vulnerability, that is why he was so popular. He came across as human. We could have fun with him, sometimes as an equal over-grown schoolboy himself, and sometimes as a victim teacher.

"No one Sir" some wag would drone in a bored and psalm-like voice, sounding completely fed-up at hearing Sir's same old tiresome hackneyed question yet again. Classrooms and lessons are sometimes a bit like that, tedious to both pupils and teachers. Like waiting for a storm to break, we boys instinctively knew it was going to be one of those days. Any minute now he would explode. If he didn't, we would make him.

"I've just about had enough of this" he would shout, throwing his chalk on the floor as his self-generated temper started rising. "I'll bloody well swing for you lot I will. I will!".

Heads would lower to hide suppressed smiles and titters as we anticipated the explosion that was about to erupt. What would he do this time, we would wonder.

"It was you again, wasn't it Jones? Get off to the Headmaster's study and tell him I bloody sent you". The swearing was part of his attraction. Not many of the other teachers swore with the dedication of Mr. Burford. And it didn't really matter whether Jones had flicked the paper or not. For various subtle reasons he was the class scape-goat. He took the blame for everything. "It wasn't me Sir..." Jones would whine, as we all knew he would.

If we were lucky it was only the chalk, or the blackboard rubber, that came flying over our heads. With considerable force I might add. It might find an unfortunate target, and it hurt. One memorable day, when his temper had reached the dangerous red-alert level, he flung the large heavy wooden T-square at the cowering class. A bit over-the-top in more ways than one.

It came whirring and whirling over our heads like a boomerang, or perhaps more like an out-of-control veering helicopter, twisting and turning close to our ducking domes. I felt the wind of it as it passed close over my own bonse. Luckily it hit the wall at the back of the class and broke into three pieces. I often wondered how he explained that to the headmaster. This was the most dangerous manifestation of Mr Burford's temper I ever witnessed. We boys were quite awed for once.

But we would never dream of reporting Mr Burford for his juvenile, grown-boy tantrums. He was too popular and too much like one of us for us to betray him. Again, there was that unwritten code of honour among types. It wouldn't have been ethical.

Mr Burford's temper would subside as suddenly as it had begun and he would carry on with the lesson, chalking on the blackboard, as though nothing had happened. This was part of his charm and what endeared him to his class. Unlike some other teachers, there would be no sulking and no threats or punishments for revenge. Though a mediocre teacher, he was a remarkable man - or so we considered him. We were all very fond of him, and I suspect he left a more lasting impression on us than did many other excellent, but more conscientious and serious-minded teachers. He certainly did on me.

As my term at the school and in Mr Burford's class approached its end, I was considered an old hand - a senior pupil. And for reasons I've never really understood (though it happens in most establishments) I was allowed to get away with almost anything.

Physical training was one of my most hated lessons. The nuisance of having to completely undress, the smell of sweat and thudding flesh, the hard discipline of exercise and the undignified open showers at the end of the instruction - I hated the whole scene. The unscrupulous and hated gardening teacher, Killer Prince, was also the gymnastics instructor. I'd do anything to wangle out of P.T.

I was getting cheeky and wangling my way blatantly by now, but (honestly) not understanding how I got away with it all. It just seemed to happen.

There came this time when all I needed was an obviously faked headache and Mr Burford would excuse me P.T. without further question. As a change, now and again I would forge a note saying I'd got a contagious skin rash, or was sick. He'd always make excuses for me and I soon cottoned on to this. Instead of physical training I was given the task of marking my own form's exercise books, sitting in a small room on my own at the back of the class. And indeed, many times I've marked my own books and given myself enhanced marks. It was this sort of guile, mentioned earlier (cheating) that helped keep me in the 'A' stream and near the top of the class!

The words 'Teacher's Pet' might spring to mind, but really it wasn't like that at all. There was no particular rapport between me and Mr Burford. Not that I was aware of anyway. I have always had an innate feeling of distaste for any sort of familiarity or favouritism, more so if directed specifically towards myself. No, I think it was just Mr Burford's basically easy-going and tolerant nature. I took advantage of it and he was just too world-weary to object.

Despite his startling outbursts of apparent temper, Mr Burford appeared as basically a kind and placid man. And, speaking for myself, I was glad I had him as my form master. (And it isn't just because he let me off P.T.!) A teacher should be able to influence a pupil's outlook for the rest of his life, preferably for the better. But it is sometimes for the worse. Mr Burford influenced mine in subtle ways that even I do not understand. And that is how it should be.

Another eccentric teacher was the art master, Mr Parry Evans. But his was an eccentricity that, although comical in the extreme, for some reason didn't endear us to him one bit. We found him rather pathetic and he was treated as a figure of fun (he was given to long periods of sulking).

But he was a brilliant artist and sculptor, or so we thought. Sculpture was not in our curriculum. But it was Parry Evans' personal hobby. He did it privately, ostensibly in his own time but quite often during class periods when he should have been teaching, in a small ante-room just off the classroom. Here he had fashioned many clay busts of famous people (I wonder what happened to them?). I can remember a brilliant one of Shakespeare: it was his best. And it was rumoured Mr Evans conversed with his Shakespeare's clay head at times of sulk or classroom stress, and in view of what used to happen during his lessons, it wouldn't have surprised me if this rumour were true.

He had this odd punishment of making class troublemakers stand on their chairs with their hands clasped on top of their heads (a rather dangerous wobbly punishment that wouldn't be allowed today) while the rest of the class sat likewise in total silence.

One day, at the beginning of the hour-long art lesson, somebody let off a loud fart. Farting in class was a common ploy of attention seekers, and a lesson- delay tactic. Evans seemed to take this as a personal insult and after the usual "who did that?" and the also usual deafening silence in place of an answer, he stated grimly, "right then, until the culprit owns up you will all sit in silence with your hands clasped on top of your heads".

Although it made our arms ache, this suited most of the lads as they thought doing nothing for an hour was great, but I've never contributed to this line of thinking. I hate having nothing to do. I was annoyed as I liked art (but not the teacher). We sat like this almost the entire hour while Mr Evans sat on the corner of his desk sulking and swinging his legs and occasionally saying petulantly "I can sit like this the whole hour...it doesn't bother ME" whilst trying to look as though he couldn't care less. He eventually retreated to his ante-room, possibly to commiserate with his Shakespeare's head, and to work on his latest clay-bust project.

This might have been his idea from the start for all I know, and the fart was just the excuse he had been looking for. Teachers can be as crafty and as devious as any pupil if it suits them, and they have more freedom to be so being in charge of the whole thing.

There was also another episode that turned me against Mr Parry (as he was known). We were doing free-style, that is drawing whatever and however we wanted to draw, but it had to be about our summer holiday recess, from which we had recently returned.

I decided to draw a scene of me and my country pals enjoying a day swimming and paddling in the river Blythe. An innocent enough idea you might think, and quite a difficult choice.

Being a country crowd, and away across the fields, if someone had forgotten to bring something to swim in, or maybe had just decided to join in anyway, we swam either naked or in our underclothes. Nobody bothered. It was all quite spontaneous and natural to us. We never even thought about it.

In my pastoral drawing of fields and youngsters having fun, some kids were swiming, some were lounging on the grass, and one girl was changing out of her clothes behind a bush. I was attempting to draw this very difficult bit of the girl struggling to pull her dress over her head (an awesome sketch even for an accomplished artist, I would think) when I felt an almighty thump on the back of my head (you don't forget whacks out of the blue like that, even in a lifetime).

"Ouch! Wha...?" I exclaimed, glancing round. Mr Parry was standing there with a disgusted look on his face.

"What's up Sir?"I asked, hurt (in more ways than one) "What was that for? What did you hit me for? What's the matter...?" I was referring to the smack.

"You don't draw naked women in MY class" he stormed. A strange attitude for an artist teacher who had probably drawn more naked women than most, and had a breasted bust of a woman in his private modelling room. But this really happened.

I forget what little Miss Handley taught, she wasn't with us for long, but I remember her vicious and unusual method of punishment, known by us recipient victims as ruler-rapping.

I remember her as an obnoxious stocky little woman with short stout business-like muscular legs, who strutted briskly about her teaching through the desk-aisles like an overblown prize bantam-cock, checking our work every few minutes. She always looked cross and critical and very intimidating. No one escaped her scrutiny or was overlooked. If you misbehaved, or made a stupid measuring mistake, she wedged your hand under her stumpy but surprisingly strong little arm and rapped your knuckles like a machine-gun with the sharp edge of a ruler clutched in her podgy-fingered hand. It almost broke your knuckles and really hurt, which I suppose it was intended to do. I have always suspected stumpy brisk-walking little women since, though no doubt many of them are grand people. Which goes to show how we are influenced and affected by certain people and their ways during our formative developing years.

The most unpopular teacher in the school was our history teacher. To be fair, this was partly due to the subject matter (which, second to maths, was the next most unpopular lesson - though I never understood why) and partly due to her own grim, unsmiling and severe physiognomy and expression, and her method of teaching. She had an unusual almost plastercast-white frozen face, etched by a deep scar which still showed the stitch marks, down one lumpy cheek. She looked like one of Mr Parry Evans' less successful alabaster faces.

I seem to remember being told she had been in a nasty road accident some time before: but as her pupils we wouldn't have had any sympathy for her anyway even if we had known this to be true. Cruel as it may seem, most ignorant youngsters see facial ugliness as something to mock, and not always only youngsters.

But Miss Cartwright knew her subject well and strode up and down the desk aisles rapping desktops (and the occasional pupil) with a thin switch, trying to emphasise and drive home boring dates and events with which history is peppered. (I could never understand why we needed to know these precise dates of hundreds of years ago. What relevance had they to our lives, then or now?) But nothing she said seemed to penetrate our obstinate and obtuse skulls. Whether she was a poor teacher and just hadn't got the knack, or whether it was our unpenetrative brain boxes, I was never quite sure. It was probably a bit of both.

Excuse my ignorance but I remember learning some king hid in an oak tree, and that another burned the cakes, and that another died horribly clutching an arrow sticking oddly out of his eye. I wondered if it was the same accident prone king who got himself into all these scrapes. It seemed odd that only kings got into trouble and were worth remembering. Where were all the other folk, the ordinary people, I wondered. These knights and kings all wore funny hats, helmets and clothes, or were encased in armour, and stood or rode on horseback, in peculiar poses, with their heads twisted sideways in profile and with sharp metal beaks like birds. I often wondered if these peculiar old pictures were the result of ancient artists who just didn't know how to draw three-dimensional characters, though I don't know why.

And that was about the extent of my learning history over many, many long boring hours spent with that horrible history teacher, and I'm sure my lack of historical knowledge hasn't affected or impeded my progress in life. In fact I have learnt much more since, and become interested in it.

We had woodwork and metalwork lessons which, because I've always liked making things, I really enjoyed. After much measuring and struggling we made a dove-tailed jewellery box and a pair of book-ends that you wouldn't be seen dead with now and which you couldn't even sell at a car-boot sale. The same can be said for a coal shovel I made in metalwork. Machines have made dove-tailing unnecessary now and very few people use coal shovels any more. So much for education and progress. Ah well...I suppose it taught me something.

I have already mentioned Killer Prince who was the feared Physical-training cum Gardening Instructor. Mr Prince was a fit, lithe, handsome, no-nonsense rangy-looking man who viewed us school-lads phlegmatically as all being potential trouble-makers or mischevious villains. He was a no-nonsense teacher and to him, boys equalled trouble. There is a teacher like this in most schools, and they are probably the most astute.

When Killer told you to jump, in P.T., you jumped, and high. He was rumoured to be shagging the delectable Miss Cogle, the double-jointed athletic girl's-school Gym Mistress, though this might just as well have been our fertile teenage imaginations again. We lecherous young lads loved a bit of juicy sexy gossip, especially if it concerned the teachers.

In gardening class I remember Killer Prince once holding a youth upside down by his ankles and shaking him until his small change, pen-knife and chewing gum dropped out of his trousers' pocket. We well knew not to mix it with Killer. He'd earned a certain awesome respect among us bothersome boys, a respect based on fear. Of which respect he was well aware, and fostered.

Another youth, another day, stuck a gardening fork through his foot whilst turning over the compost heap, and had to go to hospital. Small anecdotes to be sure, but as we're looking through school snapshots of old memories, I thought I'd tell you.

My days at this school could fill a book in themselves. For me it was a time of great change and development of my personality and character, not always for the better. I was still struggling to make sense of the world and my own thoughts and feelings in relation to the world, when I left. I was a medium to average scholar, abysmal in history and maths. My personal education was more successful in the cunning and craft I learnt from my peers in the playground, and through trying to survive and keep my sanity, than anything the teachers taught me. School is more of an attempt to prepare us to earn a living in the factories, offices and work-places of this capitalist society we have created for ourselves, than to inform us of the pitfalls and the minefields that the real world is pitted with. Democracy was mentioned at school in social studies but very few of us ever understood the concept of it, at that time. These are the type of subjects they should have concentrated on.

Surely the complex nature of our society, questionable to its roots, that man has created and is full of danger, is more of a puzzle to the young fledglings about to set out in his strange new world, than the mere workings of a machine, or a mathematical formulae, or a computer or the latest high-tec gadget from Japan? They might concentrate more on how we got here in the first place and how we've made, and are still making, such a mess of everything. And who is responsible, and why? And where are we heading? Are we advancing - as we are always being told - or are we destroying ourselves and the world? And if we are, how the hell do we put the brake on and get out of the mess we, ourselves, mankind, have created. And does anybody really care about all this anyway?

CHAPTER 18

Snapshots from the playground

Spikey and his bullying were only a small part of our play-time diversions. Most of the lads played healthy, competitive playground games, and occasionally the odd silly trick caught on, that could sometimes give rise to an accident.

The old favourites, top-spinning, tick, hop-scotch, marbles, fivestones and leap-frog all had their day. Skilled top-spinners developed their spinning to a fine art. It is wrong to decry or mock these simple games of yesteryear. They required practice and skill, co-ordination and dexterity, and most were energetic games that kept you warm outside in any sort of weather and gave both fun and exercise, things sadly lacking in today's non-participative couch-potato pastimes. With top-spinning the art was to keep your top going as long as possible. Experts could lift the spinning top with a curling whip and put it down exactly where required, still spinning furiously. As the playground became more crowded (and the teachers' responsibility for safety more onerous) top-spinning was banned as it was recognised at being dangerous. With the advance of modern safety awareness, litigation and whatever, this has happened in many areas that once gave great fun,freedom, amusement and entertainment.

Marbles were still played occasionally but seemed to be going out of fashion. The balls of coloured glass were once prized and avidly coveted (like Indians who collected cheap coloured beads) and this was the motivation for the game. But what lad today would want a pocketful of balls of coloured glass? Marbles were now being produced commercially on a large scale and therefore they all looked the same. The fun of the game had been in winning the many different variegated colours and sizes, or going after someone's special marble, or a particularly unusual set. Standard marbles killed all that. Who wanted a bag full of marbles that all looked the same? It's strange that the only people interested in marbles now are grown-up collectors who will pay high prices for rare specimens. And the marbles most sought after are those made before standardisation killed the variety. The same can be said for cigarette cards. It's a funny old world.

Cigarette card games had largely taken over from marbles when I was at school as they had a similar goal, i.e. that of winning as many of your opponent's desirable and rarish cards as possible. Certain sets of cards were very sought after and became collectable. I find it strange that us kids hurled cards across the playground dust until they fell to pieces, when they were ripped up and put in the dustbin. The same cards would fetch a fortune at today's antique fairs. I wish I still had the fistfuls of cards I used to win in the old playground games. You felt strangely rich when you had won a huge pile. And you WOULD be rich today, with the same pile.

The cigarette card games were quite skilful. There were two main games. The simpler game consisted of two players with their own cards trying to knock over a card that had been placed against the wall by flicking another card at it. This might sound easy but it was, in fact, quite difficult. Cards had to be skimmed quite a distance and, like paper aeroplanes, they would veer in all directions. Whichever player dislodged the leaning card, claimed all the cards on the ground at the time.

The second card game was much more exciting and could take on the dimensions of a high-stake roulette game as a much greater number of cards could be at stake. In fact certain games went on throughout the hour long dinner break and ended up attracting a large goggle-eyed awed playground audience. The rules of the game were simple and any number of players could participate. Like roulette too, the lad with the largest quantity of 'chips' (cards) stood the best chance of winning, as he could play longer. The cards were flicked against the school wall and fell back flat on the ground. Every time one card overlapped another (it had to go over the margin onto the picture) all the cards on the ground went to the last 'flicker' whose card had overlapped another. A large crowd would start to gather if many cards fell and none had overlapped, as this was - in view of the large number of cards at risk - a serious matter to whoever it was who would lose that particular game. If you'd flicked all your cards anyway, that was it. You retired from the game leaving your cards to be picked up by whoever won that particular game. Sometimes complete sets of cards that had taken months to save were lost in a flick like this. If a lad lost a massive number of cards, a breathless cry of "Crikey!" went up by the fascinated crowd as they turned and walked away, muttering and whispering to each other (commiserating with the loser, usually). If I became enmeshed in a game that wouldn't come to an end, and hundreds of cards lay like confetti across the concrete playground, I would silently pray that the whistle would go and playtime would end. For then, as no one had won,the game was considered null and void and we retrieved our own cards and kept them for another day. Phew, saved by the whistle again! When most cigarette companies stopped putting cards in packets, folks started hanging on to the valuable sets and this particular playground game died out as adult collectors started paying for and commandeering all the cards.

There must be a moral here somewhere, and a sign of the times we live in, that we kids owned hundreds of cigarette-card sets that got grubbier and grubbier as we won and lost them in games like these. Had we saved and kept the cards clean they would be worth many hundreds of pounds now.

The ancient game of five stones had a resurgence and became very popular for a while. The rules were complicated and had so many variations the game got harder and harder as it progressed. There must be a book on the rules of this game somewhere as no one could possibly remember all the rules. It could go on almost for ever and required real skill and dexterity. Some kids had their own stones which they carried around in their pockets. They had been specially collected for their flatness and were polished smooth with years of use. Like marbles, you could at one time purchase stones from the shops, but these were boring and all the same shape. Most playground games have two things in common: they must require very little equipment (if any at all) and the gear must be small enough to fit quickly into a school-boy's pocket - so when the whistle blows, you are able to pack up the game immediately and go back to your class in seconds.

This is partly why the game of 'Tick' is so eternally popular. "Let's play tick" someone yells, and off you go. It is energetic and keeps you warm on frosty mornings. It can be started or terminated at will and it can last two minutes or ten. Almost everyone gets a chance to be 'it' at least once and there is a great element of competition in it. And of course, it's fun.

Hopscotch is still played and is one of those games that can be carried on from break to break and day to day and requires only a piece of chalk, two legs, a stone and bags of energy. You don't see a lot of skipping now, especially multiple skipping with a long rope. Skipping requires masses of energy and appeals to the very young who have amazing reserves of this particular asset and are agile and lightweight. Perhaps it is too energetic for most of today's podgying youngsters.

The conker season also had its devotees and champions. Notorious conkers - with a record (always unproven) of many conquests of smashing other famous conkers, were called thirtyniners or fiftytwoers or whatever, depending on what their tally was rumoured to be, and were regarded with great respect...by the gullible. Stories of secret methods of hardening conkers such as baking them in ovens, circulated the school, as did rumours of the great age of some of the iron-hard shrivelled up old champions. I could never see the fascination with conkers myself. To me, the credibility of a famous conker seemed to rest entirely on the integrity and the veracity of its owner, and all schoolboys are notorious lead-swingers anyway. Like most popular but risk-laden games, conkers were eventually banned at our school after someone was almost blinded by a flying conker chip.

We are now into the age of the computer. Many expensive simulations (and then some) and complicated variations of boy's games are now available on computers, and a certain type of intelligence and great keyboard skill is required to proceed through these games.

But I can't help wondering...surely something is missing? The camaraderie of the playground for instance and the fresh air and exercise. The computer buff sits hunched-up alone for hours in a stuffy room, with his eyes glued to a flickering screen. Is this progress? Or natural? Or good for the young? Or as much fun? It certainly isn't healthier, as far as physical fitness is concerned.

At our school the game of leap-frog was superseded by a much more energetic, advanced and superior game we called dolly-pegs, which, although it was very rough and tumble and sometimes caused back and other injuries, was never actually banned (well, not in my time anyway). This was my favourite game, requiring bounding energy, great jumping ability, a bit of body weight and a bony bottom. And the more players in a team the better. It was a typical real boy's game, very boisterous, very athletic, and not a little dangerous.

It went like this: one unfortunate boy was picked by coin-toss (there were never any volunteers for this particular unpopular and painful position) to stand akimbo against the wall with his legs spraddled open.

Here, between this poor unfortunate lad's legs, bending down and clasping his knees - like in leapfrog, the first stooping player of his team thrust his head and in turn opened his legs to receive another stooping player's head, and so on and so forth, until there was a long 'crocodile' or 'snake' of stooping boys, each clasping the legs of the boy in front.

The secret was to get the best jumpers and the boniest bottoms and the largest and heaviest lads on your side. If you think about it, huge giants of lads haven't usually got bony bottoms or much jump in them, and good jumpers with bony bottoms haven't usually got much weight. So you had to be a bit crafty and selective and use your loaf who you picked for your team. The criteria was big, AND bony bottoms, or both if this rare species existed.

Les Harvy was our gentle playground giant. Completely brainless and placid, he was only popular when we wanted his weight. We always tried to get him on our team. He was too big and heavy to jump far, so he was kept back till last. As long as he could clamber onto the back of the last unfortunate crouching man in the line, the snake would inevitably collapse.

This was the goal: to pile the multiple spine of the long line of interlocked backs with the complete combined weight of the jumping team, and to make the crouching team collapse on the ground.

Those who could jump best went first because they had to jump as far along the line as possible, to leave room for the rest of the team to get on. It was considered cheating to jump without using your hands but everyone who could manage this particularly difficult and athletic manoeuvre cheated and did so, because it was here the bony bottoms scored. If you could land hard with your bony bum digging into an equally bony back, the crushing pain from the recipient's spine was excruciating and the poor fellow often collapsed immediately, yelling in agony, much to the glee of the cheering onlookers. The collapsed man had been a crucial link in the chain, and when he went down, the whole side went down with him. He was disgraced and booed and the jumping team had won that round and could jump a second time.

Failing that happening we kept jumping in quick succession, one after the other. First off went the best jumpers who could jump over say, seven men, then the bony bottoms, and finally, last but certainly not least, the largest and heaviest boy. Therefore you can imagine the pain of the spraddled 'anchor' man who stood with his back to the wall taking the punishment between his legs from both teams as they heaved, pushed, jostled and jumped. He was taking the combined weight between his legs of anything up to twenty lads! It's a wonder he wasn't ruptured. But we found his screams of agony as lad after lad jumped and landed, and the twisted expressions of anquish on his face, part of the fun and hilarious, and laughed our socks off as he grimaced with pain every time someone jumped.

Sitting astride the crocodile we clasped the backs of our boys in front and, chanting the count to ten like so many demented Aborigines in a long canoe, we would sway vigorously from side to side trying to bring down the groaning wavering line of loaded stooping boys.

It was great fun (depending on what side you were on!). And when the crocodile eventually collapsed in a seething mass of flailing arms and legs, everybody went down to loud cheers from the admiring crowd of weaklings who had refused to join in this particularly rough and back-snapping game. There was also a great sigh of relief and a "Jesus! Thank God for that!" from the suffering anchor man as he staggered away bowed low with pain, clasping his crotch and swearing that he'd never be the anchor man ever again.

The invention of games, like the invention of mischief, often springs from boredom. It was for this reason there were nearly two very nasty accidents in our science room.

The room had a large bay-windowed construction that jutted out over the playground and was designed specifically to catch the sun's heat for the propagation and nurturing of plants and specimens.

When the teachers weren't about it became a game and a challenge to us lads to see how many of us could squeeze into this conservatory window, unfortunately we didn't realise how flimsy it was.

We were clambering and packing ourselves inside it one day and trying to beat the record, when there was an ominous creaking sound followed by an almighty crack, and the whole edifice broke off from the wall and fell into the playground below. Wood and glass and writhing screaming bodies lay in a struggling mess on the concrete below. Luckily, apart from some nasty cuts and grazes, no one was seriously hurt. But Tricky Smith, the head teacher, was none too pleased and we received a stern lecture in the school hall assembly the following morning. He liked to publicly rebuke offenders in front of the whole school, probably believing it would warn others to behave.

Each desk in the science room was fitted with a gas-tap (coal gas). It was the teacher's responsibility to keep the gas turned off at the mains when it wasn't being used for bunsen-burner experiments.

At one time, during heavy rain we were allowed to stay in the classrooms during lunch breaks. One day someone (there's always one) fiddled with the main gas tap and, as half of the antiquated desk taps were either leaking or had been left turned on, about five pupils passed out with gas poisoning. The alarm was quickly given and teachers came running from all directions. An ambulance carted the victims off to hospital and we were all called once again into the hall by a shaken Tricky, and given another lecture. Thereafter no one was allowed in the classrooms during breaks, whether it was raining or not. Now, during cold and wet periods we crept about or huddled beneath the draughty glass verandas in the corridors that bordered the internal walls of the rectangle at the centre of the huddle of school classrooms. Shortly after this the gas-taps were welded shut as a temporary safety measure, and a bit later they were removed for good. A classic case of a good idea having to be abandoned because of a handful of stupid idiots. School history is peppered with examples of similar stories of good ideas going wrong, or being spoilt and abandoned because of hooliganism.

Silly phases, silly phrases, and stupid tricks and pranks - like fashions - came and went, much as they do now and always will do. One jape was to run towards an unsuspecting chum and kick his legs from under him and shout "Wow! Just saved you" as you simultaneously grabbed him, to save him crashing to the ground. This particular day I was unaware that my pal was sucking his fizzy 'Kalie' powder through a straw, when I played this trick on him, and kicked his legs from under him.

"You silly bastard" he exploded as the straw went up his nose, and the fine acidic powder shot into his eyes, mouth and nostrils and started fizzing and foaming in all these facial orifices. As soon as he could breath again, he gave me a terrific thumping. It was a classic lesson of how not to win friends and influence people.

You would have thought I'd have learnt my lesson but I was passing through a stupid practical-joke big-headed and clumsy phase and stage. Another time I whacked a mate on the back as I was pushing my way through the narrow aisles between the desks on my way to the toilet. He was concentrating on a drawing with his head bent down and, as I thumped him, the pencil went right up his nose which started pouring with blood. The teacher caught me and I was sent to the headmaster's study to have the stick across my hand. The teachers weren't handicapped by politically correct dictums then, and were allowed to use a modicum of violence on us. And unruly kids expected it. Having the stick was a quick, clean and easily understood punishment. It left no grudge and was soon forgotten. It never bothered or harmed me or any of my mates, that I can remember. Tricky's thin bamboo cane came down swift and hard on the hand and he carried out the punishment in such a polite way you almost felt sorry for him having to carry out a punishment he didn't really want to. I suppose that is why most of us said "Thank you Sir" as we walked out of his office clasping our stinging hand. We would inspect it craftily in the passage outside to see how red it had gone.

I am not proud of these silly tricks. Like pulling the proverbial chair from under someone, or shouting boo, I soon realised they could lead to serious accidents. But the kid who hasn't pulled a few daft thoughtless tricks on his classmates hasn't been born yet.

Above and beyond these childish games and playground pains and pleasures, loomed the growing realisation and fascination with girls and sex. I had fixed my eyes on a beautiful and delectable blonde bombshell named Jean Bland, who was worshipped from afar, by every red-blooded lad in the school. Trust me to set my sights on the unattainable. That was a portend of the story of my life. My later efforts to introduce myself to this apple of everyone's eye was to end in deep embarrassment and ignominious failure, which gave my confidence in future amorous pursuits a severe dent from the word go. A bad start on the rocky road to getting to know (and to understand) the supposed mysteries of the opposite sex. I'll tell you about this little faux pas later on.

It was rumoured that an elderly biscuit-factory worker sold bakery chocolate (unlawfully) through the factory railings bordering the cinder-path that ran alongside our school and lead to the girls' school. This was just the excuse I needed to go and gawp at Jean through the school railings during the dinner hour.

The chocolate story was true. You hung around the rumoured spot at a given time and this shifty old codger suddenly appeared clutching a handful of brown paper bags stuffed full of sub-standard, greasy chunks of trade-quality chocolate. It was threepence a bag and we loved it. Where or how he came by it can only be guessed at.

I went to work at the biscuit factory in later years and the old fellow was still trading his illicit chocolate to the school kids. Most of his fellow workers were aware of his little scam, but obviously his bosses weren't. He was an inveterate gambler on the horses and, apparently, this nice little extra earner funded his gambling. It was an early lesson to me what went on in the nation's factories, and opened my eyes to the bribery and corruption that was rife at the time, and probably still is. Human nature doesn't change that much.

It was time to be moving on again. I was growing up and girls were beginning to take up most of my thoughts and dreams: and my mischiefs and escapades were becoming more serious and risky. This was that age when we begin to develop in all directions at once. It is a dodgy age as we stand at the junction of a many-laned crossroads, zigzagged by numerous blurred signposts, and not sure which one to follow. Life is like that, more so when we are young, and there are none so blind as those that cannot see. And that was me, at this particular, awkward, hiatus of my life.

So I took to buying these bags of greasy chocolate (with money pinched from Grandad's till) just as an excuse to walk down the cinder path to the girls'school to stand with the row of lads gawping at the girls giggling and playing in their playground. Each oggling and goggling pair of lascivious male eyes sought out the object of his own private fantasies and desires. With me (and with many others I'm afraid) it was the gorgeous Jean Bland.

Having no gymnasium of their own the girls had to come down the cinder path to our school and use ours. This suited us boys fine. In their P.T. gear - white blouses, gym slips and pumps - these long-legged and super fit girls had to jog along the aforementioned cinder-path that ran alongside and lead to our school. They couldn't have displayed themselves better to the gawping boys if it had been planned. Different classes came at different times but our main attention was reserved for the senior girls, for obvious reasons (they were more 'developed'). The word would spread like wild-fire, "C'mon quick. The girls are coming for their P.T. It's 4A". "Jean Bland's with that lot. Let's go and have a gander!" The excited crowd of boys would turn from their games like a swarm of distracted hornets and head for the iron railings bordering the cinder-path. Here they would stand gripping the rails like excited jabbering monkeys in a cage, whisperng lewd and corny remarks to each other and drooling lecherously as their imaginations went into over-drive. We weren't allowed to cat-call, whistle or call out to the girls - so we had to keep our dirty remarks among ourselves.

The young Miss Cogle herself attracted much admiration. She was the girl's Gym Mistress so you can imagine that in our minds and - in fact - she was a very desirable creature. Killer Prince, our own much feared Gym Master fancied Miss Cogle himself, and it was rumoured (well, it would be wouldn't it?) that he was 'knocking her off'.

The windows of our wooden Gymnasium were high, but conveniently bordered our playground (what were the planners thinking of?). While the girls were doing their gymnastics a line of boys hung by their fingertips on the cills of the windows like a row of peeping-tom chads gawping at the loose-limbed scantily clad school-girls, and particularly at Miss Cogle and Jean Bland. Jean Bland was reputed to be double-jointed and able to do extraordinary things with her body, and we fought to get a glimpse of this beautiful exercising contortionist creature in action. She won most of the competitions on sport's day and became head girl of the school. This excited the imaginations of the lads still more and many lurid fantasies and rumours circulated the school about her. I doubt whether she had the faintest idea of the fuss and emotional sexual turmoil she was causing among us pubescent immature sex-mad boys. And then again, maybe she did. Glamorous girls are almost always aware of their universal sexual power over men, part of which is their ability not to show this awareness. We are a knowing lot, us humans.

CHAPTER 19

Precariously poised

This chapter, like my life at this time, will be a hotch-potch of unrelated experiences, pleasant and unpleasant, legal and illegal, and moral and amoral. Myself and my life felt all jumbled up, like a bagful of allsorts, which is just what it was.

Vanishing were the innocent pastimes of the yesteryear of my youth of idly roaming the fields and woods, when I had time to pause on the bridge of life and to stand and stare and to lazily survey the world around me. Now, through the dark mirror of my destiny, I glimpsed the shadowy and more serious visage of the future, beckoning to me that I was next in line to grow up, and to face the real world of adulthood. All our lives we have this capacity: quite aware, up to a point, what is going to happen to us, but, understandably, most of us prefer to push it to the back of our minds and look the other way, and bury our head like an ostrich, hoping and praying that what we most fear, is just not going to happen.

When we are young, like little fledgling birds in the relative safety of their nest, we have an inborn instinctive feeling that we are not quite ready to stray too far beyond the boundaries of this secure protective cosy nest. We can sense unknown dangers beyond our ken and immediate perimeters and have this intuitive feeling that we haven't yet the physical, spiritual, or emotional strength to cope with these dangers. It is this feeling that (hopefully) holds us in sway from taking the next stepping stone on our passage through life's dangerous eddying currents and whirlpools. This is as it should be. It is nature's safety net.

But nature also pushes us forward, to take our chances in the risky world, otherwise we should never learn to fend for ourselves. The trick is in the timing. Recognise the right time, and you will probably be all right. Get it wrong, and you could be in mortal danger.

But I digress.

The eccentric Tricky Smith, our headmaster, was viewed with giggles and amusement by most of his charges. This was simply because he cut a comical figure as he ambled about the school. He was getting on and was a balding, absent-minded, stooped old fellow, and given to patches of odd behaviour. Just the way most of us become as we grow older. In truth, he appeared to me as a rather timid, gentle, shy, quaint, and likeable old man (kids often view headmasters as intimidating creatures). I only crossed swords with him twice, on a personal level: once when I brought some gun cartridges into school, and once when I had the cane (he even gave you the cane in an apologetic manner - as I have mentioned).

We rarely saw him during the day but he appeared each morning in the school assembly hall to conduct prayers and to give us lectures, and any other business relating to school matters. Here, among the restless lads, much shuffling, sniffing and coughing took place. Tricky presaged the coming highlights and problems of the school, and drew attention to top achievers and occasional culprits of silly, reprehensible and sometimes downright dangerous behaviour. And, at the appropriate time, when we were about to leave school, lectured us solemnly on our future prospects in that alien scary adult world beyond the school gates.

You had to commit a pretty awful crime to be dragged onto the rostrum in the school hall at morning assembly. Such a crime sometimes involved the police, and in those days the sight of a uniformed police sergeant striding across the playground struck fear into the hearts of many secret guilty consciences.

The fine dividing line between what was and was not a crime was more indefinite, more blurred and misunderstood then than it is now. Coppers were called in simply to strike fear into the hearts of miscreants, though in law perhaps no crime as such had been committed. Were it that way now. Calling in police to put on the frighteners wouldn't work with most of today's hard-faced, street-wise youngsters - or anyone else for that matter.

I myself had the dubious honour of being one of the few to stand on stage one morning convention, between the sweet-smelling, fragile and grey-pin-striped suited Tricky Smith, and a larger-than-life walrus-moustached police sergeant. And I never forgot the experience. Being now of the older generation I still have a sneaking respect and fear of the cops.

Since quite an early age I had been allowed to go shooting on my own with Grandad's twelve-bore shot-gun, limited not by the danger aspect, but by the cost and availability of cartridges for the gun. This rather dangerous leniency (for some strange historical macho reason) was a long-standing tradition in the countryside at that time, and almost taken for granted - and might be still for all I know, but I doubt it. Adults are generally more aware of the aptitude of youngsters for getting themselves into dangerous life\death situations nowadays. Anyway, the shot-gun privilege was one of the very few grown-up perks I was allowed.

Finding a spare cartridge left inadvertently in my jacket pocket one day, I was casually showing it to my curious town-dwelling class-mate as we sat at our desks during a particulary boring lesson.

"Cor" he exclaimed, in typical schoolboy idiom. "How's it work? What makes it go off?"

"Gunpowder!" I emphasised dramatically. "The hammer hits this brass bit in the middle, the powder packed inside explodes, and millions of lead pellets fly out and pepper the rabbit". To impress our mates, we were given to excessive exaggeration.

Parents reading this might feel their hair bristle in fright and teachers might recoil in horror, but this is true.

"Can I see inside it?" my fascinated towny pal inquired. "Can you get it open?"

Sure I could. I was a curious bugger myself and had opened them many a time. I glanced at the teacher who was preoccupied chalking a long explanation on the blackboard and took out my pen-knife. It surprises me even to this day the amount and extent of mischief a kid can get up to while the teacher's back is temporarily turned. Kids, like young cats, are extraordinarily wily, swift and agile, when it suits them. And, being natural actors and liers, can resume immediately the attentive mode when the teacher turns to face them again. It's amazing really. It isn't only the quickness of the hand that can deceive the eye.

I swiftly prised off the cardboard cap that held the contents of the cartridge inside...then, "Damn!"

I dropped the cartridge and the hundreds of tiny lead-shot pellets spilled out and rolled across the class-room floor, like tiny marbles spreading in all directions. There was nothing I could do. There was no way of stopping them. Dumb struck, as if in slow motion I watched those bloody pellets travel slowly but surely between the desks and shuffling feet towards the front of the class. They reached the bemused teacher just as he turned round to face us again.

"What the hell...?"

"And what idiot is responsible for this!?" he yelled, duly appalled. "Now I've seen everything. Whose are these? Who's playing about?"

That's one thing about classroom mischief, the culprit can rarely hide. He is definitely out there somewhere...cringing, hoping...

I decided to raise a limp hand and admit my guilt. It was pretty pointless denying it. I had picked up the cartridge and was holding it in my hand and the seemingly endless pellets were still pattering from it and were obviously radiating out from where I sat. All heads turned and looked at me. Classroom peers are a curious lot if someone is in trouble (what are they thinking?) In my panic I'd closed my penknife on my finger, and was surreptitiously trying to see if I'd cut myself and was bleeding. I was caught bang to rights, as they say.

The upshot was, I was escorted smartly to Tricky's office where I had to try and explain my possession of these dangerous 'bullets' as he called them. I realised, with a sinking heart, it was a particularly serious business when he made a telephone call to the local police, instead of caning me. We weren't on the phone at home, but he promised to get a letter to my "mother" demanding to know how I came to be carrying these dangerous 'bullets' to school, and where I'd got them from. He really meant business.

The following morning, in assembly, I was called out to stand in between the aforementioned authorities and held up as a prime example of idiocy, naughtiness, and reck-lessness. "This boy's foolish behaviour was dangerous in the extreme" Tricky intoned. "And he is lucky he hasn't blown his hands off, or worse". The listening lads tittered, they were thinking I might have blown something else off! The police sergeant endorsed the headmaster's words and gave his own sermon, the meanwhile holding his heavy hand on my shoulder and making me feel about two inches tall. Naturally, being now a parent myself, I am inclined to agree with them and all they said, but at the time I couldn't understand what all the fuss was about. I had spare cartridges in all my pockets at home, and they lay about the house like discarded fag-ends. I'd even tried to bang the end of one with a hammer once to see if it would detonate that way, and what damage it would do!

But I didn't laugh when I got home. 'Em (and Grandad) were understandably disgusted that I should have let them down, and I was banned from using the twelve-bore ever again. And this was punishment enough. The odd thing was, they weren't horrified by the danger I was in, but annoyed that

I should have been so stupid as to take a cartridge to school in the first place.

Feeling grieved over this shot-gun ban, about eighteen months later, with earned and stolen pocket money, I bought my own second-hand gun. This was more dangerous than ever, as (unbeknowns to me, at that age) second-hand guns are notoriously suspect, more often than not being sold because they aren't functioning properly or are faulty. And who needs a faulty gun of all things?

It was a .303. Much smaller than a twelve bore and it felt like a kid's toy to me. I soon discovered it was becoming obsolete and I had a job finding cartridges for it, and even when I did find some the price was forever increasing. So I couldn't use it much anyway. It's killing power was so weak I had to stick it almost into the rabbit's ear-hole to kill it. After years of using a twelve-bore the .303 was a disappointment and I soon sold it on to some other equally unsuspecting wally like myself. It is trade like this that makes the world go round, or so they tell me. And therefore I have no conscience at all about this shameful memory. Why should I have? I was taught by the world!

I trod the boards of the school stage on one other occasion, more traumatic possibly than the cartridge incident.

Each christmastime we put on a show in the school hall for the benefit of parents and to raise funds for the school. I have never been one for being in the limelight. Until now, by keeping a low profile (hanging about at the back, so to speak) I had managed to avoid being conscripted (volunteered) for the school play.

But this time my skulking ways were noticed by a more observant teacher who was looking for a skulker and narrator at the same time, to link the acts together. My part would be to appear at intervals throughout the play, dressed like a prosperous wild-west gentleman, to explain the continuity of the story-line of the play. The author of this play must have had doubts as to the clarity of its plot, to have to explain it as it went along - or perhaps he was trying to be innovative and make it look like a comic-cartoon. I don't know. It's been tried before. I think one of our teachers had written it. The play was a Cowboy-and-Indians affair (very much in vogue with lads at the time). Really corny in fact as many school plays are. At the very end, when the warring parties were about to scalp or shoot each other, they were to suddenly freeze solid in mid-action, tomahawks raised and guns ablaze, in a sort of classic tableau vivant of the Wild West. This clever ploy would signal the grand-finale of the play...with the hinted promise of a later conclusion. Sometime never I hoped. Very subtle.

At this point the only thing that moved was overdressed and over-dramatic little me. I pirouetted onto the stage superfluously waving a wooden six-gun and addressed the stunned and hushed audience as follows:

"Ladees and Gentlemen: All the best stories finish in the most exciting situations. Our story is no exception to the rule, and this enthralling narrative will be continued in our next..."

And that was it. You don't forget profound lines like those.

Who wrote this stuff? It was only a tiny speech - but I was a tiny boy with a very weak and nervous voice, and that had a frog in it. It was quite enough for me. It took great courage and the audience politely clapped like hell. During the following year the nightmare that the teacher-cum-writer might write the continuation of "our next" of this childish play haunted my worst dreams. Luckily I was nearing leaving age and was already working on ways to escape many bits of unpleasant and unfinished business, like math's exams and unresolved playground fights and rivalries. It was ever thus. If you're going to move on - like moving house - leave your shameful bits-and-pieces of rubbish behind I say, and good riddance too. And if you've made a mess of things, now's a good a time as any to turn over a new leaf and to try and get it right the next time round. I was glad to leave school and contrary to what my elders were always telling me, my schooldays were not the happiest days of my life.

During my last year at school, along with my cronies in crime, about now we entered that silly and somewhat anarchic teenage stage when all we seemed to do was to fool around, waste time, get into further mischief, and mock the rest of orthodox society for just getting on with their lives. It did not pass our notice that the teachers also seemed to be losing control (or was it interest?) over us. Something (not verbalised) happens between teenagers and their elders at this stage in a teenager's life. I have often mused on this at different periods throughout my life, and can only guess at what it is. At a certain age many teenagers become virtually unmanageable and, being in the prime of life, they have boundless energy (a bit like young monkeys being let out of their cage). Also they are viewing the society they are now expected to join - rightly or wrongly - with a rather critical and cynical eye. The 'Grown Ups' see and feel this and stand back a bit to give the new arrivals a bit of space (or are they scared!). They are a new generation and might, just might decide something is very wrong with the status quo as they find it, and decide it is time for a change. This is were the young rebels come from. And what is worse, it could be proved that they are right and the adults are wrong. So the old generation is wary of the new. The young newcomers have the energy and the capacity for taking a fresh look at and of altering things, and who is going to be the one to challenge them? Being short of nothing they haven't got, the youngsters also have little to lose if they speak their minds or decide to act in a belligerent fashion. Life has always been like this. The young challenging the old. The new order taking over from the status quo. It is what I said previously: nothing stands still. Nothing is so safe and so cosy as we'd like to believe.

I am not saying this situation is right or that the youngsters could do any better than the oldies, I am merely pointing out what I believe to be the reason for this wary respect shown to youngsters at this particular age. It is a bit like the ageing leader of the lion pride who views the lithesome young newcomer prowling around with a bit of respect. He know there is a challenge to his power here, and treads warily least the young challenger decides to make a few changes around the place, and the old lion's bluff (whose roar is probably now worse than his bite) is called.

It is at this age that youngsters usually begin to separate into their various multifarious strata of society depending on how and where they were raised, how intelligent and mature they are, and how their education has progressed. Trying to find their natural level: fit into their pecking order: find their status in life. Unfortunately, lacking in most of these handy life-skills I belonged to that vast majority, that lost legion of no-hopers, who hadn't a clue where they were going and were ill-equipped anyway to be going anywhere profitable at all. Things have changed that much in the last fifty years, I suspect present day teenage rebels and lost-causes commit much more serious 'crimes', not only against society and the status quo, but against each other and themselves as well.

During this last year at school, girls, thieving and derring-do (showing off) occupied most of our thoughts and time. At just the time when we should have been taking stock of, and brushing up on, our education, we were acting like stupid kamikazee pilots. We oggled and fantasised about girls, but rarely had the courage to approach them and to get to know them properly or to do what we so ardently dreamed of doing. There was the odd reputed handsome lady-killer (as there always is) who was rumoured to have no trouble at all in scoring with the ladies, left, right and centre. The thieving, I think, was a phase, though a long drawn-out one, and was probably tied up with the derring-do thing as it seemed almost compulsory to out-shock your rivals and to impress your peers. Psychologists would use words like macho, teenage rebellion, streetwise, and pecking order. My own contribution to this immature behaviour was classically and typically stupid and hardly bears thinking about now, let alone writing about it!

Many of our escapades took place during the dinner hour when we were now allowed complete freedom to go into town or anywhere else that took our fancy, like dogging girls about the streets. It was surprising the amount of mischief we could cram into one hour of freedom and eat our dinner at the same time.

My friend at this time was a boy named Cyril Brownley. He was a thief and kleptomaniac extrordinaire. I felt he was a particularly good friend as he courageously accompanied me into town on my embarrassing expeditions to fetch Mrs Bateson's notorious currant bread. Most so-called mates wouldn't be seen dead with me while I was lugging the hated brown leather shopping bag around town, and it also cramped my style with the girls.

My attention was first drawn to Cyril's shop-lifting habits whilst we were walking around Woollies, the dime-a-dozen store, as we American apers called it then.

One day, on coming out of the store, I was ferreting in my clumsy shopping bag for the sixpences hidden there by the careful Mrs B. My next port of call was to purchase her currant bread.

"What the hell is this?" I exclaimed, surprised at finding a large packet of mushroom spawn in my bag.

"It's mushroom spawn" commented the smirking Cyril superfluously, in a pseudo-innocent matter-of-fact tone. Just as if I should have known what it was, and how it had appeared miraculously in my bag.

"I can see that" I said crossly and not a little peeved, as it was slowly dawning in my dim brain-box that maybe he'd pinched it, and it was a cheek putting it in my bag without my permission. Or maybe I was impressed and a little jealous at his expertise in getting the spawn into my bag without me seeing him. "But where's it come from" I continued, knowing, by now, full well where it had come from.

"I put it there" Cyril said calmly. "As you come from the country Mick, I thought you'd like to try growing mushrooms yourself". Like most thieves, he was always very considerate and generous with other people's property.

"I didn't see you pay for it: you didn't buy it" I said, as if stating a known fact. It had never occurred to me until then that town boys pinched their stuff from large town stores, just the same as we village kids robbed our small village shops. It was a matter of scale, and no more serious (or just as serious) than what us village rascals got up to. As a village lad I wouldn't have dared shoplift from a large town store. The whole scene was just too intimidating. We knew old Harry Mould the baker, and considered him a friend and fair game! The large town stores appeared immense impersonal places and were run by serious looking managers in posh suits. They were an unknown entity: anything could happen and we wouldn't take the risk. Things could become nasty.

But it was derring-do you see. Cyril was out to impress me that the mere size and importance of the place meant nothing. It was just more of a challenge. If you could pinch from a village shop, why not from a big store? And if from a big store, why not a warehouse, or even a bank? This is how crooks graduate.

"Buy it? ...Buy it?" Cyril scoffed in answer to my accusation that he hadn't paid for it. "I never buy ANYTHING! Only fools pay for things!" He seemed really surprised that I should even think he'd paid for it.

"You pinched it!" I exclaimed, with something like hypocritical mock-horror. My apparent self-righteousness was more than a little sanctimonious. I mean, consider: I'd long pinched things myself, and if I could get something for nothing I would. Like ninety-nine per cent of my mates would, at that time.

"Well, let's say it fell into your bag as we walked by" chuckled Cyril, as we continued on our way to fetch Mrs Bateson's currant bread and a couple of buckshee cream cakes I've no doubt, if Cyril had his way.

You see Cyril was a compulsive thief. He took anything, whether he wanted it or not. Opportunity was the only criteria. And I was too much tainted by the schoolboy ethos of mild corruption myself to be overawed by his casual shoplifting habits. It was his consumate skill, combined with his nonchalant attitude that amazed me. He seemed to have no fear of ever being caught (and he never was, incidentally). Actually, I remember, I grew the spawn and it was a surprising success. Thereafter, whenever I needed another packet, Cyril would oblige, whether I was with him or not. And he never asked any favours in return.

Why do I remember this particular little piece of knavery so well? I remember it because it struck me at the time how artlessly nice, kind and considerate Cyril was being to me! He must have espied the mushroom spawn, I ruminated, and thought "Ah, mushroom spawn. Mick comes from the country. I bet he'd like some of that". And without further ado he'd got some. Really, how thoughtful and considerate of him. The fact that it was shoplifting and morally wrong didn't seem to enter the equation at all. That just goes to show how amoral many of us youngsters were at that time.

Cyril would also steal to order. It was like a business arrangement. The bargain would be struck in minutes in the school playground. "I'd like one of those army knives. You know, one of those with a thing for getting stones out of horse's hooves with" a lad would say, meaning he wish he could afford one. Cyril would overhear him...

"I'll get you one" he'd say, in a pleasant and obliging manner. "It'll cost you though".

"How much?"

"Oh...a couple of bob".

"O.K. then." And, without question, the thing was settled. They'd slap each other's hands, like a couple of roquish horse dealers, and the bargain would be struck. Without further comment the thing was as good as done.

Repeat orders would follow. And in due course would be fulfilled. There was never any rush. Wednesday was Uttoxeter's market day and a certain stallholder always had plenty of these ex-army knives out on display on his stall. He must have been doing a roaring trade as Cyril pinched no end of these knives, and the stall holder never seemed to miss them. Bang goes another old wive's tale: in Cyril's case, crime certainly did pay!

Another racket (which I tried myself) concerned our canteen dinner tokens. These were little tin discs that (fortunately or unfortunately - depending on what side of the counter you were on) closely resembled the old silver shilling of the time. Quite a handy sum of money to us in those days. The tokens - which cost sixpence (half a shilling) had been introduced in a vain attempt to prevent us youngsters from spending our dinner money on 'rubbish' in the town instead of in the school canteen on a proper lunch. But, like most rules designed to thwart malpractice, we soon found a way round it and turned the little discs to our advantage. The powers-that-be had done us a favour - we could double our money!

The trick was to purchase exactly a shilling's worth of goodies, sweets or cakes or whatever. When the bags were packed we took them from the assistant's hand, quickly handed over our 'shilling' and ran from the shop before she discovered it was only a tin canteen token. The trouble was, this little scam had a limited 'shelf-life', so to speak.

After we had played it on almost every shopkeeper in town they became aware and the word got round. The school was informed. It meant another lecture from Tricky Smith and the tokens were clipped (by ourselves in the metal-work lesson) from being round to a hexagonal shape to make them more identifiable.

But it didn't bother us. The ideas of schoolboys are like the many heads of Medusa's snakes, cut one off and another immediately grows in its place. Our ingenuity knew no bounds. It's a shame it was misplaced. And that is a condemnation of the schooling system of that time, that they didn't recognise this, and use our wit and cleverness to everyone's advantage, meaning society's in general.

It was also round about this time that I made a brave but tremulous and pathetic attempt to woo the first love of my life, the delectable teenage temptress of the girl's school, the gorgeous Jean Bland. This pitiful, fumbling amateurish attempt ended in a dismal and embarrassing rebuttal, and shook my confidence with the girls for years to come. She was probably completely unaware that I had fallen in love with her anyway, and even if she had known I was soon made aware my advances weren't welcome in any case.

My whole plan depended on a Mars bar (yes, they had their uses, even then). Along with my fantasising day and (wet) night dreams, I had carried this Mars bar around for days in my trouser's pocket waiting for the opportune moment to present itself to the object of my desires. Like the Black Magic chocolate man, I must have had an overwhelming faith in the power of chocolate to win over a woman's heart. I've learned different since. It takes more than a chocolate mars bar.

Along with my faithful partner in crime, Cyril the Klepto, we had 'dogged' Jean and her mate around town for ages. Whether we were spotted or not, I was never quite sure. This peculiar time-honoured Modus Operandi seemed to be to get yourself noticed without it appearing obvious you were chasing the girls, a seemingly puzzling and contradictory performance that I never quite understood. I'm not much given to subterfuge in any circumstance as it smacks too much of premeditated cunning. Be that as it may, looking back now with the experience of age it was most certain that the young ladies did notice us following them. Girls are never as daft, or as naive or unobservant, as ignorant lads imagine. The slower maturing male of the species is putty in the hands of his more alert and sophisticated female counterpart. Like a spider, a boy chases a girl until she catches him.

In those days of rather strict segregation of the sexes we just hadn't the nerve and experience to simply approach a girl and talk to her, like most lads do now. Females were almost a mysterious alien species. And if you were naturally shy anyway the problem was compounded and the very idea became a formidable problem. I was shy, but I was always prepared to take the plunge and try anything once. I just needed to muster up the courage.

My chance came one day when Jean and her friend stopped to admire the photos of newly married wedding couples in the town photographer's window. (How we remember the details of traumatic moments of our lives).

With thumping heart I realised the moment for action had arrived. This is it I thought, beginning to panic. It's now or never. It's a bit like learning to swim isn't it? If you won't take that first plunge, you might never know what it's all about, or learn, or join the dance. The heartbeats of panic have the same intensity whether you're terrified of a dinosaur or a mouse, and by the way, I never did learn to swim either. Another thing I always felt ashamed of.

Cyril nudged me. I was always being egged into doing something. What was it about me that mates always wanted me to make the first move? Was I a gullible pushover? "They've stopped" he said excitedly. "Now's your chance. Get in there Mick. Ask her for a date!" Like most people who aren't personally involved in the problem at hand, he couldn't see what all the fuss was about. See girl. Want girl. Approach and win or lose girl. As far as he was concerned, it was as simple as that. Some folk never suffer from nerves at all, or so it would appear. Perhaps they have their own private Achilles-heel. Cyril was a bit disgusted that it had taken me this long anyway. I had to act now, to save face.

"Go on then Mick. Speak to her" he urged, with not a little secret vicious amusement, I would imagine. He gave me another shove.

Clutching the much squeezed softening Mar's bar in my pocket - as much as for comfort as anything else - I stopped behind the girls. I poked the apparently unsuspecting Jean Bland in the back with the squidgy bar, like a wilting gun. "Here Jean" I croaked. "I've bought you a Mars bar". It was as clumsy a primary chat-up line as one could imagine and they were the first words I'd ever spoken to her. (And the last no doubt!) And it was probably the first time she'd ever noticed me. Hardened lady-killer cynics might roar with laughter at this pathetic charade but, believe you me, at the time it was no laughing matter. I was choked and trembling with embarrassment and the jitters.

With a girlish toss of their burnished curls, both girls turned their pretty heads to glance curiously at this weak-voiced, white-faced, odd little squirt who was butting into their private conversation. I was completely aswamp with heart-thumping emotion and feelings. I mean, there is just so much fear and emotion the body can cope with all in one go. Jean's calm, limpid blue eyes seemed to envelope and swallow me whole. For one heavenly moment in time nothing else existed except those wonderful whirlpool eyes, framed in a sea of voluptuous blonde curls and an angelic face, drawing me in. I was mesmerised, hypnotised ... and probably terrorised. And deeply, deeply in love. I just couldn't say anything else. I was tongue-tied. Completely speechless and gobsmacked, as they say.

"Go on... GO ON" prompted the super-cool Cyril. "Don't give up now. You're halfway there. Ask her for a date". His urging voice sounded far behind me, distant and unreal, drowned by the thumping in my ears of my out-of-control beating heart. I was locked into a panic-stricken world of my own making.

Well, you can guess the rest: as it is written and well chronicled in the accounts of comic stories of those shy calf-love encounters and botched first approaches in the annals of first love. In my defence, I must remind you that even Superman is shy and has his failures. So I make no excuses for my inexperienced ineptitude at that delicate and sensitive age. Given half a chance, I would learn. And I did.

So, much to the disgust of Cyril, I chickened out and didn't ask her for a date. Jean gave me one of those quizzical, amused and withering looks that only young girls can give from their knowing aware pubescent eyes, and nudged her companion.

The two girls then turned smartly away and continued on their brisk giggling journey into town.

I never ever spoke to Jean again. I daren't. There is nothing like a failed attempt with the opposite sex to throw a lad into a period of self-critical introspection and confusion. I must have looked really stupid, I said to myself. And, I'm not good enough for her anyway: she is too beautiful. Or, I can't go through that ordeal again. Or, she'd probably say no anyway, even if I did ask her. And so on and so forth. I realise now this was all a completely unnecessary post-mortem on my cowardice, and unnecessary pain and heart-ache too. But tell that to a teenager who has just botched his first attempt at asking a girl for a date.

I had fluffed it, as millions of would-be suitors had before me and would continue to do, though I never realised this then but do now. I would never have the nerve or opportunity again. Time would move on and loves would come and go. Slowly I would learn the rules of the game. And finally, at the appropriate time, when nature decided I was ready, I would succeed. But sadly, I was not to know all this at that terrible - even tragic - moment in my life. Like in the song, all I was aware of at the time is that I was all shook up. I might just as well have been facing a firing squad, I was that scared. Such a powerful emotion is young love and its attempts at changing fantasy to reality.

Alone that evening I had a little cry. Was I crying because I had lost my first love? But how can you lose something you never had in the first place? Or was I crying because I felt such an abject coward that I could not even capture a butterfly? In retrospect, I was merely your average mixed up teenager, but knowing this now was no consolation to me then.

I realise now, in view of present wisdom drawn from life-experience and age, I really should have felt proud that I had found the courage to make the approach in the first place. Without courage, without that first plunge into the waters of life, and without the tempering shock of rebuttal, failure and disappointment, we will achieve nothing and will go nowhere at all. It is a necessary, hard and often brutal, learning curve.

According to our natures, we all have our private waterloos to overcome. The hurdles facing us, and our ability to jump over them, are different for every one of us. It is not so much the difficulties we face in life that are daunting, but our capacity to overcome them. The problem is really in ourselves.

For whatever reason, I cried myself to sleep that night. But not before I had unwrapped my now misshapen excuse for a Mars bar and, for comfort and consolation, gobbled it up under the bed sheets. It was Jean Bland's loss I told myself between the sobs. She had missed out on a perfectly good chocolate bar. It was many years before I realised it takes more than a bar of chocolate to win a woman's heart. It takes guile, and many more subtle things besides, not least courage and sincerity.

I was long in the learning. A couple of years later I had another fiasco with a girl. After a fair few moderate successes with the opposite sex, I think I started to get too big for my boots. It happens to the best of us.

I went through a spell when my tastes in girls changed like the seasons. There was this lithe and long-legged Geraldine who was my flavour of the month (boys can be just as fickle as girls). It was summertime. I remember her auburn hair, her slenderness, her youthful fitness, her beautiful fawn-like shot-silk brown eyes, and her outstanding lovely sun-tanned skin and slim figure. Young girls are like fruit. They come to ripeness and a man knows when the fruit is ready for plucking. Although delicious ripe fruit does not stay ripe for long. I had gained confidence with the girls, and could now boast a chat-up line second to none. I was getting on well with Geraldine. I asked her for a date.

"Uhu" she said non-committedly, like they do in American comics but rarely in real life. "Uhu. I mi...ght".

"Well, that's it then" I chirped brashly, cheekily assuming she was saying yes. "I'll meet you from the bus in town on

Saturday. 2-o-clock sharp. O.K? It's a date!" I felt so cocksure of myself I couldn't even be bothered to waste words and time in a preliminary chat-up and small talk (a fatal mistake with women). I had naively adopted a popular saying at that time, "Actions speak louder than words". And I believed implicitly in this saying. It suited my big-headed ego.

Later I was talking to George, a good-looking, dark-eyed, Italian-featured boy, with sleeked-back black hair. A real Dago type in fact, but as English as they come. "I've got a date with Geraldine Smith on Saturday" I said. I couldn't help boasting. "I'm meeting her off the bus".

George looked at me oddly. "That's funny" he said with a wry smile. "I'm meeting her off the bus too". He sounded uncomfortably confident and self-assured. I was perturbed. I'd had a recent succession of successes with girls of late, and thought I was onto a winning streak. But never count your chickens: this lad sounded (and looked) something else: real competition. But, big-headed and pig-headed, I blustered on.

"No. She can't be meeting you. She's meeting me. I bet you she's meeting me."

George knew me well and must have wanted to teach me a lesson as well as getting some easy dough. A fool and his money are soon parted, especially a big-headed and big-mouthed fool like me. "O.K." He gave a disconcerting quiet smile. I should have heeded the warning. "I'll bet you three quid she's meeting me".

I blanched silently. Three quid was a lot of money but I stubbornly took him up on it. No one was to say anything to Geraldine about it: it was a macho man's thing, all to do with male chauvinism, pride, one-upmanship and competition. We would wait for the bus to arrive and stand a little way apart so Geraldine could see the both of us. Our guess was she would walk over to one of us and ignore the other. The loser would take it like a man and walk away with his tail between his legs. The winnings would be paid on the Monday, in the school playground during the first break. We would do it the

Englishman's way, no pistols at dawn, and a stiff upper lip to the loser.

I would not have bothered to tell this pathetic story if I had won the bet. Mind you, on second thoughts, maybe I would! It would make a good boast. But in the event, Geraldine completely ignored me and walked over and took George's arm, in a hurtingly familiar manner as if she had known him all her life. To put the knife in further, George gave me a running commentary on the Monday on where they had been, and what they had got up to together. That hurt. My jealous imagination painted in the rest of the details of his successful evening and I felt like a cuckolded husband. I had learnt a valuable lesson on how not to count my big-headed chickens before they were hatched.

Women can out-fickle men anytime. This experience did me good of course although it hurt like hell at the time, as all good lessons must. It taught me never to pre-judge a situation, and never to make assumptions about people (especially women), and never to get too big for my boots. And that other people can score over you quite easily and without effort, in many respects.

I'd lost three pounds due to my inflated ego. But the funny thing was, I paid up surprisingly willingly. Because I decided it was worth it to learn Geraldine didn't love or want me anyway, and I didn't really want her. There are more expensive and more foolhardy ways of learning life's lessons. I realised I only wanted Geraldine because she was physically sexy and gorgeous. I only wanted her body as they say today, and because I thought no girl could resist my good looks and charm. I wasn't in love with her. Mind you, at that sexually powerful and romantic age, what other reason was there for wanting and pursuing a girl, if it wasn't for her body! Isn't that what the sexual imperative is all about? Truly, it seemed a strange and perplexing world. And still is.

I wouldn't have stood a chance anyway. George and Geraldine must have realised they were soul-mates even then, as they later married and had three kids. I presume they were more mature than me, and knew just what they wanted and where they were going. There are folks like that. Or, to take the cynical view, they made a premature mistake and got in so deep, so fast, and so early in life, they just couldn't get back out. This happens to many married couples also. There are all sorts of ways of looking at things. Years later I bumped into Geraldine in the street. I hardly recognised her. The girl that I once would have killed for was now too tall, obese and flabby, and pasty-faced. Or was that just sour grapes? Oh, Nymph of my youth, where didst thou go!

Gone was the fit, lithe, tanned figure that had hypnotised and drawn me to her. I thought "Phew! Narrow escape". She was probably thinking the same about me!

CHAPTER 20

What now, my life?

Apart from the debacle of my abysmal failure to woo JeanBrand - Uttoxeter town centre, and especially the Wednesday market-day, with its stalls in the town square, holds many memories for me.

The town came to life on market day. The square filled up with stalls selling everything from plants and fruit to ironmongery. There was also a bustling cattle market where cattle were auctioned, and all manner of garden and farm sundries could be purchased.

Perhaps my most bizarre memory of the market square concerns a strange well-built old lady who had taken a special interest in me. Her name was Mrs Pinder.

If you could have seen me at this time I would have been proudly swaggering about the town in my long smart flannel trousers, accompanied by the carefree light-fingered Cyril. If we weren't up to any other hanky-panky we would be eyeing or following a couple of girls and, as usual, getting nowhere fast, as we were wont to say at that time. I was rapidly becoming one of the boys-about-town and integrating into the main senior stream of my peer group, with its attendant turbulent teenage heartaches, anxieties and troubles (albeit mostly self-inflicted). In fact (outwardly at least) I seemed to have almost forgotten I was ever an evacuee...which is what I needed to do. But, in reality, I realise now, within me the damage was done, and would never be totally erased from my psyche.

So it came to pass, this particular market day, I was circulating the stalls with my regular pal Cyril Kleto (who was no doubt dithering about getting ready to acquire another ordered army knife) when I became aware of this heavily built matronly-looking woman wearing a long black coat covered in dog hairs, hovering...well, tailing us really.

I nudged Cyril. "Hey, look. Who the hell's that queer old codger. She seems to be following us". Like then as like now we never bothered a lot with older people, except perhaps to snigger at them if they looked a bit eccentric. Stupid and wrong I know, but a typical teenage stance.

"Dunno who she is" Cyril replied absentmindedly, concentrating on his imminent dirty deed. He was hanging about the ironmonger's stall with his hands dangling loose and circling like a gunslinger about to draw his gun. Any moment now a knife would disappear from the stall and reappear in Cyril's pocket. Good pilferers are a bit like magicians with their skilful sleight-of-hand: now you see it, now you don't. "Dunno" he said again, trying to look casual.

The strange woman shuffled closer. Then she waved me over to her.

Bemused, I left Cyril to his shifty maneuverings and walked over to the beckoning lady.

She was an odd sight, like someone straight out of the pages of a Dicken's novel. A quaint old-fashioned vanishing breed. She looked like a female version of the Michelin man, with a stiff head set well back on her shoulders. She had swollen tree-trunk legs. Her scruffy threadbare black coat reached almost to her ancient clumpy shoes, just allowing a glimpse of her thick bulbous ankles. Her white, puffy, tired-looking face had wiry odd hairs growing in all the wrong places. I was fascinated to see she had a small moustache on her sweat-beaded upper lip.

"It's Michael, isn't it?" she asked, in a quiet friendly way as I stood before her. She obviously knew me but was confirming that she was making no mistake as to who she was talking to. I was intrigued. It wasn't often I was called by name by strangers. It wasn't often I was called by my full Christian name by anyone let alone strangers.

"Yes" I replied. What else could I say? And who the heck was she?

She introduced herself. "I'm Mrs Pinder" she stated staring at me intently, presumably trying to perceive if I knew who she was. "How are you going on Michael? Are you all right where you are? Are you happy living with Mrs Bateson?" Now, apart from Mrs Bateson, hardly anyone ever called me Michael, unless they were officials, or serious teachers.

Suddenly, somewhere deep inside me, for no apparent reason, her kindly manner and personal questions were striking at the roots of my hidden misery and my evacuee past. Since that cold evening so long ago, when I had been so indifferently dumped with the Bateson family in their isolated farmhouse, no-one had ever asked me what I thought about what had happened to me. I had felt like a animal might when it had been sent to the cattle market. Who took it home, and what happened to it afterwards, seemed of no interest or con-sequence to anyone. It was as if the world didn't care whether I was happy or not. A knot rose in my throat. I immediately sensed this woman had something to do with orphans, or deserted kids, charities and...war evacuees. For some reason she was genuinely concerned about the abandoned children of this world. In today's cynical climate she would probably be called a do-gooder. Like Fairy Godmother's in oddball disguises, these people who always seem to have an abundance of time and money and generosity, seem to appear from nowhere, wave their magic wands, shower life's sad victims with sprays of stars of kindness, and disappear just as mysteriously as they came. Whether this is a good thing, a true kindness or not, I have no idea. Charity, I had discovered, in the light of the more cynical and mature world, is a moot word. At this particular moment in time and place, in the brashness of my youth and in the stark realness of the hard and arrogant teenage world I now inhabited, I didn't particularly want to be singled out and reminded of my fading sorry evacuee status. I suppose I just wanted to be a normal, accepted teenager.

I was trying to forget my past. At some future time and age perhaps, (like now!) when I can look back calmly and reflectively, but not then, in that market square, in the middle of my school day. Not only that, but Cyril, having got what he wanted, and wishing naturally to beat a hasty retreat, was giving me urgent looks and our secret 'thumbs up' sign, indicating 'Mission Accomplished'. He was jerking his head and mouthing "Come on. Let's get the bloody hell out of here". Also, much to my shame, I did not want to be seen talking to this eccentric-looking, scruffy, old-fashioned lady. It was not my scene. It was doing my street cred no good at all.

"I have some money for you here Michael" continued the stranger in her quiet monotone voice. With curiously podgy fingers she was fumbling in her well-worn leather concertina purse and carefully extracted some small change - copper and silver. I stood wondering. I wouldn't go just yet if she was offering to give me money.

She glanced at it in the palm of her hand and did a cursory count, as if to say, "that'll do for today". She pressed the money warmly and intimately with her cold podgy hand into my hot sticky one.

"Thank you" I said, not a little surprised. I suppose I should have asked "and who are you and what are you giving me money for?" but I was so startled by this unexpected cash-windfall from a total stranger who had given me this money in such an solemn yet matter-of-fact way, that I remained silent.

"I would like you to meet me in this market-place every Wednesday Market day, Michael" the woman went on, still staring hard into my eyes. Was she trying to read my mind? She then glanced around her, as if she didn't want to be seen giving me money. Her own eyes were bulbous and edgy, but kind. Tired, yet intense. "There's no need to say anything about this Michael. Don't tell anybody I've given you money.

I just want you to be happy" she said softly. I think she was hinting not to tell Mrs Bateson. Don't ask me why. It was part of the mystery.

True unsolicited kindness calls for no reciprocal obligation, and must be offered in this undemanding and mutually understood manner to have any effect.

For some unfathomable reason I felt that familiar lump rise in my throat, and an uncontrollable surge of silent tears welled up behind my moistening eyes. Like the memories raised by an old tune, I had been stopped in my tracks, metaphorically and for real, and my soul felt laid as bare as the bright sun that lit up the world around me. These are the moments of our lives when we are caught napping. When our cosy day-to-day world is suddenly put into perspective, and our souls are penetrated without warning, like a metaphorical sniper's bullet that seeks out and hits our soul, and why and from were and from whom we have no idea.

The dam of misery that had built up inside me over the years was now overflooding its banks, and this final rain-drop of kindness was near to bursting the flimsy, fragile walls of childhood stoicism. Kindness, and expressions of love and concern regarding my health and happiness were unknown to me. No-one had ever enquired or seemed to care whether I was happy or not, or alive or dead. "Was I happy?" What did this mean? My brother Bob had been the only other person who had asked me this question, and it had had the same emotional choking effect then.

"Yes. I will meet you" I murmured to the mysterious woman. "I'll be here. About the same time. Thanks for the money". I then walked back into the real world to join the impatient, grinning Cyril.

"Who the hell was that?" he asked indifferently, more concerned with showing me the purloined knife.

Now it was my turn to shrug my shoulders and say "Dunno". Why would I be interested in a nosy old woman in the market square? Chortling and whispering excitedly at Cyril's latest successful achievement, like two knavish partners in crime we went on our way.

And thereafter, as promised, every market day the mysterious Mrs Pinder faithfully appeared in Uttoxeter Market-place and handed me varying amounts of money from the depths of her grubby but seemingly inexhaustable purse. Sometimes it was a fairly large amount, and sometimes just small change. There was no consistency and no explanation. But always a kindly enquiry as to my health and happiness.

I should have asked after Mrs Pinder's health because soon she began to look haggard and ill, but all I did was take the money and say a polite "Thank you". Who she was and from whence she came, I neither knew nor cared. I was a mercenary and hard-faced little sod ('Em had called me this so many times I now believed it myself). I was simply glad to find another source of easy, unearned money. Too many questions might have killed the golden goose.

Whether Mrs Pinder was really a representative of some charitable organisation, or just a private do-gooder, I was never to know. But it was obvious she didn't want Mrs Bateson to know, which suited me fine: I had money coming in that Mrs Bateson knew nothing about, and also I felt someone cared more about me than Mrs Bateson ever had. These thoughts and feelings are child's feelings and, as such, are probably wide of the truth. Most children are unaware of the real situation of their lives, that is why they really need protection.

At a different age I would have thanked Mrs Pinder for her altruistic and consistent generosity and would have enquired into her own happiness and health. She always looked so solemn, tired and ill. For some reason she was trying to be a friend, but I was too young to understand. As it was I merely took the money and ran, so to speak. This went on for quite a number of years and, as I watched her growing older and scruffier, I was only interested in the bizarre hormonal hairs that were now appearing on different parts of her face, where hairs normally never grow, and her upper lip which seemed always to be covered in beads of sweat. And, of course, her money. And I still hadn't thought to enquire as to who she was. It must be remembered I only saw her for a few minutes each week while on my hour's dinner break and, apart from my watching, giggling (and thieving) companion, I also had to get some fish and chips for my dinner, find time to eat them, and collect Mrs Bateson's currant Bread from the cake shop.

Now Mrs Pinder must fade from view as must we all in our own good time. I would soon be leaving school, and I would be moving on too, but where to only God and the oracles knew: I certainly had no idea.

My meetings with Mrs Pinder became less frequent as she failed to turn up so often for our rendezvous. I felt cheated over my free weekly pocket money. The last few times we met she emptied her purse in trying to double or triple her donations, to make up for the weeks she'd missed. Bless her soul.

I was annoyed when finally she didn't turn up at all. Annoyed that is, because my easy money supply was drying up. What an avaricious little devil I must have been, and how ungrateful. I wondered where she had got to. Perhaps she had been taken ill, or grown old and died. But I neither knew nor cared and hardly gave her a thought except for the money. Yet, thinking about it now, she was one of the very few people in my life who had ever showed concern and asked me if I was alright and happy in my life. It was an unsettling question, and shook me for a bit. I mean, when you come to think of it, we don't get asked that question very often in life do we? And yet, like that unexpected smile from a complete stranger, it is probably one of the few gentle daggers than can penetrate the shell most of us have built up around ourselves, and which can stir our souls in a strange and disturbing way.

On the brink of leaving school my horizons were expanding. With mates, I started going to the pictures a lot. We were too young for pubs, but if you knew where to go certain landlords turned a blind eye. So we rounded off most evenings with a pint in one of the town's boozers and afterwards followed a couple of tittering girls home, before we cycled back the five miles to our place in the country.

'Dogging the girls' was an accepted pastime then and part of the peculiar ritual of trying to 'click' and find yourself a girl-friend. Girls indulged in it too (ostensibly - to protect their female dignity I assume) and seemed to find it amusing and useful. You could make tentative approaches and 'chat-them-up' without having to make any sort of commitment if you decided you didn't like each other. You followed them around town for awhile and made one or two silly cheeky remarks - then, if there was nothing doing, you all went home, either heartbroken because you hadn't 'clicked' with the pretty one you'd fallen in love with, or relieved that you hadn't got landed with the plain one you didn't fancy at all. Occasionally your mate clicked with the one you wanted and, to oblige, you went off with the plain one. But it rarely worked out, because you felt you had been saddled with second best. Typical crass teenage thinking.

Such behaviour might be considered politically incorrect, ignorantly macho and could be construed as sexual harassment today. Somewhere along the line the thought police would be watching you. Whoever coined the phrase 'Dogging the girls' hit the nail on the head, for when you come to think of it, we were, basically, predatory young dogs on heat, chasing the young bitches. A rather crude simile but very true and apt, nevertheless.

Apart from the odd village or town-hall dance, and the pubs - the streets were about the only other place you could meet members of the opposite sex. There were hardly any big clubs like there are now. And more often than not we had spent our school years in segregated schools, and were not comfortable with the opposite sex, nor them with us.

This policy was intrinsically wrong and flawed and caused much shyness and misery, and thwarted the natural instincts of the sexes. Boy and girls have to meet sometime and somewhere, and find something in common. It is their basic nature to do so.

It is better and healthier that the adolescent sexual thing isn't allowed to grow disproportionately and swamp all other thoughts and feelings, and cause an unnecessary imbalance which will interfere with one's concentration, education and character development.

We usually went by bike to the pictures in Uttoxeter, but occasionally used the buses. A bus ran through the village on a Wednesday (Uttoxeter Market day) and a Saturday so that the country ladies could get into town to do their shopping. Any other time we wanted to use the buses we had to walk two miles to the main Stafford road and catch the Stafford\Uttoxeter service.

Because almost every family owns a car now, most village bus services have ceased operating today. It's a sign of changing times (and prosperity). Many's the time, having spent the evening at the cinema and then the pub, and 'dogging the girls', we'd 'miss' the last bus back home accidentally on purpose, especially if the girls had looked promising and had delayed us. "Blast!" we'd cry, in mock surprise, stating the obvious as the bus disappeared up the high street, "We've missed the bus!" Which we knew we would anyway. This would mean a five mile walk back home to Blythe Bridge probably lasting into the early hours as we fooled about every inch of the way. But it was a laugh. Feeling we had all the time in the world, we'd dawdle and get up to late-night mischief, shouting and singing and sometimes scrumping apples from road-side gardens. It was great fun and totally unlawful.

If we'd gone into town on our bikes, we could set off back home anytime, and this usually meant just after midnight, or even later. Whether it was pouring with rain or bitterly cold, or even if the roads were covered with snow, it didn't seem to matter. We still wasted time and fooled around. Youth, at a certain age, is amazingly tough and resilient and can abuse the body and ignore or laugh at the elements no matter how savage the weather may be. As we age most of us begin to huddle in our homes during the long inclement winter nights.

We may not like to admit it but we are very slowly running out of steam and the zest for mischevious lively living. It fades imperceptibly...slowly.

One late, cold, wet and windy night, I remember saying to my pal Olly, "Where the hell is everybody? You know, there are millions of folks out there, and yet we seem to be the only two on the face of the earth still out and about. Where the hell do they all go? They can't all be sitting over the fire"

"Well, that's probably where they are", replied Olly. "Or in bed. We're the only two silly buggers daft enough to come out on a night like this". We thought this hilarious.

But now, fifty years on, I'm one of those 'sitting over the fire'almost worn-out deadbeats myself, and there are probably new teenage 'silly buggers' out there in the blustery cold night, laughing at people like me. And so life goes on.

To hear us speak then, 'they' were all fuddy-duddy half-dead old geezers , while we two, out in the sweeping blizzards and frozen half to death, were the only two who were really alive and enjoying ourselves. There's a moral there somewhere.

We were at that crazy age. That irresponsible no-man's land age when life mocked us and we mocked life. This particularly dodgy age and time of life is unique and short-lived and so frightening, so precarious and dangerous, it probably could not be sustained without dire consequencies. Which bitter lesson we had yet to learn and understand.

It is easy (and normal) for adults to forget what it was like to be young, with all its fears and uncertainties. Yet it is the time when fresh young minds are surveying and weighing up the world they find themselves saddled with and, rightly or wrongly, finding it wanting in many respects. "What a mess grown-ups have made of everything" they think. And "And we have to live with it, or change it and make it a better place". Were it that simple. But a conclusion that each succeeding generation will naturally assume. In later years they will never again see the world in quite the same way, mainly because they have taken on their own responsibilities and have become part of the problem themselves, and are too busy trying to cope with day to day existence.

But things have to be kept in perspective. Young people are entitled to their view and may have a point. Just because it seems that many older members of the community (especially in the Western world) have carved themselves quite a smug and comfortable little niche in their cosy little world thank you, it doesn't follow that that's how it was meant to be, or that it will stay like that. The world still remains a very unstable and dangerous place, with everyone trying to carve themselves a cosy corner, and to hang on to it.

The status quo will always be subject to change, given time. The adult community might seem to have the power, and most of the property, but never forget, the young still have the strength and the speed, the energy and stamina, and most of the aspirations. This needs to be remembered. The world is now a much more complex difficult and frightening place for the young, and in some ways it is getting worse. Many own no home of their own, and never will, and many can't even get decently paid work. The mountain gets steeper and, should they fall, they fall into the abyss deeper. Apart from their ageing parents, many feel they have no security at all. The frightening reality of their situation dawns slowly in their awakening minds and awareness.

Meanwhile, what else can they do but worry, laugh, kick out against society and the system, and drink. Then panic maybe...and pray.

And so it was then. On our way back to Blythe Bridge in the early hours of the morning, Olly and I threw stones at the ceramic telephone cups (insulators) and cheered when we hit and smashed one. Often we would grab hold of the back of a lorry as it chugged in a low gear while climbing a steep hill. Occasionally the driver would spot us in his rear view mirror, do a shuddering emergency stop, and chase us back down the hill. "Silly little buggers. You'll get yourselves killed" he'd shout. Once, a driver caught Olly and boxed his ears, but I escaped laughing and shouting for Olly to break loose and follow me. It was all a big joke to us then. Everything was a laugh. The more daring and dangerous, the better. But mild stuff you may think, compared to today's teenage tearaways.

One late wet night we were scrumping apples from an orchard behind a cottage wall. I stood balancing and wobbling on the seat of my bike, held by Olly, and reached as high as I could into the tree for the biggest juiciest apple, which always seemed to be on the highest branch. A cop car went by and the cops did a double take and I fell off the bike seat. While the cops looked for somewhere to turn their car round and get back to us, we rode furiously in the opposite direction along the narrow country lane with our lights turned off. We hurled our bikes over the hedge into a rain-soaked corn field and jumped in after them.

We saw the beams of the police car headlights turning and scanning the road like searchlights, twinkling through the raindrops, looking for the enemy. In this case us. They drove slowly back and forth along the lane probably wondering where we'd disappeared to. We were crouching in the two foot high corn, soaked to the skin. We were safe. We knew the cops wouldn't get out of their comfy car to come and look for us: they'd get wet!

On these late (or rather early morning) journeys back home we jumped and whooped and paddled in our shoes in the river, or just tossed away our bikes and ran along the road like demented idiot monkeys (which, of course, we were). Decent people in their beds trying to sleep must have thought they were being attacked by wild Indians. It was not necessarily funny, nor was it very clever or smart, though we thought it was hilarious. So why did we do it? I make no excuses for this silly behaviour, nor am I ashamed to tell you about it. Even a young animal is entitled to its one short hour of fun during an otherwise, soon to be experienced, serious, worrying and tedious life. We grow up, soon enough.

Naturally, if we are wise, there comes a time in everyones' life when we (privately, at least) reassess ourselves, our position in life, and our attitudes. We think, "What the hell am I doing?" and "Where am I going?" To the outside world we might assume a nonchalant attitude that seems to say "I couldn't care less. It's everybody and everything else that is at odds, not me". We all think like this sometime in our lives, and there is an element of truth in it, as there is in most things. But then again, nothing is so black and white, and so simple. Also, we should not be so arrogant as to think we know better than all the rest of the world put together. There are a lot of clever and intelligent people out there. There are better men than we are, Gunga Din!

It was about now our headmaster, Tricky Smith, started lecturing us at morning assembly in the school hall, about our fast approaching future in the real world, beyond the school gates.

As stated previously he was a comical, eccentric, endearing old codger at times. He probably never guessed he was viewed as such by his pupils. I remember thinking he seems really honestly concerned about us and our future (the hallmark of a good and loved teacher) and, knowing him, he probably was. Yes, I remember thinking this, after almost fifty years.

Uttoxeter is a small, quiet, pleasant market town, but dubbed boring by bored teenagers - as they always are (the teenagers AND the small towns). There were only a few places where one could go to work when I left school. It is a country and county town, surrounded by green fields and farms. There was Bamford's agricultural machinery factory; Elkes, a large biscuit factory, a corset factory and a laundry, and that was about it. Otherwise you went to work on one of the farms in the countryside surrounding the town. The biscuit factory still exists today but is much larger (it began in that little cake shop where I fetched the currant bread from). Bamfords has grown into the mighty digger/earthmoving company, and the corset factory has gone along with obsolescent corsets (it's now the town's laundry). Even most of the farms have been scaled down as meat and milk sales fall, and go out of fashion.

Tricky would strut up and down the assembly hall stage like an agitated though benign Hitler. Then he would pause at the side and do a little miming act.

"For goodness sake boys, learn a trade" he would admonish earnestly. "That is the only sensible way forward. You will never get anywhere without a trade in your hands". This advice was wasted, as most of us were duffers anyway and hadn't a clue what he meant or what we were going to do when we left school.

He would take tight hold of an imaginary handle and furiously pedal an imaginary lever with his foot: "I don't want to see you end up at the biscuit factory" he would say, almost pleading with us, "stamping elephants on biscuits...like this" (he had a droll funny way of putting things across). Then his hand and foot would pump away energetically at the side of the stage on his imaginary biscuit stamping machine, and a wave of barely concealed laughter would ripple across us intently watching boys in the hall. We found these comical antics from a respectable, bespectacled old headmaster very entertaining.

I don't know what he'd got against the biscuit factory, as later, I ignored his advice and went to work there (and still do). I've spent most of my working life there, while many other places have gone bankrupt. It employs a large percentage of the town's workforce. It has paid for everything I have, my marriage, my kids, my home, and my car. It even pays for the annual Council Tax and that's saying something! It's kept me out of trouble (well, most of the time) for over thirty-five years, and will soon see me off to retirement, so it can't be all that bad. It doesn't do to scoff at so-called menial or humble jobs, some of them outlast the hi-tech new-fangled undertakings. Thank God for biscuit eaters I say. And they never did stamp elephants on biscuits, it was cows. As for his advice on learning a trade, it was well meant certainly, and true then, up to a point. But, like much advice, over simplistic. Times change, as do trades, professions and careers. Where now are your Blacksmiths, Wheelwrights and Cartwrights of yesteryear? Plumbers will one day become redundant, as will Electricians. What is wise advice today might be very unwise for tomorrow's world. Why spend most of your life learning a trade only to see it disappear before your very eyes? No wonder Tricky looked worried about his charges' futures - he had good reason to be.

Why - I have often wondered - don't they teach you more about LIFE, at school? To be able to earn your living and to compete in the economic and commercial world is, granted, now essential in the type of capitalist society we have chosen to create and live in. But what about our private thoughts, feelings and emotions? And what about the many puzzlements and pitfalls of trying to survive in civilisation's complicated social systems and conventions. We were never warned that large families and heavy mortgages or rents would almost cripple us financially and probably physically too, and commit us to a lifelong heavy burden. Nor was the concept of love spelled out to us, sexual or otherwise. And a myriad of other mysteries to do with living in a modern world. Were we expected to know these things instinctively or just find out by trial and error? Many kids left school then not even knowing what a mortgage was, or how early sexual experiment might land you in the pregnancy trap, until it was too late. And we certainly hadn't a clue what a lifetime of hard labour and worry would follow that disaster

Or did the ommission of life-skill teaching suit the system and the status quo - not to tell us? The peasant might be happy in his misery if he has never been inside the Duke's mansion, and would work all the better for that. Things haven't changed that much in the last couple of hundred years, it is just the outer trappings that are different. The more society is manipulated to suit the establishment, the more distortion of society it will cause. Distortion leads to tension, and tension to fracture.

And what about my own case and kids suffering similiar troubles? Granted, the problems of evacuees is no longer with us, but many kids are still abandoned and dispossessed - even if they have a family.

Could not someone have spelled things out for me, in big letters loud and clear, instead of allowing me to flounder on for so many troubled years in a sea of misery and perplexity until I had, more or less, sorted it all out for myself? That a tyrant called Hitler had started a world war and that war was the ultimate human nightmare in terror and pain, and destroyed everything, even our lives. I could have been told there were thousands of kids like me around the world, lost and bewildered and unhappy orphans. It might have helped, But nobody told me anything. Almost everything I know I had to find out as I went along. To a little kid of six war is just another word, and means nothing. And his miserable and hard life, in a world at war, is the only world he knows. To him, it is normal, unless he is taught and informed otherwise.

As it was, my younger years were wasted, bogged down in a sea of misery, and all because no one bothered to explain to me what the hell was going on, and why my life and the rest of the world was in such an unhappy mess, and that it hadn't always been like this. The thing that strikes me above all others, is that some things that really worry kids can be explained in a few minutes...and a few lucid sentences can perhaps change that child's understanding of things, and therefore and thereafter his outlook and destiny, for the rest of his life. Yet no one seems to bother, or to think on these things. Maybe this is why many youngsters DO get into trouble. No one explained to them the very basics of life in the modern world.

O.K. I agree, it IS difficult to explain many things to a six year old child. They are just too young to understand. But patience, perseverence and time would help. It is the will and the common-sense that seems to be missing.

And it is still the same.

Before we left school we were taken round the local iron-foundry. Here, for the first time, I glimpsed the real world that awaited us as school leavers. I witnessed workers at the sharp end, trying to earn their livings, to survive.

My eyes must have widened at the sights and sounds of this hell on earth. The factory was old and built of rusting corrugated iron. The roof leaked and the floor was uneven and, in the moulding shop, deep with the debris of swarf and black moulding soot. We couldn't hear ourselves speak as giant steam-hammers and screeching squeaking machinery blasted our sensitive ears, and ingrimed tired and gaunt-faced men ran hither and thither as if their life depended on it. Which indeed it did.

I watched an old man operating a lathe. He'd operated it most of his life. His head turned in time to the cog he was machining. I spotted the same man in town one day. He was standing in Woolworth's studying some books on a shelf. Something struck me as odd about him, and as I watched I realised his head was still imperceptibly turning. It was scary and pathetic really.

During the lunch hour hundreds of these stooping undernourished troll-like looking men flooded through the town on their bikes, blinking like bats emerging from a dark cave into the sunlight, as they pedalled furiously homeward to rush-warm a bowl of soup for their dinner. I vowed there and then I would never go to work in the iron foundry. But I did. And it was just as grim as I had imagined. I didn't stay long.

Mrs Bateson must have been thinking about my future too. I had long proved myself quite handy at mending fences and chicken houses etc, and I had built my pet rabbit sophisticated mansion-hutches and was proud of the soapbox trucks I had refined. I now turned my hand to a bit of bricklaying and concreting and she was not a little impressed.

Would I like to become a carpenter she enquired. And later, maybe a bricklayer?

The question was superfluous, and she might just as well have been talking to the chickens. In all honesty I hadn't a clue what I would like to become. Even the lifetime work-ethic was still a vague concept to me!

Do we become things, just like that? In this context, it would make an interesing debate. Did I really want to spend my life mixing cement and building walls and houses and things? Or even making tables and cupboards and screwdrivering my way through life? For this is how I thought. The world and my future seemed much too complicated for me to make any sense of the direction I should take. This is it, isn't it? The very crux of the problem.

Just what would we like to do, or become? At that age, and especially at that time, when little help or advice was available, who would know the answer to this most complex of questions? A few years later, when I joined the Royal Air Force, I discovered they trained hundreds of Barbers, Wages Clerks, Wireless Operators, Cooks and Officer's Batsmen etc. How was it I wondered that when lads joined the RAF and were asked, "What would you like to be?" they all seemed to know straightaway what they wanted to be? I was still a puzzled life-traveller. My innocent outlook on the world, like a puzzled puppy, has never changed. Most people seem to accept things as they are without question, whereas I must ask why, wherefore and how? I have a natural curiosity. I like to try to get to the heart and truth of things as you have maybe guessed by now. Little good has it ever done me!

For instance why did the RAF want so many people in these trades? How did they find room for them all? And were so many really needed? What about the taxpayer who had to foot the bill for what, to me, were superfluous artificially created jobs? At the risk of seeming to go on, I needed to know the answer to all these questions. The truth was they needed to find jobs for the boys, not boys for the jobs. Boys were not the problem, there were too many of those. Let the boys pick themselves a trade first, then the powers will fit them in somewhere later. This happens a lot now, in all walks of life - we can use up the spare labour because there is plenty of spare money about. It's a chicken and egg situation.

This is not a particularly difficult piece of reasoning to work out, nor is it a great revelation that will change the world. But

I find this thought process necessary to prevent me going mad in a crazy world. It is my attempt to satisfy myself that I know the reason for why things happen.

I picked my own RAF career out of thin air like this, as though with a pin, and became a Wireless Operator. It sounded a good, technical and respectable trade to me: I didn't even know what it entailed. I took it mainly because all the Barbers, Bandsmen and Batsmen vacancies had been taken, while I sat dithering and confused. So I took what was left. I've always been a bit of a dawdler, and only got to pick up the crumbs the other, more alert movers amd shakers had left.

I trained and passed my tests and was a W.O.P. (Wireless Operator) for five years. Then I left the RAF and went back to the biscuit factory (a much more satisfying job!). The trade of Wireless Operator is now redundant as new computerised methods of communication are vastly superior. I wasted all that time and effort on a trade that is now on the scraphead of history, like a lot of those trades Trickey Smith had recommended we learn.

Many of us become what we are because we have little or no choice in the matter. I mean, you can't just walk into the supermarket of life and pick your future off the shelf like your favourite brand of mushy peas - well, you could in the RAF. Like a perplexed and disorientated wanderer, you stand at this crossroads of life in a sort of suppressed panic, pretending you know where you're going when really you haven't a clue.

Like a castaway on a tossing raft you clutch at straws. If a factory is handy and is advertising vacancies, well, they tell you, you have to earn your living somewhere and sometime, and there just isn't time to stand dithering about like you have done throughout your growing years. The time has come... They do not intend to keep you for ever. So get out there and earn your own living. And you never even asked to be born in the first place!

And the odd thing is, you know in your heart of hearts it is true that you must move on. You have to plunge into those dangerous and unexplored waters and, in a way, you want to - or realise you have to. It is why you are here. It is elemental and destined. This is why you were born, to find your own way and to fight your own corner, to survive. A new lone warrior.

One bright, blue-hued, snow-covered early winter's morning, standing in a twinkling Christmas-card world of stars and frosted scenery, Olly and I, well lubricated with alcohol against the bitter cold, stood at the crossroads (literally and metaphorically). For the first time since we were born, we tried to look beyond our silly teenage behaviour and scanned the enormous universe above, around and beyond our ken.

"Who made all this?" I mused to Olly waving my arms around at the cosmos in general. I was asking questions even then, of man, of life...and of God. "How can it possibly be so huge? We mortals are but grains of sand on the seashore of creation" or silly wishy-washy words to that effect. I am not normally given to spouting such a load of poetic rubbish, but it was the alcohol blending with my fear of the future. Or perhaps it was my, as yet unrealised, vocation as a would-be writer beginning to surface. Would that I had recognised it at the time. It was a clue, but one I was too young to see.

Olly, who was a simpler phlegmatic country boy and not given to spouting poetical language at all, replied, "I don't know who made it, or why it is so big". Which was really the correct answer to my lofty ponderings.

"You do realise" I continued, getting into my stride, "Life means nothing really. We come and we go, and the stars and the planets roll on, and the old earth with them. Compared with infinite time, we humans are come and are gone in an instant". I thought this was originality itself, but it's been said by more perceptive and articulate philosophers and thinkers than I, since time began. Even Mr Caveman must have pondered it.

"That's all very true" agreed Olly yawning, either too tired or too bored or both, but obviously not unduly impressed with my fancy rhetoric or the incomprehensible vastness of the universe. "Let's get off home to bed, Mick. I'm bloody freezing".

So that's it for now, I'm afraid. I have, at the moment, believe it or not, despite my long gabble, nothing more profound to tell you, and I will not make it up. Later, I met my real mother, which is also a sad story. Later still, I joined the Royal Air Force, then came out and got married and went stamping cows on biscuits in the biscuit factory and not elephants.

Later, if I'm in the mood and before I die, I'll tell you about it. But, for the moment, Au-revoir, goodnight, and God Bless. I hope you've had a good read.

Lightning Source UK Ltd.
Milton Keynes UK
11 September 2010
159687UK00002B/6/P